Charting the Course to 2002: a Summary of Changes to the GED Tests

	What's the Same	What's Eliminated	What's Included for 2002
Skills ... Arts, ... (Language Arts, Writing)	45-minute essay; 3 item types (correction, revision, and construction shift); Sentence structure, usage, and mechanics; Informational documents ("passages"); Part I, multiple-choice, and Part II, essay; Examinee must complete both parts.	Spelling—except for homonyms, possessives, and contractions. Commas—only tested when they are used to eliminate confusion.	Business Communications (letters, memos, reports, applications, etc.): "How to" texts (e.g., dressing for success, leasing a car, planning a trip, etc.); both 200–300 words, 12–18 sentences. Organization—transitions, text divisions, topic sentences, and unity/coherence. Essay scoring rubric changes from 6-point to 4-point scale.
Social Studies	Multiple-choice in sets and single items; Measures comprehension, application, analysis, and evaluation; Covers history, geography, civics, government, and economics; National, global, and adult contexts; Text and visual sources.	Behavioral science—psychology, sociology, anthropology—not tested as separate content area; some concepts tested within context of other areas.	More history, civics, and government; More graphics, photographs; More analysis; More clearly defined content in U.S. and world history. Different content areas tested within same item set; More single-item questions; At least one "practical" document (voters' guide, tax form, etc.); At least one excerpt from U.S. Constitution, Declaration of Independence, Federalist Papers, or landmark Supreme Court cases.
Science	Multiple-choice in sets and single items; Text and visual sources.	More single items, fewer item sets.	Integrated with National Science Education Content Standards; Earth science includes space science; Physical science includes physics and chemistry; Increased focus on environmental and health topics (recycling, heredity, disease prevention, pollution, climate) and on science's relevance to everyday life; 50% conceptual understanding; 50% problem-solving. Increase in graphic stimuli from 30% to 50%.
Interpreting Literature and the Arts (renamed Language Arts, Reading)	Reflect diversity—gender, ethnicity, age, region; Passages range from 300–400 words; One poem (8–25 lines) and one piece of drama represented; No graphics, viewing addressed in textual manner.	Definitions; Popular Text and Classical literature redefined as time periods; "Literal comprehension" now "comprehension"; "comprehension"; "Inferential comprehension" now "synthesis."	Content areas defined by type of text: Literary (75%) and Nonfiction (25%); At least one comparison/contrast question. Nonfiction will include one business document and one selection about visual representation: 20% comprehension, 15% application, 30–35% analysis, 30–35% synthesis.
Mathematics	Measures algebra, geometry, number relations, and data analysis. 25% set-up questions—examinee must identify correct way to solve problem.	"Not sufficient Information" questions decreased from 12% to 4%.	More emphasis on data analysis and statistics; Two parts: Part I permits calculator, Part II does not; Candidate will have practice time with calculator prior to test; Alternate Format items approximately 20%; Item sets in which candidate must access multiple pieces of information—pie charts, bar graphs, tables. All candidates will use Casio fx-260 Solar.

372.83

Pre-GED Social Studies

Reviewers

Rochelle Kenyon
Assistant Principal
Adult and Vocational Off-Campus
  Centers
School Board of Broward County
Fort Lauderdale, Florida

Dee Akers Prins
Resource Specialist in Adult
  Education
Richmond Public Schools
Richmond, Virginia

Danette S. Queen
Adult Basic Education
New York City Public Schools
New York, New York

Margaret A. Rogers
Winterstein Adult Center
San Juan Unified School District
Sacramento, California

Lois J. Sherard
Instructional Facilitator
Office of Adult and Continuing
  Education
New York City Board of Education
New York, New York

STECK-VAUGHN
C O M P A N Y
ELEMENTARY • SECONDARY • ADULT • LIBRARY

Acknowledgments

Executive Editor: Elizabeth Strauss
Supervising Editor: Carolyn Hall
Editors: Susan Miller, Valerie Gammon
Design Director: D. Childress
Design Coordinator: Cynthia Ellis
Cover Design: D. Childress
Editorial Development: McClanahan & Company, Inc.
Project Director: Mark Moscowitz
Writer/Editor: Phyllis Goldstein, Mark Moscowitz
Design/Production: McClanahan & Company, Inc.

Photograph Credits:

Cover:	© TWS/Click-Chicago
p. 13	Bettmann Archive
p. 17	The Library of Congress
p. 42	U. S. Pentagon
p. 43	Bettmann Archive
pp. 58 & 64	Granger Collection
p. 70	Library of Congress
p. 90	Alan Carey/The Imageworks
p. 91	Courtesy, WANG Laboratories
p. 106 top	Courtesy, Sotheby's
p. 106 bottom	© Topps
pp. 126–127	Bettmann Archive
p. 143	U. S. Supreme Court Historical Society
p. 148	Courtesy, Wendy Langenderfer/Lorain City Schools
p. 162	© 1985 Naoki Okamoto/Stock Market
p. 163	American Museum of Natural History
p. 165	Jon Feingersh/Stock Market
p. 190	Marc Lofon/Gamma-Liaison
p. 191	David Redfern/Retna
p. 197	Steven Purcell/The White House
p. 201	International Museum of Photography, George Eastman House

Illustration Credits: Maryland Cartographics, Inc.

Credits continue on pages 232–233, which are an extension of this copyright page.

ISBN 0-8114-4488-0

5 6 7 8 9 PO 98 97 96 95

Table of Contents

Unit 1 Geography   *Page 12*

Unit 2 History   *Page 42*

Unit 3 Economics   *Page 90*

Unit 4 *Political Science*   Page 126

Unit 5 *Behavioral Science*   Page 162

To the Student

How to Use This Book

This book allows you to build upon what you already know to improve your social studies skills. You will increase your understanding of the five areas of social studies by reading interesting articles on many different topics. These topics are divided into the five units described below.

Units

Unit 1: Geography. This unit covers geography skills such as how to read rainfall, climate, and resource maps. You will use map keys and distance scales as you read maps and articles about the geography of the United States and other parts of the world.

Unit 2: History. This unit covers such history skills as reading historical and political maps, understanding photos, and using timelines. The articles you read will increase your knowledge of major events in American and world history.

Unit 3: Economics. This unit includes skills in economics. You will use graphic illustrations such as tables, line graphs, circle graphs, and bar graphs. You will gain an understanding of our economy by reading articles about supply and demand, world trade, and managing your money.

Unit 4: Political Science. In this unit, you will learn about selected concepts in political science. You will read diagrams, political ads, and political cartoons. You will also read about how laws are made and the roles of local, state, and federal governments.

Unit 5: Behavioral Science. This unit focuses on concepts in anthropology, psychology, and sociology. The graphic illustrations provide practice in skills such as understanding photos, interpreting cartoons, and reading population maps. Topics of articles in this unit include body language, how children learn male and female roles, and cultural diversity.

Inventory and Posttest

The Inventory is a self-check of what you already know and what you need to study. After you complete all of the items on the Inventory, the Correlation Chart tells you where each skill is taught in this book. When you have completed the book, you will take a Posttest. Compare your Posttest score to your Inventory score to see your progress.

Sections

All the units are divided into sections. Each section is based on the Active Reading Process. *Active reading* means doing something *before reading, during reading,* and *after reading.* By reading actively, you will improve your reading comprehension skills.

Setting the Stage

Each section begins with an activity that helps you prepare to read the article. This is the activity you do *before reading.* First, determine what you already know about the subject of the article. Then, preview the article by reading and writing the headings in the article. Finally, write the questions that you expect the article will answer.

The Article

The articles you will read are about interesting topics in social studies. As you read each article, you will see a feature called *Applying Your Skills and Strategies.* In these sections you learn a reading or social studies skill, and you do a short activity. After completing the activity, continue reading the article. *Applying Your Skills and Strategies* occurs twice in every article. These are the activities you do *during reading.*

Thinking About the Article

These are the activities you do *after reading.* Here you answer fill-in-the-blank, short-answer, or multiple-choice questions. Answering these questions will help you decide how well you understood what you just read. The final question in this section relates information from the article to your own real-life experiences.

Answers and Explanations

Answers and explanations to every exercise item are at the back of this book, beginning on page 209. The explanation for multiple-choice exercises tells why one answer choice is correct and why the other answer choices are incorrect.

Study Skills

Here are some things you can do to improve your study skills.

- Find a quiet place to study.

- Organize your time by making a schedule.

- Take notes by restating important information in your own words.

- Look up any words you don't know in a dictionary or the glossary.

- Make a list of concepts and skills on which you need to work. Take time to go back and review this material.

INVENTORY

Elevation: The United States

Use this Inventory before you begin Section 1. Don't worry if you can't answer all the questions. The Inventory will help you determine which content areas you are strong in and which content areas you need to practice further.

Read each article, study any graphics, and answer the questions that follow. Check your answers on page 209. Then enter your scores on the chart on page 11. Use the chart to figure out which skills to work on and where to find those skills in this book.

United States Elevation Map

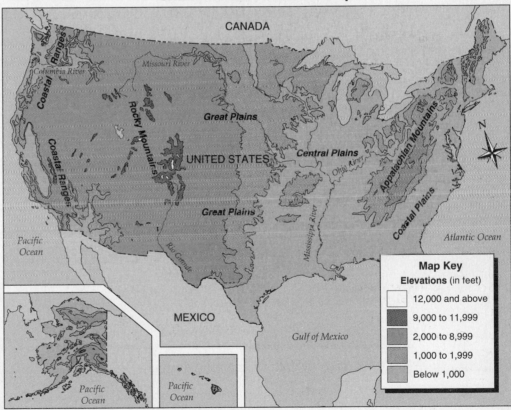

Write your answers in the space provided.

1. What is the elevation of the Coastal Plains?

_____

2. What is the elevation of the Great Plains?

_____

Desert Regions

Every continent, except Europe and Antarctica, has at least one desert region. When people think of deserts, they often picture hot, dry, empty lands. Every desert is very dry, but not all deserts are hot. Some are cold. Hot deserts are usually found at low latitudes and low elevations. The Sahara Desert in North Africa is a hot desert. Cold deserts include the Gobi Desert in Asia and the Great Basin Desert in the United States. Cold deserts are found at higher latitudes and higher elevations.

Deserts are home to many different plants and animals. The plants and animals of the desert have adapted to the harsh environment. Desert plants have tough skins and few leaves so they can keep any water they absorb. Some desert animals, like the mourning dove and the desert rat, are active at night when temperatures are cooler. Other animals conserve water. For example, kangaroo rats never actually drink water. Instead, they get their water from the seeds they eat. Other desert animals, such as the camel, are able to go for long periods without water.

People have also found ways to live in the desert, just as they have in every other environment. Some people move from place to place with herds of camels, goats, or sheep. Other people farm in the desert. To do so, they must bring water to their fields from a distant spring or river. People also look for oil and other resources in the desert. People have even built cities in the desert.

Write your answers in the space provided.

3. Name one way deserts are alike.

_____

4. Name one way deserts are different.

_____

Circle the number of the best answer.

5. Which of the following is a conclusion that can be drawn from the article?

   (1) Only animals can live in the desert.

   (2) People have developed ways to survive in any environment.

   (3) Camels can go a long time without water.

   (4) People cannot live in a desert environment.

   (5) People can survive only in a cold desert.

The American Revolution

At the start of the American Revolution, everyone in North America took sides. Those who wanted to be free from Britain were called Patriots. Those who remained loyal to Britain were called Loyalists. Most African Americans faced a hard choice. Many were slaves. They chose the side that would give them their freedom.

Even before the war began, African Americans were taking sides. There were African-American soldiers at all of the early battles in the war. Then, in November 1775, Patriot leaders said African Americans could no longer serve in the army. Those who had already joined were sent home. Slave owners did not want any African Americans to have guns. They were afraid African Americans would use the guns to fight slavery.

Then the British promised to free any slave who joined their army. Many slaves accepted the offer. As a result, Patriot leaders had to change their minds. They decided to allow only free African Americans, not slaves, to join their army. Then, in December 1777, George Washington took his army of about 9,000 men to Valley Forge, Pennsylvania. By the spring of 1778, Washington had fewer than 6,000 soldiers. Many deserted, while others died of cold or hunger.

Washington desperately needed more soldiers. So the Patriot leaders decided to allow slaves to enlist. By the end of the war, 5,000 African Americans had taken part in the American Revolution. They came from every state, and fought in every major battle. The efforts of African-American soldiers during the war helped end slavery in the northern states.

Write your answers in the space provided.

6. Why were African Americans turned away from the army in 1775?

_____

7. What was the effect of the British decision to free any slave who joined their army?

_____

Circle the number of the best answer.

8. What event allowed slaves to join the Patriots' army?

(1) the start of the American Revolution

(2) Britain's decision to free slaves that joined its army

(3) the loss of so many soldiers at Valley Forge

(4) African-American participation in earlier battles

(5) the end of the American Revolution

The Korean War

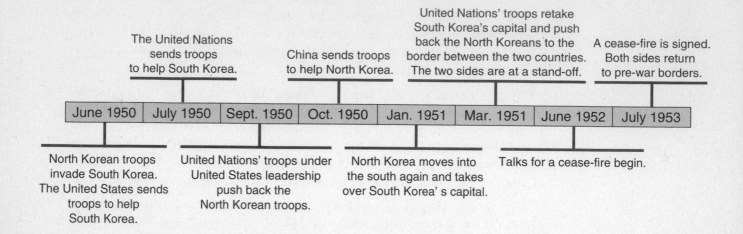

Write your answer in the space provided.

9. What event started the Korean War?

_____

Circle the number of the best answer.

10. Which event was a result of China's entry into the war?

   (1) North Korea moved into the South and retook South Korea's capital.

   (2) The Korean War ended.

   (3) United Nations' troops pushed back the North Koreans.

   (4) The Korean War started.

   (5) The United Nations entered the war to help South Korea.

11. Which of the following statements best summarizes the timeline?

   (1) South Korea, with the help of United Nations' troops, was winning the war by September 1951.

   (2) North Korea, with the help of Chinese troops, was winning the war by December 1952.

   (3) By 1951, the two sides were deadlocked, and the deadlock was not broken until truce talks began in June 1952.

   (4) The two sides tried to reach a truce for over one year.

   (5) Neither side gained from the war.

                                                                    Go on to the next page.

Buyers' and Sellers' Markets

Communities across the country are recycling. Newspapers are being separated from other trash. These efforts have had a dramatic effect on the paper industry.

Many towns are now selling tons of old newspapers to paper mills. In fact, the amount of newspaper available is far greater than the demand for recycled paper. Some cities and towns are getting only a fraction of the amount they received for newspapers in 1988. Towns near Boston, New York, and Philadelphia cannot even give away old papers. They have to pay paper mills $10 per ton to take the newspapers. It is a buyers' market. The paper mills are the buyers, and they are paying very low prices.

However, the market for old newspapers is changing. The demand for recycled paper is expected to more than double between 1990 and 1993. Box makers and countries with a shortage of trees are buying recycled paper. Together, these two groups account for about half of all the purchases of old newspapers. They are being joined by newspaper publishers across America. Recently, seven states passed laws requiring that newspapers use recycled paper.

Today Americans recycle less than 45 percent of all newspapers. To keep up with the expected demand, they will have to recycle about 57 percent by 1995. That may be an impossible goal. Within a few years, there may be a shortage of old newspapers. It would then become a sellers' market. People selling old newspapers would be able to command high prices.

Write your answers in the space provided.

12. When the paper mills pay low prices for newspapers, what kind of market is it?

_____

13. When the paper mills pay high prices for newspapers, what kind of market is it?

_____

Circle the number of the best answer.

14. When the demand for a product is low, but there is a lot of the product to sell, the price

   (1) goes up.

   (2) goes down.

   (3) stays the same.

   (4) is not affected by the demand.

   (5) is not affected by the amount of the product available.

Go on to the next page.

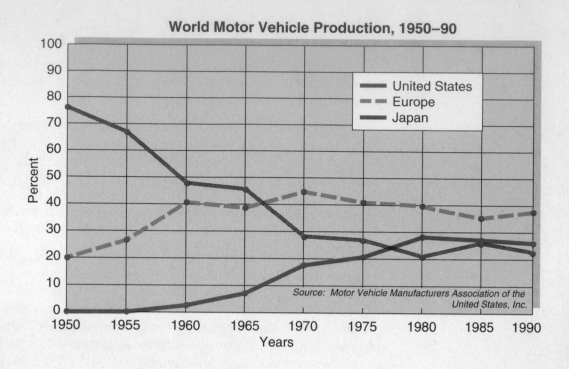

World Motor Vehicle Production, 1950–90

Source: Motor Vehicle Manufacturers Association of the United States, Inc.

Write your answers in the space provided.

15. Rank the three auto producers in 1950 from largest to smallest.

_____

16. Rank the three auto producers in 1970 from largest to smallest.

_____

17. Rank the three auto producers in 1990 from largest to smallest.

_____

Circle the number of the best answer.

18. The <u>best</u> conclusion that can be drawn from the graph is that

    (1) Japan is a threat to the United States auto industry.

    (2) European auto producers may be a more serious threat to the United States than the Japanese.

    (3) the American auto industry is beginning to make a comeback.

    (4) other parts of the world threaten the control Japan, Europe, and the United States have on the auto industry.

    (5) all auto producers had problems in 1990.

Civil Rights

After the Civil War, African Americans began working for equal rights. In the North and the South, they faced discrimination. They did not have the same civil rights as other Americans. That means they did not have the same freedoms as other citizens. In many states, schools were segregated. As a result, African-American and white children could not attend the same school. Many neighborhoods and jobs were closed to African Americans. Some state laws even kept African Americans out of places such as restaurants, public swimming pools, movie theaters, and hotels.

In August 1963, over 250,000 Americans gathered and marched down the streets of Washington, D.C. They included white people and African Americans from every state and several foreign countries. They demanded that Congress pass a civil-rights bill to end discrimination in the United States.

Dr. Martin Luther King, Jr. captured the mood of the day. He said to the crowd, "I have a dream that one day this nation will rise up and live out the true meaning of its creed: 'We hold these truths to be self-evident; that all men are created equal.'"

President John F. Kennedy supported King's cause. He called on Congress to pass a strong civil-rights bill. Kennedy did not live to see it pass. After Kennedy's death, Congress passed the Civil Rights Act of 1964. It protected the right of all citizens to vote. It outlawed discrimination in hiring and education. It also ended segregation in public places.

Write your answers in the space provided.

19. In many states, African-American children went to different schools

    from white children. The schools were _____.

20. Why did Americans march on Washington in 1963?

    _____

Circle the number of the best answer.

21. Dr. King was calling on all Americans to

    (1) change the nation's values and beliefs.

    (2) live up to the nation's values and beliefs.

    (3) march down the streets of Washington, D.C.

    (4) pass a civil-rights bill.

    (5) ignore their heritage.

Go on to the next page.

Electing a President and Vice President

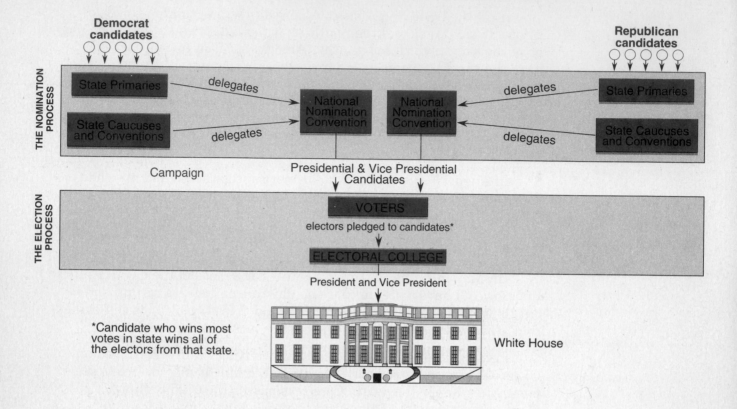

Circle the number of the best answer.

22. Based on the information provided in the diagram, whom do the voters elect?

    (1) the president and vice president

    (2) delegates

    (3) electors

    (4) delegates, as well as a president and vice president

    (5) electors and a president and vice president

23. According to the diagram, why is it possible for a candidate to get the greatest number of votes and still lose the election?

    (1) by winning by a large margin in states with few electors and losing by a narrow margin in states with many electors

    (2) by losing in states with few electors and winning in states with many electors

    (3) by winning support of the voters but not the electors

    (4) by not having enough support from his or her own party

    (5) by losing in the caucuses

Go on to the next page.

Human Behavior

Surveys suggest that 70 percent of all Americans feel that shyness has hurt them at some time in their lives. Shyness is an anxiety reaction in social situations. That means people who are shy become nervous when they are with others. These people become overly concerned with how they look and how they sound. People are afraid others will see them as foolish, unattractive, unintelligent, or in some way unworthy.

Although some people are born shy, most shyness is a learned pattern of behavior. To overcome shyness, doctors teach their patients new ways of acting in groups. They recommend one or more of the following techniques.

1. Rehearse what you want to say before going out in public. Practice the words until they become easy and comfortable.
2. Build self-esteem by focusing on your strong points.
3. Practice smiling and making eye contact.
4. Work to improve your speaking voice by talking into a tape recorder. People who sound confident are viewed as being confident.
5. Pay more attention to what other people are saying. Pay less attention to yourself.
6. Imagine being a social success. Don't think about failing.
7. Practice deep breathing and meditation to relax.

Doctors have even been successful in treating people who are so fearful that they refuse to leave home. Some believe that the key is for people to believe that they will succeed.

Write your answers in the space provided.

24. People who are nervous around others could be having an

_____ .

25. Why do doctors believe shyness can be overcome?

_____

Circle the number of the best answer.

26. According to the article, you can infer that people who are shy

   (1) do not like people.

   (2) tend to have low self-esteem.

   (3) will never be able to overcome their problems.

   (4) are unfriendly.

   (5) are comfortable with their social skills.

Go on to the next page.

Cultural Borrowing

"What I really feel like having is ham and eggs."

Drawing by B. Tobey; © 1940, The New Yorker Magazine, Inc.

Write your answer in the space provided.

27. The cartoon is set in the United States. How do you know that Americans can get foods from other cultures?

_____

Circle the number of the best answer.

28. What inference can be made from the cartoon?

    (1) The man likes and always wants to eat foods from other cultures.

    (2) The man may enjoy foods from other cultures but sometimes prefers food from his own culture.

    (3) The man eats only American food.

    (4) The man does not like Japanese food.

    (5) People do not easily accept food from other cultures.

Check your answers on pages 209–210.

INVENTORY
Correlation Chart

Social Studies

The chart below will help you determine your strengths and weaknesses in the five content areas of social studies.

Directions

Circle the number of each item that you answered correctly on the Inventory. Count the number of items you answered correctly in each row. Write the amount in the Total Correct space in each row. (For example, in the Geography row, write the number correct in the blank before *out of 5*). Complete this process for the remaining rows. Then add the 5 totals to get your Total Correct for the whole 28-item Inventory.

Content Areas	Items	Total Correct	Pages
Geography (Pages 12–41)	1, 2 3, 4, 5	_____ out of 5	Pages 14–19 Pages 20–25
History (Pages 42–89)	6, 7, 8 9, 10, 11	_____ out of 6	Pages 50–55 Pages 80–85
Economics (Pages 90–125)	12, 13, 14 15, 16, 17, 18	_____ out of 7	Pages 104–109 Pages 116–121
Political Science (Pages 126–161)	19, 20, 21 22, 23	_____ out of 5	Pages 140–145 Pages 146–151
Behavioral Science (Pages 162–197)	24, 25, 26 27, 28	_____ out of 5	Pages 164–169 Pages 188–193
TOTAL CORRECT FOR INVENTORY _____ **out of 28**			

If you answered fewer than 25 items correctly, look more closely at the five content areas of social studies listed above. In which areas do you need more practice? Page numbers to refer to for practice are given in the right-hand column above.

Unit 1

GEOGRAPHY

The World

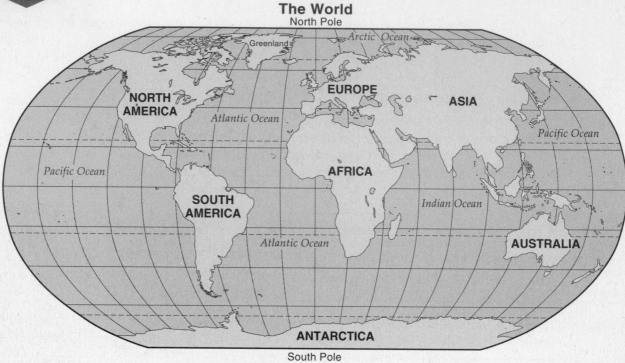

Geography is the study of Earth's surface. It includes how people use Earth and its resources. Geographers try to understand the relationship between people and places on Earth. When studying a place, geographers ask five main questions: Where is it? What does it look like? How have people changed it? How is the place linked to other places? And finally, how can the place be grouped with other places to form regions?

Geographers have learned that changes are always occurring in the environment of a place. Some changes are due to natural causes. An earthquake or a windstorm can instantly change the land. Most changes, however, are the result of human activities. These are the things people do or fail to do. Geographers realized that a change in one part of an environment affects all of the other parts of that environment.

Today, changes in one part of the world can affect people living in distant places. People all over the world depend on one another more than ever before. They trade goods, such as food or machines, with one another. They exchange ideas, too.

Geographers rely on many people for help. Explorers are among those who help geographers. They take notes and draw maps as they travel. Early explorers often took along artists to draw pictures of what they saw. Since the late 1800s, explorers have been taking photographs.

One of the most famous explorers was Robert E. Peary. He led many trips north to the Arctic, assisted by Matthew Henson. In 1891, Peary explored northern Greenland. He proved that it is an island. In 1898, Peary set out to find the North Pole. On that trip, he came within 390 miles of the pole. But he did not reach it. Hardships forced Peary to turn back.

In 1905, Peary tried again. He came within 200 miles of the pole. This time storms forced him to go home. However, Peary refused to give up. In 1908, he set out for the North Pole one more time. He was accompanied by Henson, his assistant, and four Eskimos. Finally Peary was successful. On April 6, 1909, Peary and his group reached the North Pole. They had traveled as far north as anyone can go on Earth.

For many years, people thought that Peary had figured his location incorrectly. They thought he had not really reached the North Pole. In 1989, a group of explorers used Peary's notes to retrace his route. They proved Peary and his group were the first to reach the North Pole.

Robert E. Peary

This unit features articles about geography and the work of geographers.

■ The article about regions describes how places are grouped into regions. It shows the ways people use the resources of one region.

■ The climate article focuses on how location on Earth determines climate.

■ The oil spill article explains how the parts of an environment are linked.

■ The article about the Middle East discusses the value of certain resources.

Geographic Regions

Setting the Stage

The Great Plains stretch from Canada through the United States as far south as Texas. In the early 1800s, people thought of the Great Plains as the Great American Desert. However, different groups of people have been eager to live there. Each group has valued the Great Plains for different reasons.

Past: What you already know

You may already know something about the Great Plains. Write two things you already know.

1. _____

2. _____

Present: What you learn by previewing

When **previewing** an article, look it over quickly to find out what it is about. Do not read it. Instead, look at headings, pictures, and maps to get an idea of what the article is about. Write the headings from the article on pages 15–17 below. The first one is done for you.

The Great Plains

Vegetation and Climate
_____

3. _____

4. _____

5. _____

What does the map on page 15 show?

6. _____

Future: Questions to answer

Write two questions you expect this article to answer.

7. _____

8. _____

Check your answers on page 210.

The Great Plains

As you read each section, circle the words you don't know. Look up the meanings.

The Great Plains are one of six regions within the United States. A **region** is an area that is different in some way from the places around it. There are no real lines that mark where one region ends and another begins. However, a region may be set apart by climate, vegetation, or natural boundaries. It may also be distinguished by the culture of the people who live there or by the way they earn their living.

Vegetation and Climate

Vegetation can define a region. **Vegetation** is the plant life that grows naturally in an area. For example, thick forests cover much of the eastern regions in the United States. These forests slowly give way to a huge prairie. A **prairie** is a large area covered with tall, thick grass. Farther west, the land gets higher and the grass becomes shorter. Here the Great Plains region begins. The Great Plains are a kind of dry grassland known as a **steppe**. The grass grows in short, thin clumps. Still farther west, the Rocky Mountains form a natural boundary to the Great Plains region.

Average Yearly Rainfall in the Continental United States

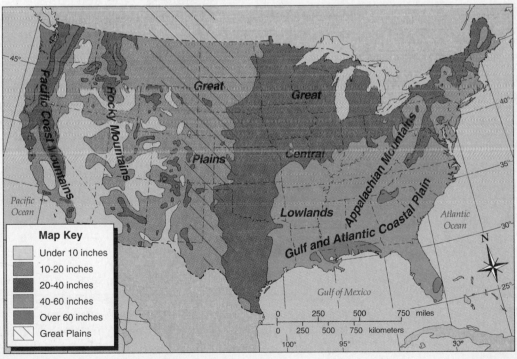

Map Key
- Under 10 inches
- 10-20 inches
- 20-40 inches
- 40-60 inches
- Over 60 inches
- Great Plains

Reading a Map Key. To study a map, look at the title first. Then look for the *map key*. Maps use symbols to tell about places. Symbols can be lines, dots, colors, or pictures. The map key explains what each symbol means.

Look at the map key above. How much rain falls on the Great Plains each

year? _____

Applying Your Skills and Strategies

Check your answer on page 210.

The vegetation of a region depends on its climate. **Climate** is the usual weather of a region over a long period of time. The climate of the Great Plains includes hot summers and long, cold winters. Drying winds blow across the open spaces all year long. Trees will not grow unless they receive at least 20 inches of rainfall each year. The Great Plains receive 10–20 inches of rain per year. That is enough water to support only a few trees.

Culture: Hunters on the Plains

Native Americans were the first people to live on the Great Plains. Although they did some farming, Native Americans on the Great Plains were mainly hunters. They traveled the grasslands in search of buffalo. They used the buffalo for more than food. They used the hides for shelter, clothing, bedding, cooking pots, and even boats. They made weapons and tools from buffalo horns and bones.

Until the 1500s, Native Americans hunted on foot. Then Spanish explorers brought horses to the Americas. In time, some of the horses broke loose and began to wander freely on the plains. Over the years, Native Americans learned to tame and ride the wild horses. As a result, their way of life began to change. Many tribes gave up farming and hunted all year long. With horses, the hunters could keep up with the buffalo. As long as herds of buffalo thundered across the open grasslands, the Native Americans thrived.

Finding the Main Idea.   One way to make sure you understand what you read is to find the main idea of each paragraph. A paragraph is a group of sentences about one main idea or topic. The main idea usually is stated in one sentence, called a *topic sentence.* The topic sentence covers all the points made in the paragraph.

Applying Your Skills and Strategies

The topic sentence of the paragraph above has been underlined. Underline the topic sentence in the first paragraph under the heading *Culture: Hunters on the Plains.*

Then in the 1860s, railroad workers began to lay tracks across the plains. Herds of buffalo blocked the trains. So, many railroad companies hired hunters to keep the animals away from their rail lines. Between 1870 and 1885, the hunters killed over 10 million buffalo. Many Native Americans did not have enough to eat.

Economics: Ranchers on the Plains

Once the railroads were built, a number of people saw a chance to get rich. The Spanish explorers brought cattle as well as horses to the Americas. These cattle also ran wild on the plains. In the West, cattle were worth only a few dollars apiece. In eastern cities, however, the cattle could be sold for as much as $40 each.

Check your answer on page 210.

Ranchers rounded up the cattle and branded them. A **brand** is a mark burned onto an animal to show who owns it. Once the cattle were branded, they were allowed to roam freely. By the 1880s, the Great Plains were crowded with hungry cattle. Ranchers did not worry about the crowding until the summer of 1886. That summer, cattle ate the grasslands bare. The next winter was one of the worst ever. One blizzard after another swept across the plains.

Economics: Farmers on the Plains

In the 1860s, the United States government offered Americans free land on the plains. Although many people took advantage of the offer, few succeeded with farming. Then in the 1880s, new inventions made farming on the plains a little easier. One of the new tools was a plow with steel blades. Earlier plows were not sharp enough to break through hard, dry earth. Giant power drills made a difference, too. Some farmers had to dig wells as deep as 800 feet to find water for their crops. To reach so far underground, farmers needed metal drills. Windmills were used to pump the water to the surface.

Heavy rains washed away the soil. Droughts killed crops, and strong winds blew away the rich topsoil. Many farmers left the plains.

Farmers who stayed on the Great Plains learned how to **conserve** land and water. *Conserve* means to "use wisely." The farmers learned to **irrigate** their fields. They dug canals to bring water to their crops. With irrigation, they could plant trees to hold the soil in place. They also learned to make good use of what little rain they got. They plowed their fields at least a foot deep in the fall and then replowed their fields in the spring. This way a fine dust formed on top of the soil and kept it from drying out quickly.

In the 1930s, scientists discovered an aquifer beneath the Great Plains. An **aquifer** is a huge underground lake. Farmers could not use the water from the aquifer on their fields until the 1940s. Then engineers developed special pumps to tap the underground water.

Today no one thinks of the Great Plains as a desert. The best land in the region is covered with fields of wheat and other grains. The farms and ranches of the Great Plains have helped make the United States a world leader in farming.

Thinking About the Article

Fill in the blank with the word or words that best complete each statement.

1. An area of land that is different from the places around it is called a

   _____.

2. The Great Plains are a kind of dry grassland known as a

   _____.

3. Farmers learned how to _____, or use their land and water wisely.

4. Hot summers and long, cold winters are a part of the _____ of the Great Plains.

5. A huge underground lake called an _____ was discovered beneath the Great Plains in the 1930s.

Write your answers in the space provided.

6. Review the questions you wrote on page 14. Did the article answer your questions? If you said *yes*, write the answers. If your questions were not answered, write two things you learned from this article.

   _____

   _____

   _____

   _____

7. According to the article, why do so few trees grow on the Great Plains?

   _____

   _____

   _____

8. Reread the paragraph on page 17 that begins, "In the 1860s. . . ." What are the three new tools that made farming on the plains a little easier?

   _____

   _____

   _____

Check your answers on page 210.

9. Name two ways that farmers on the Great Plains learned to conserve land and water.

_____

_____

_____

Circle the number of the best answer.

10. Which of the following statements is supported by the article?

   (1) People cannot live on the Great Plains.

   (2) The invention of new tools and machines helped people live on the Great Plains.

   (3) The Great Plains is still a desert.

   (4) Varying amounts of rainfall make it impossible to live on the Great Plains.

   (5) The discovery of the aquifer helped farmers in the 1930s.

Write your answers in the space provided.

11. What event or group of events do you think changed life on the Great Plains the most?

_____

_____

_____

_____

_____

12. Have you ever visited the Great Plains? If you have, did this article describe what you saw? If you haven't, describe how you would expect the Great Plains to look.

_____

_____

_____

_____

_____

Section 2

Climatic Regions

Setting the Stage

Sun, water, and wind shape the weather. Weather can change from day to day or in just a few minutes. Climate changes far more slowly. Climate is the weather a place has over a long period of time. Many different factors determine a region's climate.

Past: What you already know

You may already know something about climate. Write two things you already know.

1. _____

2. _____

Present: What you learn by previewing

When previewing an article, look it over quickly to find out what it is about. Do not read it. Instead look at headings, pictures, and maps to get an idea of what the article is about. Write the headings from the article on pages 21–23 below. The first one is done for you.

Factors Determining Climate

The Equator and Climate _____

3. _____

4. _____

What does the map on page 22 show?

5. _____

Future: Questions to answer

Write two questions you expect this article to answer.

6. _____

7. _____

                    Check your answers on page 211.

Factors Determining Climate

*As you read each
section, circle the
words you don't
know. Look up the
meanings.*

The world can be divided into many different climatic regions. Each climatic region is determined by its location on Earth. A region's distance from the equator makes a difference. The **equator** is an imaginary circle exactly halfway between the North and South poles. Nearness to large bodies of water also affects climate. The kinds of winds that blow across the region make a difference, too. Nearby mountain ranges also make a difference.

The Equator and Climate

At the equator, the sun shines almost directly overhead every day of the year. These direct rays produce warm temperatures. The amount of sunlight a place gets depends on its latitude. **Latitude** is the distance from the equator. It is measured in degrees. Places near the North or South poles are the farthest from the equator. They get very little sunlight.

Earth makes one complete circle, or **revolution**, around the sun each year. Earth tilts slightly as it revolves. That tilt causes the changes in seasons. Earth is always tilted $23\frac{1}{2}°$. So the farthest point to the north receiving direct sunlight lies at latitude $23\frac{1}{2}°$ N. The farthest point to the south receiving direct sunlight is latitude $23\frac{1}{2}°$ S. The region between those two lines is often called the **tropics**, or the low latitudes. The tropics receive the sun's most direct rays. So most places in the tropics have a warm climate.

Identifying Details. A paragraph is a group of sentences about one main idea or topic. Details, or small pieces of information, explain or support the main idea. The main idea in the first paragraph under the heading *The Equator and Climate* is "The amount of sunlight a place gets depends on its latitude." List one detail from the paragraph that supports that main idea. As you read, continue to look for details that support main ideas.

*Applying
Your Skills
and
Strategies*

_____

_____

_____

Regions with high latitudes are located near the North and South poles. These two regions have **polar climates**. Both regions receive no sunlight at all for part of the year. They get only slanting rays the rest of the year. As a result, the climate of the polar regions is cold all year, with very short summers.

Check your answer on page 211.

Between the tropics and the polar regions are the middle latitudes. These two regions have **temperate climates**. *Temperate* means "mild." So temperatures in the temperate climates are cooler than those in the tropics. But they are warmer than those in the polar regions. However, temperatures in the temperate climates are not always mild. They can vary greatly from place to place and from season to season.

Water and Wind

Latitude explains why Alaska is colder than Florida. It does not explain why winters in southern Alaska are often warmer than winters in Montana. The reason is that southern Alaska borders the Pacific Ocean. In contrast, Montana lies inland.

Oceans and large lakes keep temperatures mild. These large bodies of water do not gain or lose heat as quickly as land areas. In summer, ocean water stays cold long after the land has grown warm. Large bodies of water also hold the summer's heat as the land cools. The temperature of the water affects the air above it. So winds blowing over the water cool the land in summer. They warm the land in winter. As a result, places near an ocean or large lake have mild temperatures.

The climate in southern Alaska is mild for another reason as well. It is warmed by an ocean current. A **current** is water in motion. It is like a river in the ocean. Some ocean currents carry warm water, while others are very cold. A warm current flows along the coast of southern Alaska. Without it, southern Alaska would be icebound all winter.

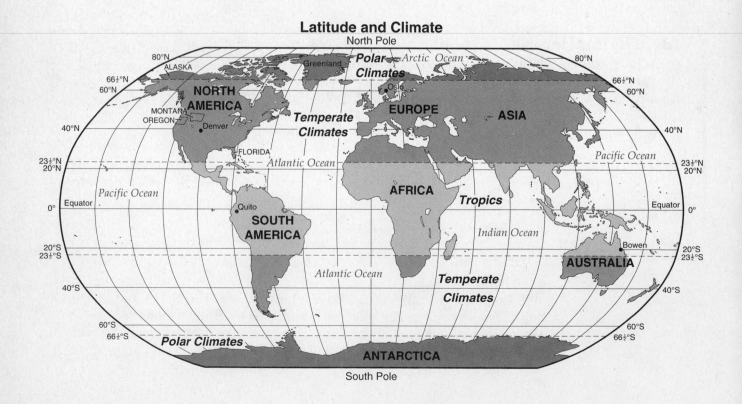

Latitude and Climate

Using Latitude. Many maps have two sets of lines. These lines cross each other to form the squares of a grid. They are used to locate places on Earth. *Parallels of latitude* measure distances from the equator in degrees (°). The equator lies at latitude 0°. All other parallels are labeled *N* or *S*. This shows whether they lie north or south of the equator. Lines of *longitude*, or *meridians*, reach from pole to pole. These lines measure distances to the east and west.

Applying Your Skills and Strategies

Look at the map on page 22. Write the name of the city that lies closest to the

following lines of latitude. 40° N _____ 0° _____

20° S _____ 60° N _____

A climate affected by an ocean is called a **marine climate**. Places with a marine climate, like southern Alaska, have warmer temperatures than their latitude suggests. Montana has a **continental climate** since it's found inland, away from large bodies of water. The winds are very cold in winter and very hot in summer.

Winds blowing over large bodies of water often bring moist air to nearby land. Dry winds tend to blow across land. So southern Alaska gets far more rain than Montana.

Mountains and Climate

Elevation is the height of the land. Mountains have the highest elevation on Earth. Mountains affect climate. They can make a difference to both temperature and rainfall. This is because air cools as it rises. So, temperatures at the top of a mountain are much colder than temperatures at the bottom of the mountain. Some mountains along the equator are snowcapped all year long. The most important factor in a mountain, or **highland climate** is elevation, not latitude.

Mountains can also affect the climate in other places. Mountains in the western United States block mild winds coming from the Pacific Ocean. Places like Montana lie east of the mountains. They have colder winters and hotter summers than places along the coast.

Mountains also influence rainfall. In Oregon, for example, there are mountains near the coast. They keep the Pacific Ocean's moist winds from reaching places farther east. These winds rise as they hit the western slopes of the mountains. As the air rises, it cools. Cold air cannot hold as much moisture as warm air. So clouds form and drop water on the western slopes of the mountains. By the time the winds reach the eastern slopes, they are dry.

Many factors determine the climate of a place. They include latitude, nearness to large bodies of water, winds, and elevation. The climate in which people live affects their way of life. Climate influences their choice of housing, food, and clothing.

Thinking About the Article

Fill in the blank with the word or words that best complete each statement.

1. An imaginary circle that is halfway between the North and South poles is called the _____ .

2. The flow of an ocean _____ helps warm southern Alaska.

3. Distances from the equator are measured by _____ .

4. Climates affected by an ocean are called _____ climates.

5. Places located inland, far from an ocean or large lake, have a

   _____ climate.

6. The height of the land is known as its _____ .

Write your answers in the space provided.

7. Review the questions you wrote on page 20. Did the article answer your questions? If you said *yes*, write the answers. If your questions were not answered, write three things you learned from this article.

   _____

   _____

   _____

   _____

   _____

8. According to the article, why do different parts of the world have different climates?

   _____

   _____

   _____

   _____

   _____

9. Reread the third paragraph under the heading *Mountains and Climate*. Explain why places on one side of a mountain range get more rain than places on the other side.

_____

_____

_____

_____

Circle the number of the best answer.

10. Which of the following explains why most places in the tropics have a warm climate?

 (1) nearness to the high latitudes

 (2) moist winds from the ocean

 (3) not enough sunlight

 (4) warm ocean current

 (5) direct rays from the sun

11. Which factor explains why southern Alaska has milder temperatures than Montana?

 (1) latitude

 (2) marine climate

 (3) continental climate

 (4) varying amounts of rainfall

 (5) elevation

Write your answer in the space provided.

12. What factor or factors best explain the climate where you live? Write your answer in complete sentences.

_____

_____

_____

_____

Check your answers on page 211.

Section

3

Rescuing an Environment

Setting the Stage

On March 24, 1989, an oil tanker struck a reef in Prince William Sound. The sound is a large body of water connected to the Gulf of Alaska. The ship tore open. Over 11 million gallons of oil spilled into the sea. Many people rushed to Alaska. They wanted to clean up the oil spill and save the wildlife.

Past: What you already know

You may already know something about the Alaskan oil spill. Write two things you already know.

1. _____

2. _____

Present: What you learn by previewing

Write the headings from the article on pages 27–29 below.

Oil Spill in Alaska

3. _____

4. _____

5. _____

What does the map on page 28 show?

6. _____

_____

Future: Questions to answer

Write three questions you expect this article to answer.

7. _____

8. _____

9. _____

Check your answers on page 211.

Oil Spill in Alaska

*As you read each
section, circle the
words you don't
know. Look up the
meanings.*

Prince William Sound is a type of environment. An **environment**
is all of the living and nonliving things that make a place. Thousands of
plants and animals live in the sound and along its shores. Plants, animals,
and people are the living parts of that environment. Soil, rocks, water, and
the glaciers that line the coast are the nonliving parts. **Glaciers** are huge
masses of ice that flow slowly over land.

Every part of an environment is closely tied to all other parts. This
was clearly seen when oil spilled into the Prince William Sound. The spill
had far-reaching effects on the environment of the sound. The effects of
the oil spill showed how the parts of this environment were linked.

Before the oil spill, people shared Prince William Sound with many
types of wildlife. Many of these people fished for their living. Others
worked in the tourist industry. Thousands of tourists visited parks,
forests, and wildlife refuges near the sound.

Some people who lived along the sound were involved in the oil
industry. They stored and shipped oil. The Alaskan pipeline brought oil
from Alaska's North Slope to Valdez. Valdez is a small port on Prince
William Sound. Over 70 huge tankers arrived there each month. They
carried the oil to other parts of the United States.

Using the Glossary or Dictionary. When you read, you may see
words you do not understand. Circle any words you do not know. Look up the
meanings of words in dark print in the glossary at the back of the book.
Other unfamiliar words can be found in a dictionary.

*Applying
Your Skills
and
Strategies*

Circle all of the words in dark print in this article. Write their definitions on
your own paper. Then look up any other words you do not know. Write their
definitions on your own paper, too.

Disaster in Prince William Sound

It was Thursday evening, March 23, 1989. An oil tanker called the
Exxon Valdez left port. The ship had a five-day run to Long Beach,
California. Shortly after midnight, the ship turned sharply to avoid an
iceberg. An **iceberg** is a huge block of ice that has broken off from a
glacier.

The tanker missed the iceberg but hit a reef. The smell of untreated
oil, called **crude oil**, filled the air. The ship was leaking. By dawn on
March 24, an oil slick had formed. A thick oily film now covered six square
miles of Prince William Sound. By early evening, about ten million gallons
of oil were in the sound. The oil slick stretched over 18 square miles.

Check your answers on page 211.

Within days, wind and water carried the oil farther into the sound. Then a storm hit just four days after the spill. High winds and strong waves carried the oil into tiny inlets and coves. After the storm, the oil slick covered 500 square miles. And it was still growing. By this time the oil spill had polluted over 1,100 miles of coastline. It was a serious threat to the coastal environment.

The Cleanup

The oil spill in Prince William Sound was huge. No one had ever cleaned up a spill that large. So no one knew exactly what to do. The Exxon Corporation played a leading role in the cleanup. It owned the *Exxon Valdez*. The company that managed the pipeline also took some responsibility for the cleanup. So did the state of Alaska, the Coast Guard, and several United States government agencies. But it was not always clear who was in charge. As a result, sometimes the cleanup effort did more harm than good.

The Alaskan Oil Spill

The cleanup crews tried everything they could think of to remove the spilled oil. They tried to contain the spill using floating barriers called booms. Then they set the oil on fire. Crews also tried to skim the oil from the water. They wanted to transfer it to barges. Some experts wanted to spray the sound with chemicals. These chemicals act much like a detergent. They would speed up the natural process of breaking the oil into tiny droplets. Some scientists think the sound should have been sprayed right away. They believe cleanup crews could have stopped the spill before it reached the coastline.

Why didn't Exxon use chemicals? One reason is that the company did not have enough of the chemicals. They could not treat the whole spill. Another reason is that state and federal officials were slow to permit the spraying. By the time everyone was ready to act, it was too late. The storm had begun. The storm caused the spill to spread far beyond Prince William Sound.

Many workers continued to clean up the oil spill from the water. But other workers attacked the spill on the beaches. Some crews tried to blast the oil from rocks. They sprayed the beaches with hot water. This did more damage than the oil had done. The hot water killed some wildlife. It also sent oil deep into the gravel beaches. Then workers were not able to reach the oil. Other crews had better luck spraying a fertilizer mix on some beaches. The fertilizer encouraged the growth of bacteria that eat oil.

Workers rescued some of the many fish, birds, and animals from the oil. They also protected several fish hatcheries. Most important of all, they managed to unload the remaining oil from the tanker. They did this without dumping more oil into the sound. However, crews were not able to clean up all of the oil spill. Workers recovered only about twenty percent of the oil that coated the shoreline. They recovered less than ten percent of the oil from the sound itself.

Using a Map Scale.   A map is always much smaller than the area it shows. You can figure out real distances by using the *map scale*. Find the scale on the map on page 28. It shows the distance on the map that equals 150 miles. Place the edge of a piece of paper on the map between Valdez and Kodiak on Kodiak Island. Make a mark at each location on the edge of the paper. To measure this distance, see how many times the map scale will fit between the two marks. Multiply that number times 150. What is the distance between these two areas?

Applying Your Skills and Strategies

The Effects of the Oil Spill

Just after the oil spill, many people believed that Prince William Sound was dead. They did not think wildlife would ever return to the sound. Yet less than a year later, the air and water were clear again. Fish and whales that had survived the spill returned to the sound. They came back the next spring just as they always did. Plants sprouted again as well.

Although the sound was not dead, the environment had changed. In April 1991, the United States government issued a report. It was based on scientific studies of Prince William Sound. These studies show that the oil spill continues to affect the sound. Many populations of sea birds have not recovered from the spill. Scientists say their recovery will take from twenty to seventy years. Injuries to other wildlife are just beginning to show up. The studies also show that some oil is still there. It is at the bottom of the sound. That oil is still hurting marine life.

Alaskans want people to learn from what happened to Prince William Sound. No one person caused the mess. We are all responsible for the environment. So we must take steps to protect it. One Alaskan says, "The environment is a reflection of who we are. We can't ignore the reflection we see. We have to live with it—today, tomorrow, and forever."

Thinking About the Article

Fill in the blank with the word or words that best complete each statement.

1. An _____ consists of the living and nonliving things that make a place.

2. _____ are huge blocks of ice that fall into the sea.

3. Oil that has not been treated is called _____.

4. A huge mass of ice that moves slowly across land is known as a

   _____.

Write your answers in the space provided.

5. Review the questions you wrote on page 26. Did the article answer your questions? If you said *yes,* write the answers. If your questions were not answered, write three things you learned from this article.

   _____

   _____

   _____

   _____

   _____

6. Describe the environment of Prince William Sound before the oil spill.

   _____

   _____

7. What were two effects of the storm on the oil spill?

   _____

   _____

8. Why did the cleanup sometimes do more damage than the oil spill?

   _____

   _____

Check your answers on page 212.

9. What happened to the land around Prince William Sound as a result of the oil spill?

_____

_____

_____

Circle the number of the best answer.

10. Which of the following was not used as part of the cleanup effort at Prince William Sound?

   (1) The oil-covered beaches were sprayed with hot water.

   (2) A fertilizer mix was sprayed on the oil.

   (3) Oil was skimmed from the surface of the water.

   (4) Workers pushed the oil onto the beaches.

   (5) The oil was contained with booms and then set on fire.

11. Which of the following is an example of the way the oil spill changed Prince William Sound?

   (1) The oil-thick water of the sound killed many types of wildlife.

   (2) Huge blocks of ice fell into the sound.

   (3) Many types of wildlife lived in the sound.

   (4) Over seventy tankers used the harbor at Valdez.

   (5) Many people work in the fishing and tourist industries.

Write your answer in the space provided.

12. What did the Alaskan mean by saying, "The environment is a reflection of who we are?" How does your environment reflect who you and others in your community are?

_____

_____

_____

_____

_____

A Matter of Resources

Setting the Stage

In the early 1900s, people in the Middle East discovered the value of oil. That discovery has turned the Middle East into one of the richest regions in the world. Yet to the people of the region, oil has never been as valuable as water. Since ancient times, water has been the Middle East's most important resource.

Past: What you already know

You may already know something about the Middle East. Write two things you already know.

1. _____

2. _____

Present: What you learn by previewing

Write the headings from the article on pages 33–35 below.

The Middle East

3. _____

4. _____

5. _____

What does the map on page 35 show?

6. _____

Future: Questions to answer

Write three questions you expect this article to answer.

7. _____

8. _____

9. _____

Check your answers on page 212.

The Middle East

As you read each section, circle the words you don't know. Look up the meanings.

The Middle East lies at the crossroads of three continents: Africa, Asia, and Europe. It was once thought of as a poor region. Today, some countries in the Middle East are among the richest in the world. The change is a result of the growing importance of oil from the Middle East. Oil is one of the most valuable resources in the world today. A **resource** is any part of an environment that people can use to meet their needs. Although rich in oil, the Middle East has a great shortage of water.

Water: A Scarce Resource

To help solve the water problem, countries of the Middle East are building **desalination plants**. In these plants, salt is taken out of seawater using special machines. Then the water can be used for drinking and watering crops. However, the machines are very expensive. Countries in the Middle East are willing to buy these machines anyway. This is because water is a scarce resource. It is in short supply.

Water supplies limit where people live in the Middle East. Very few people live in the desert. Those who do, live near an oasis. An **oasis** is a place in the desert with an underground spring for water. Most people in the Middle East live in river valleys and along the coast. However, only a few countries are lucky enough to have flowing rivers. Egypt has the Nile River. Over 90 percent of the Egyptian people live in the Nile River Valley. Most people in Syria and Iraq live between the Tigris and Euphrates rivers. But some parts of the Middle East don't have any lasting rivers or lakes. For example, part of Saudi Arabia is called the Empty Quarter. It does not have any water or people.

Getting Meaning from Context. As you read, you may come across unfamiliar words. You can often figure out their meaning from the *context*, or the rest of the words in the sentence. Find the word *scarce* in the second paragraph on this page. Use context to figure out the meaning of this word. Then write a definition for *scarce* in the space below.

Applying Your Skills and Strategies

_____

_____

Summers in the Middle East are very dry. It rains only in the winters, and even then, many places get very little rain. So people must make the most of what little water they have. They have developed many different tools and methods for getting and using water. Farmers **irrigate** their fields. They dig canals or build pipelines to carry water from rivers and wells to their fields. People in the region tap aquifers and other sources of underground water.

Check your answer on page 212.

Middle Easterners also dam their rivers. This way they can store water for use in the dry season. The largest of these dams is the Aswan High Dam in Egypt. Before the dam was built, the Nile River flooded every summer. Egyptian farmers would plant their crops in the fall. The land was too dry for farming during the rest of the year. Since the dam opened, the Nile River no longer floods. The dam traps the water in a large reservoir called Lake Nasser. Today, farmers have water whenever they need it. The dam also produces water power to make electricity for Egypt's factories.

The Aswan High Dam was very expensive to build. Other ideas for controlling the region's water supply are far less costly. Some are very old. Long ago, people farmed using a network of trenches and raised terraces. Terraces are large, flat steps of earth. Then people forgot about this method of farming for about 1,500 years.

About fifty years ago, a scientist decided to try this method of farming. He rebuilt some of the trenches and terraces in what is now Israel. It rained not long after he finished. It rarely rains in the desert. When it does rain, the water cannot soak into the hard ground. Most of the water runs off. The run-off washes away any loose soil from the hillsides. However, this time the rainwater and the loose soil ran into the scientist's trenches. The trenches brought the rainwater and loose soil down the hillsides to the terraces. The water collected on the terraces and soaked into the ground. The scientist called this method of farming run-off agriculture.

Many people did not believe this kind of farming would work in the desert. They thought it was impossible to collect enough water to grow crops. So the scientist tested the idea, and it worked. Today, some farmers in Israel use this method. They are able to grow fruits and vegetables in the desert.

Black Gold in the Desert

The Middle East has over 60 percent of the world's known oil reserves. This oil is mainly found in countries along the Persian Gulf. Saudi Arabia has 20 percent of the world's reserves. The United Arab Emirates, Iran, Iraq, and Kuwait each have 10 percent.

Reading a Resource Map.   A map can show the resources of a region. *Resource maps* use symbols to show where those resources are found. The map key tells the meaning of each symbol. Study the map on page 35. It shows that oil is the main mineral resource in the Middle East. List the other resources found in this region.

Applying Your Skills and Strategies

Check your answers on page 212.

People have known that there was oil in the Middle East for thousands of years. They noticed places where a sticky, black liquid seeped to the surface of the ground. But no one paid much attention to the oil then, since it had little value.

Today, oil is more valuable than gold. It is used to run machines, heat buildings, and fuel cars and airplanes. Oil and natural gas supply over half the world's energy needs. Oil is also used to make hundreds of different products, including plastic, asphalt, chemicals, paint, fertilizers, and even lipstick.

The oil-rich countries of the Middle East carefully watch their oil supplies. They know oil is a **nonrenewable resource**, so it will not last forever. These countries use some oil money to guard their future. They are building new factories that make products, such as cement, air conditioners, and toys.

Mineral Resources in the Middle East

Map Key
- Oil
- Natural Gas
- Iron
- Coal
- Phosphates

Resources and National Borders

Resources cross national borders in the Middle East. The people of Kuwait and Iraq drill oil from the same field. The people of Israel and Jordan pump water from the same aquifer. In fact, all of the countries in this region must share water supplies. A dam built in one country can affect a neighboring country.

Many people think that the Middle East can solve its water problems. They believe the countries must work together to manage the water resources. Some people in Turkey have suggested what they call a "peace pipeline." This pipeline would pump water from rivers in northern Turkey to dry lands farther south. Other people in the region have made a similar suggestion. They think Egypt should share the waters of the Nile River.

Thinking About the Article

Fill in the blank with the word or words that best complete each statement.

1. Water is a _____ that people use to meet their needs.

2. Oil is a _____ resource because once it is used up, it is gone forever.

3. A place in the desert that has water is called an _____.

4. Machines are used to remove salt from seawater at

    _____.

Write your answers in the space provided.

5. Review the questions you wrote on page 32. Did the article answer your questions? If you said *yes*, write the answers. If your questions were not answered, write three things you learned from this article.

    _____

    _____

    _____

    _____

    _____

6. Why wasn't oil considered a valuable resource before the early 1900s?

    _____

    _____

    _____

7. How does water affect life in the Middle East?

    _____

    _____

8. How has the Aswan High Dam changed Egypt?

    _____

    _____

Check your answers on page 212.

Circle the number of the best answer.

9. Which of the following best describes run-off agriculture?

   (1) loosening the soil to soak up the water

   (2) trenches direct rainwater to terraces

   (3) building a dam on a river to store water

   (4) producing water power for electricity

   (5) building irrigation ditches and canals

10. Which of the following is a reason that some countries in the Middle East are among the richest in the world?

    (1) Many new industries have been built in the Middle East.

    (2) Water is scarce throughout the region.

    (3) Oil is a nonrenewable resource.

    (4) The Middle East has over 60 percent of all the world's known oil reserves.

    (5) People in the Middle East have known about oil for thousands of years.

11. Which of the following is not yet a method for using water wisely in the Middle East?

    (1) building pipelines from rivers to dry areas

    (2) farming with run-off agriculture

    (3) pumping water from underground sources

    (4) using desalination plants

    (5) building dams for reservoirs

Write your answer in the space provided.

12. Some people fear the next war in the Middle East will be over water. Do you agree? Explain the reasons for your answer.

    _____

    _____

    _____

    _____

    _____

Unit 1 Review:
Geography

Earth Day

The first Earth Day was held on April 22, 1970. Over twenty million people gathered in parks throughout the United States. They wanted to change people's attitudes toward the environment. Earth Day 70 started an awareness of the need to protect the environment. This awareness quickly spread throughout the world.

In the 1970s, people in the United States and other countries called for new environmental laws. These people are called **environmentalists.** The laws protected wildlife, rivers, and lakes. The laws also controlled air pollution. By the 1980s, however, the laws were not always enforced. Many people were not as interested in the environment as they once were. As a result, people continued to abuse the environment.

So environmentalists organized Earth Day 90 for April 22, 1990. Over 200 million people gathered in 140 countries around the world. This time, they asked people to recycle waste and to save energy. They called for changes in the way the environment is used. Earth Day 70 called for a change in attitude. Earth Day 90 called for a change in behavior.

Circle the number of the best answer.

1. Which of the following <u>best</u> summarizes the article?

   (1) Environmentalists discuss the environment only on Earth Day.

   (2) There were no environmentalists before Earth Day 70.

   (3) Earth Day makes people more aware of their environment.

   (4) Environmentalists did not care about nature in the 1980s.

   (5) Earth Day 90 was a worldwide event.

2. What lesson did environmentalists learn from Earth Day 70?

   (1) It is best to focus only on passing new laws.

   (2) Laws are not important in solving environmental problems.

   (3) Environmentalists cannot change people's attitudes and behavior.

   (4) Environmentalists should focus on changing people's behavior.

   (5) Solving environmental problems requires people to change their attitudes and behavior.

Robert E. Peary Reaches the North Pole

Write your answers in the space provided.

3. Where did Robert E. Peary's final trip to the North Pole begin?

_____

4. What latitude did Peary reach on his trip in 1902?

_____

5. What latitude did Peary reach on his trip in 1906?

_____

Circle the number of the best answer.

6. Which of the following was the most important to Peary in terms of direction to the North Pole?

   (1) depth of the ocean

   (2) knowing his location in terms of latitude

   (3) weather conditions

   (4) knowing his location in relationship to Greenland

   (5) speed of travel

Go on to the next page.

The Geographic Regions of Texas

Texas is so large that geographers divide it into four regions. Each region has different resources. Those resources help make Texas one of the richest states in the country.

One region of Texas is called the Gulf Coastal Plain. It covers eastern and southern Texas. The climate in this region is warm and wet. Long ago forests covered the Gulf Coastal Plain. Today, much of the land has been cleared for farming and ranching. Farmers grow cotton, vegetables, rice, and fruit. Oil and natural gas are important resources of this region.

Another region of Texas is the North Central Plains. Here the climate is drier. Grasslands make up a large part of the North Central Plains. Ranchers graze cattle and sheep on the grasslands. Farmers in this region grow cotton. The North Central Plains are rich in resources such as coal, oil, and natural gas.

The Great Plains region is colder and drier than the other two regions. Farmers must irrigate their wheat fields. Irrigation also helps supply water to ranchers. Some of the richest oil fields in Texas lie beneath the Great Plains.

The Basin and Range region is the mountainous area in western Texas. Miners have found resources such as gold, copper, and silver in these mountains. Like the Great Plains, the climate is dry. Ranching and farming are possible only through the use of irrigation.

Circle the number of the best answer.

7. The farmers and ranchers of the Great Plains region of Texas use irrigation

    (1) as a way to get to the rich oil fields.

    (2) to help them find gold.

    (3) as a way to get to the natural gas.

    (4) to get water for their crops and animals.

    (5) to get water from other regions.

8. Which of the following best explains why Texas is divided into four regions?

    (1) Texas is one of the richest states.

    (2) Texas has different climates.

    (3) Texas has many resources.

    (4) Texas is large, with many resources throughout the state.

    (5) There are farms and ranches throughout Texas.

Top Ten Cattle-Ranching and Oil-Producing States

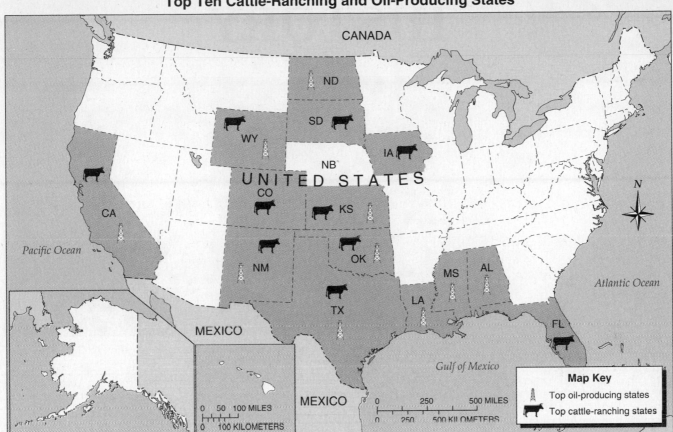

Write your answers in the space provided.

9. Which symbol on the map is used to show the top oil-producing states?

_____

10. Which symbol on the map is used to show the top cattle-ranching states?

_____

Circle the number of the best answer.

11. Which of the following cannot be determined from the map?

   (1) how many southern states are top oil producers

   (2) how many western states are top cattle producers

   (3) how much oil is produced in the top oil-producing states

   (4) how many states are the top producers of both oil and cattle

   (5) where the top cattle-producing states are located

HISTORY

Secretary of State Dick Cheney administers the oath of office to General Colin L. Powell, USA, Chairman, Joint Chiefs of Staff.

History is the study of the past. Historians try to understand the ways that people are connected to past events. In studying an event, historians ask: What happened? When did it happen? Why did it happen? What difference did it make? The last question is the most important. The past shapes who we are today and how we approach the future. Sometimes the ties between the past and the present are hard to see. At other times, the connections are very obvious.

On October 3, 1989, General Colin Powell made history. He became the first African American to head the Joint Chiefs of Staff. He is the nation's top military officer. It was General Powell who directed the war in the Persian Gulf in 1991. He has had a long and successful career in the army.

In 1936, when Powell was born, African-American soldiers usually served in all-black units under white commanding officers. Until World War II, very few African Americans had a chance to become officers. There were no African-American generals. Yet African Americans had fought bravely in every war in the nation's history, including the American Revolution. However, they did not have the same opportunities as other Americans. During the Civil War, African Americans had to fight for the right to join the army. Once they were in, they had to fight for equal pay. Over the years, African Americans have demanded equal rights in every part of American life. They have had many victories.

On October 6, 1940, B.O. Davis, Sr. became the first African-American general in the regular army. Powell was four years old at the time. He was a teen-ager in 1951 when the army disbanded the last all-black unit. By the time Powell joined the army, the military offered young African Americans more opportunities than businesses did. Powell made the most of that opportunity. When Powell speaks to students, he is careful to remind them the struggle is not over yet. He is aware that his success will open new opportunities for young men and women. Every generation opens doors for the next generation.

African-American troops training in Northern Ireland during World War II

This unit features articles about many events in history and the way they shape our lives.

■ The article about the North American colonies tells how people built a new life in a new land.

■ The American Revolution article focuses on the events that led to the fight for independence.

■ The article about the Civil War tells how African-American soldiers came to join the army and fight bravely.

■ The reform movement article tells how labor reformers fought for better working conditions and child labor laws.

■ Contributions by women and African Americans to the war effort are the focus of the article about World War II.

■ The article about the cold war focuses on the importance of freedom to people everywhere in the world.

■ The article about the Persian Gulf War in 1991 describes the participation of American troops in an Allied victory.

Section 5

English Colonies in North America

Setting the Stage

People from England built their first lasting settlement in North America in 1607. That first colony was located in Virginia. By 1700, there were hundreds of English towns and villages. They were located all along the Atlantic coast of North America.

Past: What you already know

You may already know something about English settlements in North America. Write three things you already know.

1. _____

2. _____

3. _____

Present: What you learn by previewing

Write the headings from the article on pages 45–47 below.

Establishing Colonies

4. _____

5. _____

6. _____

What does the map on page 46 show?

7. _____

Future: Questions to answer

Write three questions you expect this article to answer.

8. _____

9. _____

10. _____

Check your answers on page 213.

Establishing Colonies

As you read each section, circle the words you don't know. Look up the meanings.

Beginning in the 1500s, Europeans started colonies in the Americas. The Spanish were the first to build a colony across the ocean. A **colony** is a settlement or group of settlements far from the home country. **Colonists**, or settlers, are ruled by the home country. People in other European countries had watched Spain grow rich from its colonies. They wanted to share in that wealth. By 1600, other European countries were planning colonies of their own. England was one of these countries.

In 1606, a group of people in England went to talk to King James. They asked for permission to start a colony in North America. The group called itself the London Company. Each person joined by buying stock, or shares, in the company. The stockholders shared the profits and the risks. They knew that building a colony was expensive and risky. Others had tried to build colonies in North America. They had failed. They had lost large sums of money. Some had even lost their lives.

King James told the London Company to found, or establish, a colony in a part of North America now called Virginia. The stockholders offered people free passage to Virginia. In return, these people had to work for the company for seven years. The settlers had many jobs. Their most important job was to search for valuable items. Then the company would sell these for a profit in Europe. The first colonists—144 men and boys— sailed from England in December 1606.

Sequencing Events. The sequence of events is the order in which things happen. Words like *first, second, next,* and *finally* provide clues to the order of events. Look for specific dates, too. Reread the first paragraph of this article. List at least two words or phrases that provide clues to the order of events.

Applying Your Skills and Strategies

A Colony in Virginia

After 18 weeks at sea, the colonists entered Chesapeake Bay on April 26, 1607. From there they sailed up a deep river. Within a few days, the colonists had reached a small peninsula. A **peninsula** is a piece of land surrounded on three sides by water. They built a settlement and called it "King James His Towne" in honor of King James. The name was later shortened to Jamestown.

The settlement was on low, swampy land. Mosquitoes spread disease. The water was not safe to drink. Within six months, half of the settlers were dead. By then, it was almost winter. The food the colonists had brought with them was nearly gone. Everyone had been too busy searching for gold to plant crops.

Captain John Smith decided that Jamestown needed a strong leader. He took charge of the colony. He ordered the settlers to clear land and plant crops. The settlers needed food while they waited for the first harvest. So Smith traded with nearby Native-American villages for food. By 1609, life in Jamestown was getting better. That summer, a ship came to Jamestown with more colonists. When the ship returned to England in the fall, Smith was on board. He had been injured in a gunpowder explosion.

Now the colony was without a leader. To make matters worse, there was not enough food. That winter the colonists ate dogs, cats, snakes, toadstools, and horsehides. By spring, only 60 settlers were still alive. They were about to give up and return to England, when two ships arrived. On board were 300 settlers, fresh supplies, and a new governor. The new governor forced the colonists to stay and try again.

Although the governor kept Jamestown going, the colony was still not making money. The colonists had not found any gold or silver. So they had to find something else that they could sell abroad. It had to be something of high value. It also had to be something that Europeans wanted but could not produce themselves. In 1611, a farmer named John Rolfe arrived in Jamestown. He had a solution to the problem.

English Voyages to North America

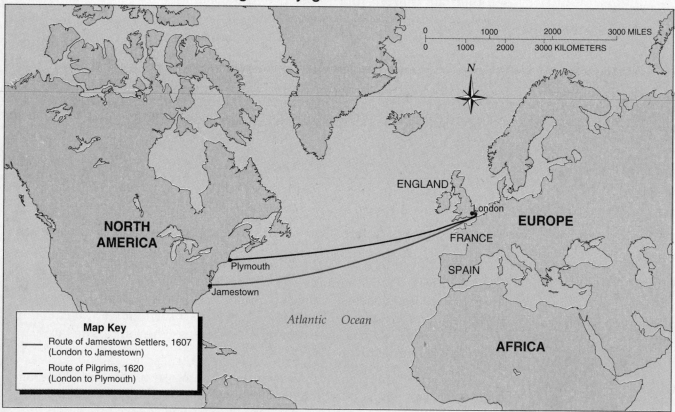

Map Key
— Route of Jamestown Settlers, 1607 (London to Jamestown)
— Route of Pilgrims, 1620 (London to Plymouth)

Rolfe thought that tobacco would grow well in Virginia. After some experimenting, he sent a shipment to England in 1614. Although the king called it a "stinking weed," Europeans were eager to buy it. Jamestown finally had a cash crop. A **cash crop** is grown to sell rather than to feed a farmer's family.

Reading a Historical Map. A map can show the routes taken by ships. The title of the map tells which voyage the map shows. Use the key to identify each route. Then trace each route from beginning to end. What two journeys does the map on page 46 show?

Applying Your Skills and Strategies

_____

_____

A Colony in Massachusetts

In September 1620, a number of families left England for Virginia. After two months at sea, the colonists reached Cape Cod in what is now Massachusetts. They had not landed in Virginia because the ship had blown off course. The group decided to stay where they were, rather than sail on to Virginia. These new colonists saw themselves as pilgrims. A **pilgrim** is someone who makes a long journey for religious reasons. These colonists left England because they were not free to practice their religion.

The Pilgrims moved quickly to build a settlement. They called it Plymouth, after the town in England from which they had sailed. Winter was coming, so they hurried to gather food and build houses. However, the cold weather arrived before the Pilgrims were ready. They did not have enough food. Their clothes did not keep them warm enough. The Pilgrims realized winters in Massachusetts were colder than winters in England.

Nearly half of the Pilgrims were dead by spring. Those who survived refused to give up. They worked together to clear land and plant crops. They got help from Native Americans, who taught them how to grow corn and trap animals for fur. The Pilgrims ate part of the corn and fed the rest to their animals. They sold the furs in England. The Pilgrims never got rich, but they did survive in their new home.

More Colonies

Jamestown and Plymouth were England's first two lasting settlements in what is now the United States. In the 1600s, the English built a number of other colonies along the East Coast of North America. By 1700, about 250,000 people lived in these English colonies. By 1775, the population was $2\frac{1}{2}$ million. The English were finding that North America was a land of opportunity.

Check your answers on page 213.

Thinking About the Article

Fill in the blank with the word or words that best complete each statement.

1. Jamestown was a _____ , or settlement, far from England but under English rule.

2. A _____ is land surrounded by water on three sides.

3. The English who traveled far from home for religious reasons to found

   Plymouth were _____ .

4. Tobacco is a _____ that is sold for money.

Write your answers in the space provided.

5. Review the questions you wrote on page 44. Did the article answer your questions? If you said *yes*, write the answers. If your questions were not answered, write three things you learned from this article.

   _____

   _____

   _____

   _____

   _____

6. Why was tobacco a valuable crop to the people of Jamestown?

   _____

   _____

7. How was the first winter in Plymouth like the first winter in Jamestown?

   _____

   _____

   _____

   _____

    Check your answers on pages 213–214.

Circle the number of the best answer.

8. Jamestown was founded

   (1) before the London Company was started.

   (2) after Plymouth was founded.

   (3) during the 1500s.

   (4) after the London Company got the approval of King James.

   (5) after John Rolfe arrived.

9. Which of the following is a reason for Jamestown's success?

   (1) Captain John Smith traded with Native Americans for food.

   (2) The colonists spent much of their time hunting for gold.

   (3) Tobacco grown in Virginia could be sold in Europe.

   (4) The London Company was interested in making money.

   (5) Hundreds of people in England wanted to settle in Virginia.

10. Which of the following is <u>not</u> true of the colony founded in what is now Massachusetts?

   (1) The colonists left England in 1620 for the colony.

   (2) The colony was abandoned the year after it was founded.

   (3) Plymouth was the name of the new colony.

   (4) The colonists there considered themselves pilgrims.

   (5) Winters in Massachusetts were colder than those in England.

Write your answer in the space provided.

11. Suppose you were asked to choose people to become colonists in North America. What qualities would you want the people to have? What skills would the people need?

   _____

   _____

   _____

   _____

   _____

   _____

Section 6

The American Revolution

Setting the Stage

Beginning in 1763, England wanted more control over its North American colonies. So Parliament became more involved in the governing of the colonies. The colonists did not welcome this new interest. They wanted to do things their own way. Parliament and the colonists disagreed about how the colonies should be governed. In time those disagreements led to a war known as the American Revolution.

Past: What you already know

You may already know something about the American Revolution. Write two things you already know.

1. _____

2. _____

Present: What you learn by previewing

Write the headings from the article on pages 51–53 below.

The Fight for Independence

3. _____

4. _____

5. _____

What does the timeline on page 52 show?

6. _____

Future: Questions to answer

Write three questions you expect this article to answer.

7. _____

8. _____

9. _____

Check your answers on page 214.

The Fight for Independence

As you read each section, circle the words you don't know. Look up the meanings.

In 1763, England won a long war with France. The American colonists were very happy to be part of England. However, within a few years, England and the English colonists in America would be at war.

Growing Disagreements

War costs money! Since the war with France was so costly, England was in debt. A **debt** is money that is owed. The government in England needed to raise more money. The only way to raise this money was through taxes. People in England were already paying high taxes. **Parliament**, England's group of lawmakers, had to do something. Parliament believed that the colonies had greatly benefited from England's victory over France. It felt that the colonists were not paying their fair share of English taxes.

Therefore, Parliament demanded that the old tax laws be enforced more strictly. In 1765, Parliament passed a new tax law called the Stamp Act. Under the Stamp Act, colonists had to buy special stamps. They used the stamps to buy things, such as marriage licenses and playing cards.

Identifying Cause and Effect.   Every event has at least one cause and one effect. The *cause* is *why* something happened. Words like *because, since,* and *reason* signal a cause. The *effect* tells *what happened* as a result of the cause. Words such as *so, therefore,* and *as a result* signal an effect. Reread the first two paragraphs under the heading *Growing Disagreements*. In the space below, write one cause and one effect of England's debt.

Applying Your Skills and Strategies

The colonists were angry when they heard about the new tax. In many colonies mobs forced tax collectors out of town. The colonists knew English law. They pointed out that people could not be taxed unless they were represented in Parliament. The colonists did not have representation in Parliament. Therefore they believed that Parliament did not have the right to tax them. They felt only a colony's legislature, or group of lawmakers, had that right.

Parliament said it represented everyone, including the colonists. But the colonists complained loudly. One year later Parliament **repealed,** or did away with, the Stamp Act. Colonists celebrated with bonfires and parades. However, Parliament still believed it had the right to tax the colonists. So in 1767 it passed a new law that taxed glass, lead, paper, silk, and tea.

All the colonies protested the new law. Some boycotted English goods that were taxed. When people **boycott** something, they refuse to buy it. England sent troops to the colonies to protect the tax collectors. The English troops also made sure the taxes were paid.

The colonists continued to get angry. The anger turned to bloodshed on March 5, 1770, in Boston, Massachusetts. What began as a group of colonists taunting an English soldier turned into the Boston Massacre. English troops killed three colonists and wounded eight others. Two of the wounded died later.

A Tea Party in Boston

A month later Parliament repealed all the taxes except the one on tea. It kept the tea tax to remind the colonists that Parliament had the right to tax them. The colonists responded to the tea tax by boycotting tea. So in 1773 Parliament passed a new law. This law kept the tax on tea but lowered its price.

Events That Led to the American Revolution

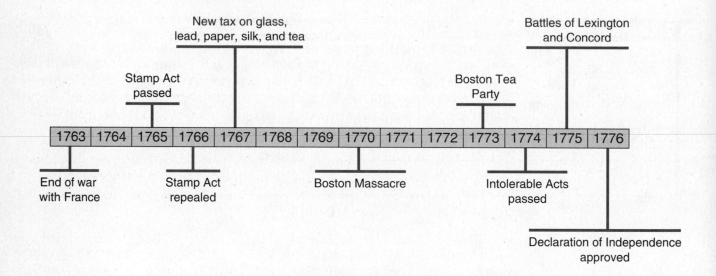

Parliament believed that the lower price of tea would cause the colonists to buy it again, even though it was taxed. To Parliament's surprise, there were more protests. On the night of December 16, 1773, a group of colonists in Boston dressed up like Native Americans. They boarded the English ships in Boston Harbor. They dumped more than three hundred chests of tea into the harbor. This event became known as the Boston Tea Party.

The English were outraged. In 1774, Parliament passed new laws to punish the colonists. One law closed Boston Harbor until the colonists paid for the tea. Another law had English governors rule the colonies instead of the colonial lawmakers. Still another law allowed English soldiers to use the colonists' homes. Colonists called the laws the Intolerable Acts. *Intolerable* means "unbearable."

Reading a Timeline. A *timeline* shows when a series of events took place. It also shows the order in which these events happened. It can be used to find the amount of time between events. Look at the timeline on page 52. What time period does it cover?

Applying Your Skills and Strategies

Because of the Intolerable Acts, representatives from 12 of the 13 colonies met in Philadelphia, Pennsylvania in 1774. That meeting was known as the First Continental Congress. The delegates at the meeting were still willing to remain part of England. But they wanted the harsh laws repealed. They also wanted Parliament to know it did not have the right to tax them. The delegates voted to meet again in May 1775. Before that meeting could be held, the American Revolution began.

The Battles of Lexington and Concord

Few colonists wanted a war, but they trained for battle. They called themselves minutemen. **Minutemen** could be ready to fight at a minute's notice.

The English also prepared for war. English troops in Massachusetts planned to capture two colonial leaders, John Hancock and Sam Adams. The English troops also wanted to take the military supplies the colonists had stored in the small town of Concord. Concord is about twenty miles from Boston.

Paul Revere and other colonists learned of the English plan. On the night of April 18, 1775, they rode ahead of the English troops to warn everyone. When the English soldiers arrived at Lexington, a town near Concord, the minutemen were waiting.

The minutemen and the English soldiers were under orders not to shoot first. Nevertheless someone opened fire. When the shooting ended, eight minutemen were dead. The battle gave Hancock and Adams time to get away. So the English marched to Concord. There they found only a few weapons. Just outside Concord, there was a brief battle in which three British soldiers and two minutemen were killed. At about noon the outnumbered English soldiers headed back to Boston. Minutemen hid behind fences, barns, and farmhouses along the road. They fired at the soldiers. By the time the English reached their camp near Boston, 73 of them had been killed. Another 200 of them were wounded or missing.

The American Revolution had begun! In the weeks that followed, the fighting spread. On July 4, 1776, the Second Continental Congress met and approved the Declaration of Independence. It told the world that the 13 colonies were independent from England. But the American colonists had to continue the fight for their independence until 1781.

Thinking About the Article

Fill in the blank with the word or words that best complete each statement.

1. _____ makes the laws in England.

2. A law that has been done away with has been _____.

3. When people refuse to buy a product, it is called a _____.

4. _____ were colonists who trained for battle.

Write your answers in the space provided.

5. Review the questions you wrote on page 50. Did the article answer your questions? If you said *yes,* write the answers. If your questions were not answered, write three things you learned from this article.

_____

_____

_____

_____

_____

6. What happened as a result of the Stamp Act?

_____

_____

_____

_____

7. What was the reason for the Boston Tea Party?

_____

_____

_____

_____

8. Which of the following was <u>not</u> a cause of the American Revolution?

    (1) tax on tea

    (2) signing of the Declaration of Independence

    (3) taxing of the colonists by Parliament

    (4) passing of the Intolerable Acts

    (5) the Boston Massacre

9. Which of the following was a result of the Battles of Lexington and Concord?

    (1) Boston Tea Party

    (2) meeting of the First Continental Congress

    (3) passing of the Intolerable Acts by Parliament

    (4) passing of the Tea Tax

    (5) beginning of the American Revolution

10. One result of the meeting of the Second Continental Congress was to

    (1) honor Paul Revere.

    (2) tell Parliament to repeal their harsh laws.

    (3) prepare the minutemen for war.

    (4) approve the Declaration of Independence.

    (5) approve the Stamp Act.

Write your answer in the space provided.

11. The first shot fired at Concord on April 19, 1775, has been called "the shot heard round the world." Why do you think it has been called that? Do you agree? Explain your answer.

_____

_____

_____

_____

_____

_____

Section 7

The American Civil War

Setting the Stage

In 1861 the Civil War began in the United States. A **civil war** is a war between people who live in the same country. The American Civil War was fought between 23 northern states and 11 southern states. There were many reasons for the war. One important outcome of the Civil War was the end of slavery in the United States.

Past: What you already know

You may already know something about the American Civil War. Write two things you already know.

1. _____

2. _____

Present: What you learn by previewing

Write the headings from the article on pages 57–59 below.

African Americans in the Civil War

3. _____

4. _____

5. _____

6. _____

What does the photograph on page 58 show?

7. _____

_____

Future: Questions to answer

Write two questions you expect this article to answer.

8. _____

9. _____

Check your answers on page 214.

African Americans in the Civil War

As you read each section, circle the words you don't know. Look up the meanings.

For more than two hundred years, most African Americans who lived in the United States were slaves. The Civil War ended the system of slavery. During the war, the northern states were called the Union, or the North. The southern states were called the Confederacy, or the South. The South no longer wanted to be part of the United States of America. Northerners wanted the United States to remain one country. They didn't think the southern states had the right to declare themselves a separate country. They were willing to fight a war to keep *all* the states together. For African Americans, the Civil War was fought to end slavery. About four million African-American slaves won their freedom as a result of the Civil War.

Lincoln's View

Just before the war started, there were 15 states where people owned slaves. Four of these slave states did *not* join the Confederacy when the war started. They were called border states. These states stayed in the Union. The president of the United States during the Civil War was Abraham Lincoln. He asked for volunteers to join the army when the war began. Thousands of free African Americans rushed to join. But they were turned away. Lincoln was afraid to let them join the army. He thought the North might lose the four border states to the South. He feared they would join the Confederacy. He didn't want the people in these states to think that the Union was fighting the war to end slavery. Lincoln explained his beliefs in a letter he wrote. The letter was to the owner of a New York newspaper. In this letter he said, "My paramount object in this struggle [the Civil War] is to save the Union, and is *not* either to save or destroy slavery. If I could save the Union without freeing *any* slave I would do it; and if I could save it by freeing *all* the slaves, I would [do] it; and if I could do it by freeing some and leaving others alone, I would also do that."

Understanding the Main Idea. The main idea of a paragraph is often stated in a sentence called the *topic sentence*. It is often the first sentence in a paragraph. It tells what the paragraph is about. Underline the topic sentence from Lincoln's letter. Then in your own words, write what you think is the most important point Lincoln made.

Applying Your Skills and Strategies

_____

_____

_____

_____

The Emancipation Proclamation

Early in the war, many people in the North didn't care if slavery was ended. They were fighting because they didn't think the South had the right to separate from the North. But by 1862 many people in the North were in favor of ending slavery. Lincoln decided it was time to do something. He decided that all slaves in the South should be freed.

Lincoln thought he should wait for a Union victory before announcing his decision. The North won a battle at Antietam, Maryland, in September 1862. Five days later Lincoln issued a written statement freeing all slaves in the South. The statement said that on January 1, 1863, all slaves in states fighting against the United States would be "forever free." This statement was called the **Emancipation Proclamation**. Lincoln was still concerned that the border states might leave the Union. So he did not free the slaves in those states.

After the Emancipation Proclamation, the war took on new meaning for many people. African Americans and white Northerners who were against slavery celebrated. People from Europe also welcomed the news. Many people from Europe supported the war when ending slavery became a goal.

The proclamation did not officially end slavery in the United States. It was not a law. It was an order by the president acting as head of the Union army. It also did not end discrimination. **Discrimination** is the unequal and unfair treatment of a person or group. African Americans were still treated differently than other Americans. Even free African Americans did not enjoy the same rights other Americans enjoyed. In most states they could not vote or attend public schools. Many states did not allow them to own property.

The 54th Massachusetts Regiment attacking Fort Wagner, July 18, 1863

The Fight for Freedom

The Emancipation Proclamation opened the door for former slaves to join the Union army. By the end of the war, about 200,000 African Americans had served in the Union army and navy. Most of them had been slaves in the South.

African-American soldiers faced discrimination. They had white officers, but they were not allowed to fight with white soldiers. At first they were paid only half as much as white soldiers. But by the end of the war both groups were paid the same amount.

Massachusetts was one of the first states to have African-American regiments. A **regiment** is a large military group. The men of the 54th Regiment refused to be paid until they received the same pay as white soldiers. But the 54th Regiment was willing to fight, with or without pay. In July 1863 they attacked Fort Wagner near Charleston, South Carolina. The regimental commander, most of the officers, and nearly 50 percent of the men were killed.

Identifying Point of View. Everyone has a point of view. Writers express their point of view using words. Artists use pictures to show how they feel. Look at the picture on page 58. It shows the 54th Regiment at Fort Wagner. Do you think the artist sided with the Union or the Confederacy? Explain your point of view.

Applying Your Skills and Strategies

A Proud Record

The fighting record of African-American soldiers in the Civil War was outstanding. The Congressional Medal of Honor is given only to the bravest members of the armed forces. Twenty-three African Americans received this honor during the Civil War.

A small band of slaves in South Carolina took over a Southern ship, *The Planter*. Robert Smalls was the slave who led the band. Later he said, ". . . Although born a slave I always felt that I was a man and ought to be free, and I would be free or die. While at the wheel of *The Planter* . . . it occurred to me that I could not only secure my own freedom but that of numbers of my comrades. . . ."

One of the most remarkable African Americans was Harriet Tubman. At one point she went into South Carolina to guide Union raids deep into Confederate territory.

The South surrendered in April 1865. The Civil War was over. African Americans had won their freedom. However, the fight to end discrimination in the United States was just beginning.

Check your answer on page 215.

Thinking About the Article

Fill in the blank with the word or words that best complete each statement.

1. A war between people of the same country is called a

    _____.

2. To treat one group of people unfairly and unequally is called

    _____.

3. The slave states that remained with the Union were called

    _____.

Write your answers in the space provided.

4. Review the questions you wrote on page 56. Did the article answer your questions? If you said *yes,* write the answers. If your questions were not answered, write three things you learned from this article.

    _____

    _____

    _____

    _____

    _____

5. Why weren't African Americans allowed to join the Union army at the beginning of the Civil War?

    _____

    _____

    _____

6. Give two examples of how African-American soldiers were discriminated against during the Civil War.

    _____

    _____

    _____

Circle the number of the best answer.

7. Which sentence best expresses the main idea of the picture on page 58?

    (1) African Americans fought bravely for the Union.

    (2) Confederate soldiers won the battle.

    (3) African-American soldiers pushed back Confederate soldiers as they attacked the fort.

    (4) Union ships supported the attack on Fort Wagner.

    (5) The American flag is at the center of the picture.

8. Which of the following events came first?

    (1) Lincoln issues the Emancipation Proclamation.

    (2) The battle is fought at Antietam.

    (3) African-American soldiers attack Fort Wagner.

    (4) African Americans are allowed to join the Union army.

    (5) Lincoln decides to free the slaves in those states that were fighting against the United States.

9. Which of the following was a result of the Emancipation Proclamation?

    (1) Discrimination against African Americans ended.

    (2) The Union won a victory at Antietam.

    (3) Slave states left the Union.

    (4) Slaves in the South were freed by Lincoln.

    (5) The Civil War began.

Write your answer in the space provided.

10. What are two ways to fight discrimination in your community?

_____

_____

_____

_____

_____

The Reform Movement

Setting the Stage

In the 1700s, American families made most of the everyday things they used. By the 1800s, families were buying more goods made in factories. A growing number of Americans were working in those factories. Thousands of children were among those workers.

Past: What you already know

You may already know something about the growth of factories and child labor. Write two things you already know.

1. _____

2. _____

Present: What you learn by previewing

Write the headings from the article on pages 63–65 below.

Child Labor

3. _____

4. _____

5. _____

6. _____

What does the photo on page 64 show?

7. _____

Future: Questions to answer

Write three questions you expect this article to answer.

8. _____

9. _____

10. _____

Check your answers on page 215.

Child Labor

As you read each section, circle the words you don't know. Look up the meanings.

The first cotton mill in America opened in 1791. It was in Pawtucket, Rhode Island. Most of the workers were children under 12 years old. As factories grew in the United States, so did child labor. **Child labor** is the practice of using children as workers.

Learning a Trade

Child labor was not a new idea in 1791. Since Colonial times, children had worked with their parents. A family worked as a team. Each family member was expected to do his or her share of the work. Children worked from sunup to sundown. They worked six days a week. Few children went to school.

Often children learned a job, or trade, at an early age. Many went to work as apprentices by the time they were 12 years old. An **apprentice** is someone who learns a trade from an expert called a master. Apprentices worked long, hard days. Being an apprentice was an opportunity for boys to get ahead. Girls, on the other hand, rarely had the chance to become apprentices.

At the age of 12, Benjamin Franklin became an apprentice to an older brother. The older brother was a printer. He agreed to teach Benjamin how to become a good printer. He also provided Benjamin with food, a place to live, and clothing. In return, Benjamin had to work hard for five years. He also agreed not to waste his master's goods. Benjamin had to promise not to give away any of his master's printing secrets.

When Benjamin Franklin finished his apprenticeship at age 17 he had a valuable trade. Then he went to work for a printer in Philadelphia. He started his own printing shop when he was 22. Benjamin Franklin became one of the best-known men in America. He was an outstanding writer and inventor. He was also an important leader.

Comparing and Contrasting. *Comparisons* show how people, events, or things are alike. Words like *also*, *as well as*, and *like* signal a comparison. Contrasts show how things are different. Words that signal a contrast include *however*, *on the other hand*, *although*, and *yet*. Reread the third paragraph. Does it compare or contrast opportunities for girls and boys? What phrase gives you a clue?

Applying Your Skills and Strategies

_____

_____

_____

The Growth of Factories

In the 1700s, most Americans were farmers. By the 1800s, hundreds of new inventions were changing the way people made things. More and more people were working in factories and mines. Many of these new jobs required little or no training. A ten-year-old child could handle the work. So many ten-year-old children did!

The members of a family often worked side by side in a factory. The families that had the greatest number of children were hired first. Some factory owners hired only children. They claimed that children could do certain jobs better than adults. It was also cheaper to hire children. They were paid less than adults. Children worked for as little as fifty cents per day.

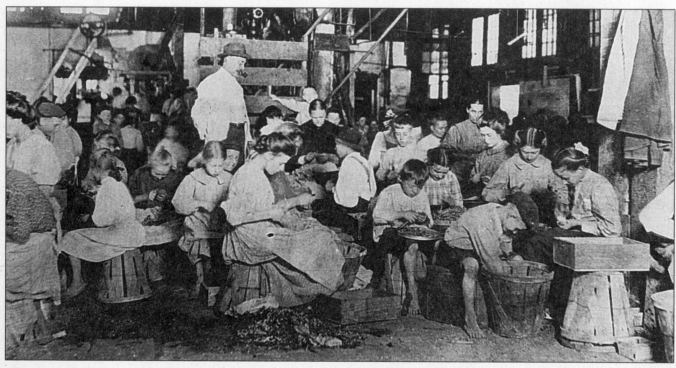

Children working in a cannery. The photograph was taken by Lewis W. Hine in 1912.

Most parents wanted their children to go to school. By the late 1800s, many states had free public schools. However, factory jobs paid so little that some parents needed to have their children work. They could not manage without the money their children earned. These parents could not afford to let their children go to the free schools. Other parents were able to send only one child to school. Some parents tried to give all of their children a few years of schooling.

Children did not work only in factories. They worked in other places as well. Some worked in coal mines. Others worked in stables or sold newspapers. By 1900, nearly two million children under the age of 15 had jobs. Some of these children worked 12 hours per day, six days a week.

The Push for Reform

After the late 1800s, many Americans worked hard to improve the lives of children. People who work to change things for the better are called **reformers**. These reformers wanted laws that set a minimum working age. They wanted to limit the number of hours children could work. They felt children should be kept out of dangerous jobs. Most reformers believed that every child should have the chance to go to school.

Reformers worked to make people aware of the conditions under which children worked. They hired people as investigators to look into the problem. The investigators visited factories and mines. One of these investigators was Lewis Hine. He wrote about the children he met. He also took photos of them at work. In 1910, he took the photo shown on page 64. The children in this photo are preparing beans for canning.

Hine's work was often dangerous. Factory owners hired guards to keep him away. They did not want anyone to take pictures of their workers. They were afraid to let people see what conditions were like. But Hine found ways to get inside the factories. He often disguised himself as a Bible salesman or as a fire inspector. Sometimes he pretended to be a photographer eager to take pictures of the latest machines. He always kept his notebook hidden in a pocket. He used his notes to write many articles. His photographs, however, were more powerful than any words he could write.

Understanding a Photo. Hine took photos such as the one on page 64. He used them as proof of the need for laws to protect children. How does this photo show the need for child-labor laws?

Applying Your Skills and Strategies

New Laws

A number of states passed laws to protect children. This was the result of the work of Lewis Hine and others. By 1914, every state but one had child-labor laws. But many Americans wanted a common law for all states. They wanted a national law.

Finally a national law was passed in 1938. Congress made it illegal for most businesses to employ children under the age of 16. Children under the age of 18 could not work at dangerous jobs. But the law did not protect all children. Farm work was not covered by the law. Today every state requires children under the age of 16 go to school. Every state also protects the health and safety of all workers.

Check your answer on page 215.

Thinking About the Article

Fill in the blank with the word or words that best complete each statement.

1. The practice of using children as workers is called

   _____.

2. Someone learning a trade from an expert is an

   _____.

3. People who work to change things for the better are called

   _____.

Write your answers in the space provided.

4. Review the questions you wrote on page 62. Did the article answer your questions? If you said *yes*, write the answers. If your questions were not answered, write three things you learned from this article.

   _____

   _____

   _____

   _____

   _____

5. Why did some parents have to send their children to work?

   _____

6. Why did so many factory owners hire children?

   _____

   _____

7. Why do you think factory owners tried to keep Lewis Hine from visiting their factories?

   _____

   _____

   _____

8. Which of the following was <u>not</u> one of the responsibilities of the master trade worker to the apprentice?

    (1) train for a trade

    (2) provide food

    (3) provide clothing

    (4) give a place to live

    (5) teach reading and writing

9. Which of the following applied to Benjamin Franklin?

    (1) He became one of America's most important leaders.

    (2) He was a carpenter's apprentice.

    (3) He was a shoemaker's apprentice.

    (4) He finished his apprenticeship at the age of 12 and went to work for a printer.

    (5) He was the first apprentice in Philadelphia.

10. Which of the following was <u>not</u> a goal of the reformers?

    (1) setting a minimum working age

    (2) limiting the number of hours children could work

    (3) keeping children out of dangerous jobs

    (4) giving every child a chance to go to school

    (5) creating a minimum wage for children

Write your answer in the space provided.

11. There is a Chinese saying that "one picture is worth a thousand words." How does this saying apply to Hine's photograph on page 64? Explain your answer.

_____

_____

_____

_____

_____

Section 9

World War II

Setting the Stage

The United States entered World War II in 1941. American industry was able to make war supplies quickly. This was a major reason the war was won by America and its allies. Before entering the war, American industry was already making war supplies for some countries. After entering the war, production increased. It was as much as ten times greater than what it had been before the war.

Past: What you already know

You may already know something about the part American workers played in World War II. Write two things you already know.

1. _____

2. _____

Present: What you learn by previewing

Write the headings from the article on pages 69–71 below.

The Search for New Workers

3. _____

4. _____

5. _____

What does the graph on page 70 show?

6. _____

Future: Questions to answer

Write three questions you expect this article to answer.

7. _____

8. _____

9. _____

Check your answers on page 216.

The Search for New Workers

As you read each section, circle the words you don't know. Look up the meanings.

On December 7, 1941, the United States was attacked by Japan. The next day the United States declared war on Japan. Thousands of young men left their jobs to join the armed forces. Many other workers were drafted into the service. This meant there were fewer workers in the factories. Yet skilled workers were needed more than ever before. American factories had to make military supplies for the troops. The United States also produced most of the military supplies for its allies. **Allies** are friends. They help each other. During the war the Allies fought together against Germany, Italy, and Japan. Enemy bombs had destroyed thousands of factories in Allied countries. So the Allies depended on American military supplies. As a result, the American defense industry had more work than ever. The **defense industry** is made up of companies that produce military supplies. New workers had to be found.

The Doors Open

For years employers had discriminated against hiring African-American workers. But **civil rights** allow every person certain freedoms and the right to be treated equally. So African-American leaders worked to end discrimination. They convinced President Roosevelt to do something. In 1941, he issued a presidential order. It was the first time since the Emancipation Proclamation that a president's order protected civil rights. The order was for factories working on national defense contracts. These factories were ordered to end discrimination in hiring and promoting. They could no longer refuse to hire or promote workers because of their race or religion.

An African American who found a job in a shipyard described her feelings about this change. "When we first got into the war, the country wasn't prepared. And as the manpower in the country was getting pulled into the service, all of the industries were wide open. So they decided, 'Well, we better let some of those blacks come in.' Then after the source of men dried up, they began to let women come in. The doors were opened."

Summarizing Information. When you *summarize* something you condense, or shorten, a larger amount of information into a few sentences. You state the major points of a larger body of information in your own words. Reread the text under the heading *The Doors Open* and summarize it.

Applying Your Skills and Strategies

_____

_____

_____

_____

Check your answer on page 216.

Soldiers Without Guns

The United States government helped the defense industry. They recruited workers by creating an advertising campaign. The advertisements encouraged everyone to help in the war effort. They showed how people could help win the war by taking factory jobs. Government posters and movies called defense-industry workers "soldiers without guns."

Early in the war, an airplane company created a poster. It showed a woman named Rosie working as a riveter. Riveters together joined large airplane sections. The idea of a woman putting together an airplane was new to Americans. The poster was an overnight success. Songs were written about Rosie. She appeared in movies. Her picture was put on the cover of a magazine. Rosie became a symbol of all the women who worked in the defense industry.

Some women worked in steel mills. Others made guns or bullets. Some helped build airplanes and ships. Women drove buses, trucks, and trains. They flew airplanes from factories to battlefields. Many women served in the armed forces. No job seemed too tough.

When the war began, women made up about 25 percent of the labor force. The **labor force** is all of the people who are capable of being employed. Most women had low-paying jobs in offices and shops. Some worked in low-paying factory jobs. The war opened the door to higher paying jobs. By the end of the war, women made up 36 percent of the labor force.

A poster honoring women in the labor force

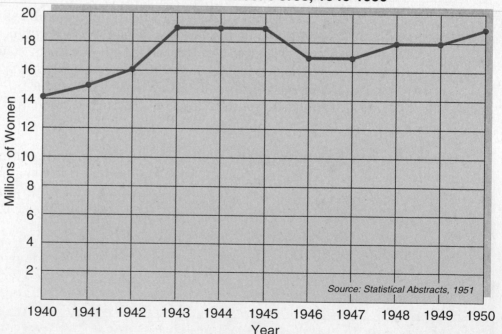

Women in the Labor Force, 1940-1950

Source: Statistical Abstracts, 1951

Reading a Line Graph. A *graph* is a special kind of drawing. It uses lines, bars, pictures, or parts of a circle to compare information. The title tells what the graph is about. The labels along the side and bottom of a graph tell how the graph is organized. The graph on page 70 is a *line graph*. Line graphs often show how something changes over time. Study the line graph on page 70. Did the number of women in the labor force increase or decrease from 1940 to 1950?

_____

How do you know?

_____

_____

If the line graph were extended to 1951, do you think the line would rise or fall? Explain your answer.

_____

_____

A Changing Labor Force

American workers did an amazing job! During World War II, they produced twice as much military supplies as Germany, Italy, and Japan combined. In 1939, about 6,000 planes were built. By 1944, almost 100,000 planes were being made each year. American workers made military supplies in less time than ever before. The time for making an aircraft carrier was cut from 35 months to 15 months. Factories were open day and night.

World War II affected the wages of American factory workers. Women and African Americans earned more than they had before the war. But women still earned less than men who were doing the same job.

The work these Americans did was valued. It was critical to the war effort. It was an experience many workers would never forget. A welder in New York explained the change. She said, "Rosie the Riveter was the woman who got up early in the morning when it was still dark and went to work and came in smiling, drinking coffee, working hard, finding herself as a new person."

Yet many of these new workers were unemployed within a year after the war was over. Still more women and African Americans were employed than before the war. Neither group was willing to go back to the way things used to be. An African-American woman recalled, "A lot of blacks . . . decided they did not want to go back to what they were doing before. They did not want to walk behind a plow, they wouldn't get on the back of the bus anymore."

Check your answers on page 216.

Thinking About the Article

Fill in the blank with the word or words that best complete each statement.

1. Nations that help each other during war are _____.

2. Companies that make military supplies are part of the

   _____.

3. People who are employed are part of the _____.

4. Every person has _____ that allow for certain freedoms and the right to equal treatment.

Write your answers in the space provided.

5. Review the questions you wrote on page 68. Did the article answer your questions? If you said *yes*, write the answers. If your questions were not answered, write three things you learned from this article.

   _____

   _____

   _____

   _____

6. What do you think the African-American worker quoted on page 69 meant when she said, "The doors were opened"?

   _____

   _____

   _____

7. Name two causes of the changes in the labor force.

   _____

   _____

Check your answers on page 216.

8. President Roosevelt issued a presidential order in 1941. Why was it important?

    (1) It ended all discrimination against African Americans.

    (2) It ended discrimination in all factories.

    (3) It protected the rights of women.

    (4) It raised the pay for women and African Americans.

    (5) It ended discrimination in companies with national defense contracts.

9. Which statement best expresses how women who were defense-industry workers thought about themselves during World War II?

    (1) We are too delicate to do the really tough jobs.

    (2) We are not capable of doing the work that men do.

    (3) We are not very important to the war effort.

    (4) We are working to help win the war.

    (5) We are working only for the pay.

10. Which of the following best states what Rosie the Riveter symbolized?

    (1) women driving trucks

    (2) women in the movie industry

    (3) women building planes

    (4) women working in the defense industry

    (5) women in magazines

Write your answer in the space provided.

11. Suppose you lived during World War II. How would you have helped in the war effort?

_____

_____

_____

_____

_____

The Cold War

Setting the Stage

During World War II, the United States and the Soviet Union were allies. They fought together against Germany. But soon after the war ended, they were no longer allies. The struggle between them was known as the cold war. It lasted from 1945 until 1989.

Past: What you already know

You may already know something about the cold war. Write two things you already know.

1. _____

2. _____

Present: What you learn by previewing

Write the headings from the article on pages 75–77 below.

A Divided Europe

3. _____

4. _____

5. _____

What does the map on page 75 show?

6. _____

Future: Questions to answer

Write three questions you expect this article to answer.

7. _____

8. _____

9. _____

Check your answers on page 217.

A Divided Europe

As you read each section, circle the words you don't know. Look up the meanings.

After World War II, Americans were very worried about the safety of their country. Those fears grew out of different ideas held by the people of the United States and the Soviet Union. The struggle between them was called the cold war. A **cold war** is fought mainly with words and money. At the same time, each side prepares its military for a war that it hopes will never come.

The Iron Curtain

The cold war began as World War II was ending. In February 1945, the president of the United States met with leaders of Great Britain and the Soviet Union. They agreed that for a while Germany would be divided into four parts, or zones. One zone would be under the control of the United States. Another would be controlled by the Soviet Union. The remaining two zones would be controlled by Great Britain and France. Berlin, the capital of Germany, was in the zone controlled by the Soviet Union. Berlin was also divided into four parts.

Europe During the Cold War

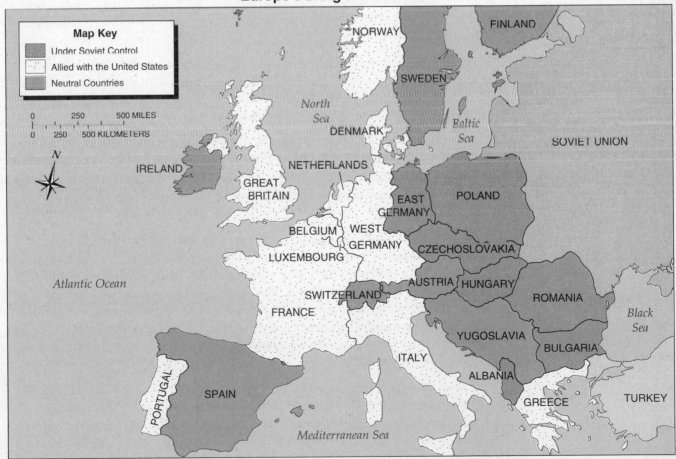

Map Key
- Under Soviet Control
- Allied with the United States
- Neutral Countries

0   250   500 MILES
0   250   500 KILOMETERS

It soon became clear that the Soviets were ignoring the agreement. They set up their own governments in Eastern Europe. It was obvious the Soviets did not intend to leave the countries they controlled.

In March 1946, Winston Churchill made a speech in Fulton, Missouri. Churchill had led Great Britain through World War II. He watched the spread of Soviet power with alarm. He warned that an "iron curtain" was falling across Europe. He believed it was separating the Soviet-controlled countries of Eastern Europe from the democratic countries of Western Europe. But Western European countries did nothing to stop the Soviets because they feared another war.

Reading a Political Map.   There are many different kinds of maps. Those that focus on showing boundaries between countries are called *political maps*. The map on page 75 is a political map. Study the map and its key. Which countries were under Soviet control?

Applying Your Skills and Strategies

_____

_____

Two Germanys

After World War II, countries all over the world were taking sides in the cold war. Some took a strong stand with the United States. Others sided with the Soviet Union. Some tried to be **neutral** by not choosing sides. Some countries, such as Germany, could not be neutral.

The United States, Great Britain, and France were still allies. Often they are called the West. The West believed that a rich Germany was the best protection against another war. The Soviets thought a poor Germany was their best protection. So they stripped their zone, East Germany, of its factories and other resources.

In 1947, the West combined its three zones to make West Germany. Life in the combined zone was returning to normal. Factories were open again. The United States gave the people a great deal of financial help to rebuild their homes and shops. The West Germans elected their own leaders. The Soviets were angry that the zones of West Germany had been combined. They decided to protest this action by forcing the West out of Berlin. The next year the Soviets closed all roads and railroads from East Germany into West Berlin.

The only way to reach West Berlin was by air. So the West rounded up all the airplanes they could. These airplanes brought food, clothing, fuel, and medicine to the city each day. In 1949 the Soviets realized that the West was not going to back down. Roads and railroads into West Berlin were reopened. That same year, the West made West Germany an independent nation. Shortly thereafter the Soviets made East Germany an independent nation.

Check your answer on page 217.

In the years that followed, West Berlin became an island of freedom within Eastern Europe. To the people of East Germany, it was their best route to freedom. By 1961, three million East Germans had escaped to West Berlin.

Drawing Conclusions. A judgment made from facts is a *conclusion*. To draw a conclusion, read for the main idea. Then look for supporting statements. These are the details that lead to a logical conclusion. Then ask yourself what point the author is making. Reread the last paragraph under the heading *Two Germanys*. What conclusion can you draw from it?

Applying Your Skills and Strategies

_____

_____

The Berlin Wall

In 1961, the East German government decided it was time to stop its people from fleeing to West Berlin. At midnight on August 13, work began on a concrete and barbed-wire wall. The wall separated East from West Berlin. It was called the Berlin Wall.

The Soviet-backed East German government achieved its goal with the wall. Very few East Germans were able to escape in the years that followed. Almost thirty years later, Soviet control over Eastern Europe, including East Germany, decreased. Mikhail Gorbachev became head of the Soviet Union. He faced many problems in his own country. So he decided to let Soviet-controlled countries make some of their own decisions. In doing so, he set off a chain of events. People in these countries decided to have elections. By 1989, they had voted out leaders with ties to the Soviet Union. They opened trade and travel with the West.

On November 9, 1989, the East German government allowed its people to travel to places in the West. This included West Berlin. Within minutes, thousands of East Berliners gathered along the wall. The guards opened the gates and in that instant the city was united. Within days, people tore down the wall itself. Within months, Germany became a single country once again. The cold war was ending. Willy Brandt was the mayor of West Berlin when the wall was built. After it was torn down he wrote, "Once again, Berlin has become a symbol, but now it has become a symbol of hope."

Changes continued to take place, not only in Eastern Europe but in the Soviet Union itself. The Communist Party had ruled the Soviet Union for 74 years. But by the fall of 1991 it was crumbling. As a result, three former republics of the Soviet Union became independent countries. The Soviets realized they could no longer dominate other parts of the world.

Check your answer on page 217.

Thinking About the Article

Fill in the blank with the word or words that best complete each statement.

1. A war that is fought mostly with words and money is a

    _____.

2. Germany was divided into four parts called _____.

3. A country that does not favor one side over another is

    _____.

Write your answers in the space provided.

4. Review the questions you wrote on page 74. Did the article answer your questions? If you said *yes*, write the answers. If your questions were not answered, write three things you learned from this article.

    _____

    _____

    _____

    _____

    _____

5. According to Winston Churchill, what was one cause and one effect of the iron curtain that fell over Europe after World War II?

    _____

    _____

    _____

6. Study the map on page 75. How many countries were controlled by

    the Soviet Union? _____

7. How did the West respond to the closing of land routes into West Berlin?

    _____

    _____

Check your answers on page 217.

Circle the number of the best answer.

8. Which of the following is the best reason the West combined their three zones in Germany?

    (1) The West believed that a rich Germany was the best protection against another war.

    (2) The West believed that a poor Germany was the best protection against another war.

    (3) The West wanted to make the Soviets angry.

    (4) The West wanted life in its zones to return to normal.

    (5) The West wanted the Soviet zone to join the combined zone.

9. Which of the following was a reason the Soviets in East Germany built a wall through Berlin?

    (1) ending the Berlin airlift

    (2) protesting the creation of West Germany

    (3) stopping the escape of East Germans to West Berlin

    (4) keeping people from West Berlin out of East Berlin

    (5) celebrating the creation of East Germany.

10. Which of the following conclusions can be drawn from the article?

    (1) Walls cannot keep people from seeking freedom.

    (2) The iron curtain is too strong to be torn down.

    (3) Germany will always be divided.

    (4) Walls unite people.

    (5) East Germans preferred living behind the wall.

Write your answers in the space provided.

11. Why were Germany and Berlin symbols of the cold war?

    _____

    _____

    _____

12. What do you think people can do to make sure there isn't another cold war?

    _____

    _____

Section 11

War in the Persian Gulf

Setting the Stage

Iraq and Kuwait are two countries in the Middle East. In August 1990 soldiers from Iraq invaded the neighboring country of Kuwait. People throughout the world were outraged. A number of countries, including the United States, prepared for war. On January 16, 1991, the fighting began. When it ended six weeks later, Kuwait was free.

Past: What you already know

You may already know something about the war in the Persian Gulf. Write two things you already know.

1. _____

2. _____

Present: What you learn by previewing

Write the headings from the article on pages 81–83 below.

Victory in the Gulf

3. _____

4. _____

5. _____

What does the map on page 82 show?

6. _____

Future: Questions to answer

Write three questions you expect this article to answer.

7. _____

8. _____

9. _____

Check your answers on page 217.

Victory in the Gulf

As you read each section, circle the words you don't know. Look up the meanings.

On August 2, 1990, Iraqi troops marched into Kuwait. General Colin Powell, the highest ranking general in the United States, heard the news. Powell was head of the Joint Chiefs of Staff. So he made a telephone call to a military base in Florida. The man he called was General H. Norman Schwarzkopf. Schwarzkopf directed a special unit in the military called the Central Command, or CentCom. It included officers from the army, navy, air force, and marines. These officers were responsible for the nation's military activities in nineteen countries. The countries were located in Africa and the Middle East. CentCom's mission was to **deter**, or prevent, war in these regions.

Schwarzkopf at CentCom

Schwarzkopf was not surprised by Iraq's invasion of Kuwait. Earlier in the year, he met with reporters. He said that local conflicts were the main threat to peace in the Middle East. Such a conflict could easily get out of hand. He continued with the following statement. "We came to the conclusion that one of the things that would threaten Free World interests more than anything else was if Iraq decided it was going to come down here [to the Gulf] and take over the oil fields. That's the one we developed a plan for."

Identifying Point of View. A *point of view* is the thoughts and feelings of a person or group of people. Words or phrases often provide clues to a point of view. Reread the quote in the previous paragraph that tells what Schwarzkopf said. Which words show the point of view of Schwarzkopf's special unit?

Applying Your Skills and Strategies

Back in July 1990, CentCom had scheduled a computer war game. A war game is a "what if" kind of exercise. The game creates different situations that may happen in a war. Officers decide what they would do in each situation if it were actually to take place. Schwarzkopf wrote much of this war game himself. One situation the game created was of a dictator threatening neighboring oil fields. A **dictator** is someone who has total power over a country.

The game did not name any specific country. Still, the officers quickly identified Saddam Hussein of Iraq as the dictator. They also identified the country under attack as Kuwait. In the past, Hussein had made no secret of his interest in Kuwait's oil fields. Just days after the game ended, Kuwait was invaded by Iraqi soldiers. Suddenly the CentCom officers faced a real war, not a game.

Check your answer on page 217.

Three days after the invasion, the United Nations called for economic **sanctions** against Iraq. That means members of the United Nations agreed not to trade with Iraq. The sanctions would stay in effect until Iraq's troops left Kuwait. At the same time, CentCom prepared for war in case the sanctions did not work.

President George Bush agreed that the United States should prepare for war. He asked other countries to prepare for war as well. He wanted them to join a coalition against Iraq. Members of a **coalition** join together to meet a goal. In this case the goal was to free Kuwait. Among those joining the United States in a coalition were Saudi Arabia, Great Britain, France, Egypt, and Syria.

From Plan to Action

On August 7 the first American troops left for the Gulf. CentCom also moved to Saudi Arabia. Schwarzkopf and his staff faced an awesome task. They had to turn a training exercise into a battle plan. Schwarzkopf was a good choice as commander for this job. He was a professional soldier who had grown up in the military. His father was also a general. Although Schwarzkopf had a temper, he was popular with his troops. They nicknamed him "Stormin' Norman" and "The Bear."

Within weeks of CentCom's arrival in the Middle East, the general took charge of more than 500,000 American troops. Schwarzkopf also co-commanded 200,000 allied forces. He and his staff did more than bring a military force together in the desert. They also arranged to house, feed, and arm these troops. They planned the mission and commanded the attacks. From August through January, Schwarzkopf worked around the clock to put it all together.

The Ground War Against Iraq February 24-28, 1991

Operation Desert Storm

The sanctions caused hardships in Iraq. Yet the Iraqis refused to leave Kuwait. The allied forces told the Iraqis to leave Kuwait or there would be war. The war began on January 16, 1991. Bombs dropped by the allied forces lit up the skies over Iraq and Kuwait for forty days. The Iraqis responded by firing missiles at Israel and Saudi Arabia. The Iraqis hoped these attacks would draw Israel into the fighting. Israel and its Arab neighbors do not get along. The Iraqis thought that the Arabs would leave the coalition of allied forces if Israel got involved in the war. Israel refused to fight. The coalition stood firm.

As CentCom prepared for a ground war, the allies gave Iraq one more chance to get out of Kuwait. There was no reply. So the ground war began on February 24. The plan was simple. Schwarzkopf led the Iraqis to believe attacks would come from the south and the sea. The map on page 82 shows what really happened. The plan worked better than expected. In less than 100 hours, the troops were in Kuwait City and the war was over.

Reading a Historical Map.   Historical maps show what happened in a particular time and place in the past. The title of the map tells when and where the event took place. It also tells what the map is about. Study the map on page 82. The attack on Iraqi forces came from which directions?

Applying Your Skills and Strategies

By March 8, the first American troops were going home. General Schwarzkopf spoke to them before they left Saudi Arabia. He told the troops that he knew they would have many tales to tell. He went on to ask that they tell the whole story.

"Don't forget to mention the great Air Force that prepared the way for you and was overhead the entire time you fought. Don't forget the great Navy pilots that were there and the great ships that were at sea.... And don't ever forget to say that the 1st Tank Division of the United Kingdom was protecting your right flank. And don't ever forget to say there was an Egyptian corps protecting their right flank. And two divisions of Marines out there making a hard push into Kuwait City with a fine Saudi Arabian force protecting their right flank. And don't ever forget to say in your story, there were Kuwaitis, Omanis, French Foreign Legion involved because you were part of the great coalition determined not to let a petty dictator no matter what size his army, no matter how many tanks he had...get away with bullying his neighbors.... Don't forget to make sure that everyone understands that we did it as part of a joint team, as part of an international team. We all did it together, we all paid the price, we all shared in the victory."

Check your answer on page 217.

Thinking About the Article

Fill in the blank with the word or words that best complete each statement.

1. The United States tried to prevent, or _____, a war.

2. Saddam Hussein had total control over Iraq. He is a

    _____.

3. When the United Nations refused to trade with Iraq, members were

    applying economic _____.

4. Members of a _____ join together to meet a goal.

Write your answers in the space provided.

5. Review the questions you wrote on page 80. Did the article answer your questions? If you said *yes*, write the answers. If your questions were not answered, write three things you learned from this article.

    _____

    _____

    _____

    _____

    _____

6. Why wasn't Schwarzkopf surprised by the invasion of Kuwait?

    _____

    _____

    _____

7. Name two ways the United States responded to the invasion of Kuwait.

    _____

    _____

Check your answers on page 218.

8. Why did Iraq bomb Israel?

_____

_____

Circle the number of the best answer.

9. CentCom officers played computer war games because

    (1) they were afraid sanctions would not work.

    (2) it is a good way to prepare for a possible war.

    (3) they knew Iraq was going to invade Kuwait.

    (4) they did not trust Saddam Hussein.

    (5) they wanted to be ready when Iraq attacked.

10. Which statement best expresses Iraq's response to economic sanctions?

    (1) The Iraqis left Kuwait.

    (2) The Iraqis continued to occupy Kuwait.

    (3) The Iraqis attacked Israel.

    (4) The Iraqis asked for more time.

    (5) The Iraqis attacked Saudi Arabia.

11. Which statement best expresses the way Schwarzkopf viewed the victory in the Gulf?

    (1) American troops were responsible for the victory.

    (2) It was an air force victory.

    (3) Troops from many countries made it a team effort.

    (4) CentCom did it alone.

    (5) It was a naval victory.

Write your answer in the space provided.

12. Do you think the United States should have gotten involved in the War in the Persian Gulf? Explain your answer.

_____

_____

_____

Unit 2 Review:
History

The Colony of St. Augustine

Juan Ponce de León, a Spaniard, was one of the first Europeans to explore the Americas. While living in Puerto Rico, he heard about a fountain that restored youth. The Fountain of Youth was supposed to be in what is now Florida. In 1513, Ponce de León went to Florida, hoping to find the Fountain of Youth. Although Ponce de León never found it, he claimed Florida for Spain. During the next several years, he tried to start colonies in the newly claimed land. Each time, however, the Native Americans drove him out.

In 1565, the king of Spain found out the French were building a colony in northeastern Florida. He was angry because he believed all of Florida belonged to Spain. Pedro Menéndez de Avilés was sent by the king to destroy the French colony. Menéndez de Avilés and his soldiers wiped out the French colony and built a Spanish colony called St. Augustine.

St. Augustine became an important military base for the Spaniards. The soldiers guarded the Spanish ships carrying gold and silver from Mexico to Spain. They also kept out the French and English settlers.

Circle the number of the best answer.

1. The king of Spain wanted to build a colony in Florida to

    (1) keep the English and French out and protect Spanish ships.

    (2) protect Spanish ships and help the French build a colony.

    (3) honor Juan Ponce de León.

    (4) improve relations with the English.

    (5) honor Pedro Menéndez de Avilés.

2. Which reason best explains why Pedro Menéndez de Avilés was sent to Florida?

    (1) to find the Fountain of Youth

    (2) to guard the Spanish ships going from Mexico to Spain

    (3) to drive out the English colonists

    (4) to drive out the French colonists

    (5) to search for gold and silver

Go on to the next page.

The United States in 1862

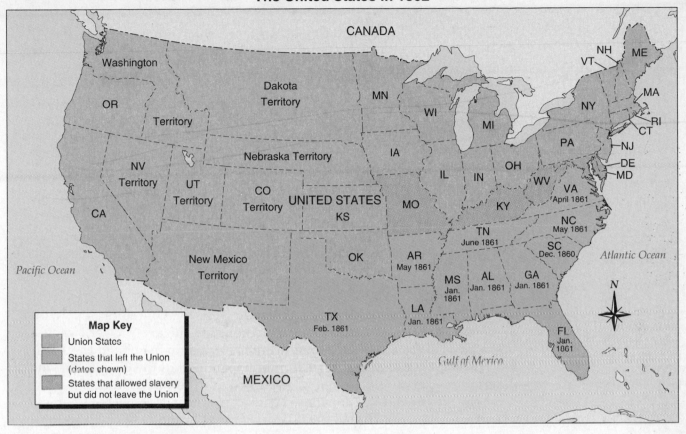

Map Key
- Union States
- States that left the Union (dates shown)
- States that allowed slavery but did not leave the Union

Write your answers in the space provided.

3. The first state to leave the Union was

   _____.

4. The last state to leave the Union was _____.

5. How many states left the Union?

   _____

Circle the number of the best answer.

6. States that allowed slavery but did not leave the Union were called border states because they

   (1) lay along the southern border of the United States.

   (2) lay along the northern border of the United States.

   (3) separated the eastern states from the western territories.

   (4) separated the Union states from the Confederate states.

   (5) lay along the eastern coast of the United States.

Go on to the next page.

The Internment of Japanese Americans

On December 7, 1941, Japan attacked the United States at Pearl Harbor. The next day, the United States declared war against Japan. After Japan's attack, it was feared that Japanese Americans would become spies for Japan. In March 1942, the United States government began to move Japanese Americans away from the west coast. Over 120,000 Japanese Americans were forced to sell their property. Then they were interned. **Interned** means they were sent to camps and forced to stay there.

Sheila Hamanaka, a Japanese-American writer, wrote about the internment camps. She told how families were rounded up and sent to remote places, often in the middle of a desert. She described how one or two families had to live in a single room. Often there was no running water. Japanese Americans were treated as prisoners. Hamanaka wrote, "Anyone, including the elderly and children, who wandered too close to the barbed-wire fences surrounding the camps risked being shot by the guards who sat in towers, armed with rifles and machine guns."

Yet Japanese Americans remained loyal to the United States. In 1943, Japanese Americans were permitted to enlist in the army. Over twelve hundred men from the internment camps signed up. Although their war records were outstanding, their families remained in the camps. The last Japanese Americans were not allowed to leave the camps until six months after the war ended. No Japanese American was ever convicted of spying. Finally in 1988, the United States government formally apologized to the Japanese Americans.

Circle the number of the best answer.

7. Japanese Americans were interned because

   (1) the Japanese attacked the United States.

   (2) the United States declared war on Japan.

   (3) of the fear that Japanese Americans might be spies for Japan.

   (4) the Japanese Americans were not allowed to join the army.

   (5) of the fear that Japanese Americans would move to Japan.

8. The <u>best</u> conclusion you can draw from the article is that

   (1) Japanese Americans were spies for Japan.

   (2) the internment of Japanese Americans was an injustice.

   (3) Japanese Americans didn't mind the internment camps.

   (4) the United States won the war with Japan.

   (5) Japanese Americans should have joined the Japanese army.

Go on to the next page.

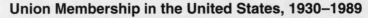

Union Membership in the United States, 1930–1989

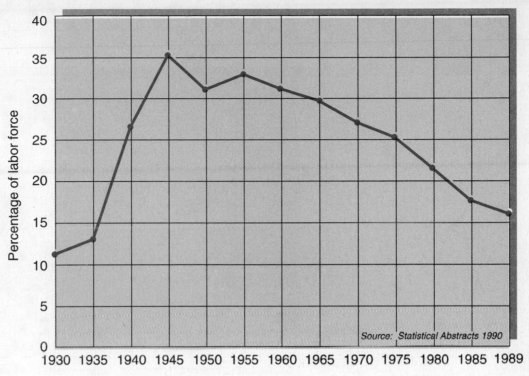

Source: Statistical Abstracts 1990

Year

Write your answers in the space provided.

9. Union membership kept increasing until what year?

_____

10. What happened after union membership increased in 1955?

_____

11. What happened after union membership reached its peak in 1945?

_____

Circle the number of the best answer.

12. Which of the following is a <u>true</u> statement based on the graph?

    (1) Union membership was greater in 1989 than in 1930.

    (2) Union membership grew rapidly from 1965 to 1970.

    (3) Union membership continued to decrease after 1950.

    (4) Union membership continued to increase after 1955.

    (5) Union membership was highest in 1955.

ECONOMICS

The market is where buyers and sellers meet. Here people are shopping for electronic equipment.

Throughout the world, resources are limited. Yet the list of the things people want and need is unlimited. So people have to make choices. **Economics** is the study of how people use their resources.

Economics is an important part of life. People make economic decisions all the time. They buy one product over another. They pay cash rather than use a credit card. They take a new job or leave an old one. These choices not only affect the individual. They also affect the economic system of the United States.

The economic system of the United States is called the free enterprise system. In a **free enterprise system**, buyers affect what goods and services are produced, how much is produced, and how much the goods cost. People are also a part of the production process. Workers use tools to turn natural resources into goods that consumers buy. In addition, someone has to come up with new ideas and turn these ideas into goods and services. This person is called an **entrepreneur**.

In a free enterprise system, entrepreneurs play a leading role. They invest their time and money in hopes of making a profit from their business. Without their willingness to take risks and explore new ideas, the United States would not be as rich a country as it is today. An Wang is an example of how entrepreneurs have helped the nation prosper.

An Wang

An Wang came to the United States from China in 1945, just after World War II. He was 25 years old. While Wang studied physics at Harvard University, he became interested in a new invention called the computer. In 1951, he decided to design and build computers. With $600, Wang set up a laboratory in an old store over a garage. For the next forty years, Wang Laboratories grew into a business with sales over two billion dollars.

When Wang put all of his money into a new business in a brand-new industry, he was taking a risk. The free enterprise system rewards entrepreneurs like Wang for taking risks. It does so because the whole country benefits from their efforts. Among those who benefitted were the thousands of people who worked for the company over the years. His machines helped many other businesses grow and expand as well. For example, some companies produce parts for Wang computers. Others provide software needed to run the machines.

This unit features articles about economics.

■ The article about the free enterprise system uses farming as an example of how the system works.

■ The article about managing money explains how budgets help people make decisions about how to spend their money.

■ In the article about supply and demand, the baseball card market is used to explain these important concepts of economics.

■ The article about inflation and recession explains the causes of these problems and ways of managing them.

■ The kinds of jobs people have and where these jobs are located are the focuses of the world trade article.

The Free Enterprise System

Setting the Stage

The United States has an economy based on the free enterprise system. Buyers and sellers determine the type of goods produced, the amount produced, and the price.

Past: What you already know

You may already know something about the free enterprise system. Write two things you already know.

1. _____

2. _____

Present: What you learn by previewing

Write the headings from the article on pages 93–95 below.

How Free Enterprise Works

3. _____

4. _____

5. _____

What do the graphs on page 94 show?

6. _____

_____

Future: Questions to answer

Write three questions you expect this article to answer.

7. _____

8. _____

9. _____

How Free Enterprise Works

As you read each section, circle the words you don't know. Look up the meanings.

The United States has an economic system called the free enterprise system. In a **free enterprise system**, people respond to opportunities in the market. A **market** is a place where buyers and sellers meet. It determines the goods and services that will be produced. The market also determines how goods will be produced and who will buy them. Farming is a good example of how free enterprise works in the United States.

Farming for a Market

How do farmers decide what crops to grow? How do they decide what animals to raise? How do farmers know how much to produce? Farmers try to find answers to these questions by watching consumers. **Consumers** are the people who buy and use goods and services. For example, suppose consumers are buying fewer potatoes than they did in the past. Stores will order fewer potatoes. So the potato farmers will grow fewer potatoes. On the other hand, if consumers begin buying more potatoes, stores will order more. Then potato farmers will increase their potato crop.

Farmers have a good reason, or an **incentive**, to produce the kinds of goods people want. The incentive is simple. Farmers want to make as much money as possible. By looking at what consumers buy, farmers learn what to produce and how much. The **price** is the amount of money a consumer pays for goods.

Farmers earn more when they produce goods that are in demand. **Demand** is the amount of goods or services consumers are willing to buy at a certain price at a given time. If people prefer beets over potatoes, then the demand is higher for beets. Farmers have an incentive to grow beets.

An incentive for the consumer is the price. The price helps to determine who buys the goods. For the most part, goods go to the people who have money to buy them. If the price is low, more people are able to buy the goods.

Making Inferences. It is important to look for main ideas and details as you read. Sometimes you can use that information to figure out things that are not actually stated. This is called making an inference. Reread the last paragraph under the heading *Farming for a Market*. Write the detail that tells what happens when the price is low.

Applying Your Skills and Strategies

_____

Make an inference about what happens when the price is high.

_____

The Effects of Competition

Farmers sell their goods in a market where there is competition from other farmers. The farmers sell similar goods. Consumers, or buyers, look at the price to decide what to buy. There are many buyers and sellers in the market. So no one buyer or seller can affect the price. Also, buyers and sellers are free to enter and leave the market at any time.

In a competitive market, sellers have an incentive to keep prices low. Suppose one farmer's price for beets is higher than another farmer's price. The consumer will buy the beets at the lower price. So the farmer has to sell goods at the lowest possible price. But the price can't be too low because the farmer must make some money.

A competitive market requires efficiency. Over the years, no group has been more efficient than American farmers. In the 1850s, one farmer could produce enough food to feed five people. At that time about 50 percent of all Americans worked as farmers. Today the average farmer feeds 65 people. Yet less than 3 percent of all Americans are farmers.

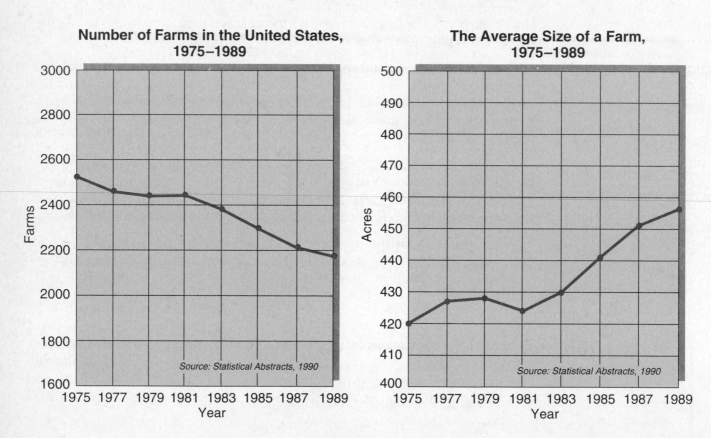

Source: Statistical Abstracts, 1990

How do so few farmers produce so much food? The answer lies in efficiency gained through technology. **Technology** is the tools and methods used to increase production of products for people. Today, farmers have machines. They also have special seeds, fertilizers, and weed killers. As a result, fewer farmers can supply more food efficiently. No other country can grow, process, and market food products as efficiently as American farmers.

The farms today are larger than the ones in the past. But there are fewer of them. Many farms are now owned by corporations rather than individuals. A **corporation** is a business that is owned by stockholders. Each stockholder shares in the profits and the risks of the business. Since a corporation may consist of many people, it is able to raise large sums of money. Today, large amounts of money and skill are needed to run a farm.

Comparing Line Graphs. *Line graphs* are often used to show changes over a period of time. If there is any change, it may be an *increase* or a *decrease*. Look at the two line graphs on page 94. They show the changes in the number and size of farms in the United States. How has the number of farms changed from 1975–1989?

Applying Your Skills and Strategies

How has the size of the farms changed over the same time period?

Responding to Change

Competing with large farms owned by corporations is not easy. As a result, some individual farmers have left the market. Others have made contracts with canneries, frozen-food companies, and other food processors. These farmers know how much they will get for their crop before it is harvested. Some earn extra money by growing crops to meet a company's special needs.

Other individual farmers form cooperatives. A **cooperative** is a group of farmers who join together to ensure the quality of their crops. They work as a group to obtain the best price. California raisin growers belong to a cooperative. Many orange and grapefruit growers in California and Florida do, too.

Some cooperatives advertise to encourage consumers to buy their products. For example, people are eating less beef and pork. That is because these consumers feel that beef and pork contain too much fat. So certain cooperatives try to persuade consumers to buy more beef and pork. They say these meats can be part of a healthful diet. They explain that new technology is helping to produce pork and beef that is lower in fat.

Competition benefits consumers in many ways. In 1900, the average American family spent over 45 percent of its income on food. Most families could afford chicken once a week. Today, the average family spends only about 19 percent of its income on food. They can have chicken or oranges as often as they like. Competition has kept prices down and given consumers more choices. It has also provided incentives to expand the nation's food supply.

Thinking About the Article

Fill in the blank with the word or words that best complete each statement.

1. An economic system in which the market decides what goods will be produced and how these goods will be distributed is called a

   _____.

2. People who buy goods and services are _____.

3. The _____ is where buyers and sellers meet.

4. The tools and methods used to increase production of products for

   people is _____.

Write your answers in the space provided.

5. Review the questions you wrote on page 92. Did the article answer your questions? If you said *yes*, write the answers. If your questions were not answered, write three things you learned from this article.

   _____

   _____

   _____

   _____

   _____

6. Why do farmers try to develop better tools and experiment with new methods of farming?

   _____

   _____

   _____

7. Name two ways consumers benefit from competition.

   _____

   _____

    Check your answers on page 219.

Circle the number of the best answer.

8. Look at the graphs on page 94. The graphs suggest that by the year 2000 there will be

   (1) fewer farms, and they will be smaller.

   (2) more farms that are the same size as farms today.

   (3) fewer farms, but they will be larger.

   (4) farms that are owned by corporations only.

   (5) a need for Americans to buy all of their food from other countries.

9. Based on the article, which of the following is an effect of a competitive market?

   (1) Many people are selling similar goods.

   (2) People are always entering and leaving the market.

   (3) Sellers can charge any price they want for their goods.

   (4) Price is a major factor when people decide what to buy.

   (5) Producers must be more efficient when producing goods.

10. Which of the following is the best reason for pork cooperatives to advertise to the consumer?

    (1) developing new technology in pork production

    (2) increasing the demand for pork

    (3) charging a higher price for pork

    (4) encouraging pork producers to join the cooperative

    (5) reducing the cost of producing pork

Write your answer in the space provided.

11. Long-distance telephone companies are in a very competitive market. How does that competition help you choose which telephone service to use? How would you be affected if there were less competition in this market? Explain your answer.

_____

_____

_____

_____

_____

Money Management

Setting the Stage

Most people want more things than they have the money to buy. Very few people have enough money to satisfy every want or need. So choices have to be made. People try to find ways to make the most of the money they have.

Past: What you already know

You may already know something about managing money. Write two things you already know.

1. _____

2. _____

Present: What you learn by previewing

Write the headings from the article on pages 99–101 below.

Getting the Most for the Money

3. _____

4. _____

5. _____

What do the chart and graph on page 99 show?

6. _____

_____

Future: Questions to answer

Write three questions you expect this article to answer.

7. _____

8. _____

9. _____

Check your answers on page 219.

Getting the Most for the Money

As you read each section, circle the words you don't know. Look up the meanings.

Few people have as much money as they would like. So people try to use their money wisely. People who manage money well create and follow a plan for spending it. They consider all the costs before deciding whether or not to buy something. Good money managers do not borrow money often. If they do need a loan, they borrow carefully.

Follow a Plan

People who manage their money often make a budget. A **budget** is a detailed financial plan. It shows how much money comes in each month. It also shows how much money is spent each month. To prepare a budget, first list the net income. The **net income** is money left after taxes are paid. Then list all expenses, or money that is paid out. Start with fixed expenses. **Fixed expenses** are payments that stay the same each month. Rent and car payments are fixed expenses. Next list expenses that vary from month to month. These are **flexible expenses**. Clothing is a flexible expense.

The chart below is an example of a budget. The amounts the family planned to spend in the month of May are in the left-hand column. The amounts actually spent are in the right-hand column.

BUDGET FOR THE RIVERA FAMILY		
NET INCOME $2,000		
Expenses	Planned	Actual
Housing	$500	$500
Utilities	140	160
Food	340	320
Transportation	440	440
Credit cards	300	200
Medical	80	100
Clothing	100	200
Other	100	80
TOTAL EXPENSES	**$2,000**	**$2,000**

How the Average American Family Spends Its Income

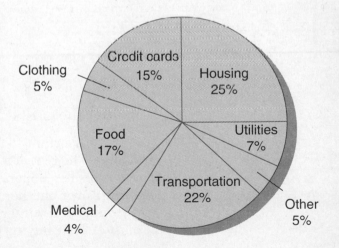

Clothing 5%
Credit cards 15%
Housing 25%
Utilities 7%
Food 17%
Transportation 22%
Other 5%
Medical 4%

Fixed expenses are usually easy to budget. However, sometimes fixed expenses are due only a few times a year and are forgotten. Property taxes are an example of this type of expense. It is important to set aside money each month. Then bills can be paid when they are due. It is harder to budget for flexible expenses. The best way is to make a prediction. Base it on how much was spent during the past year.

A budget helps people decide what they can and cannot afford. They see how a purchase could affect other things they want or need. They may find places where they can cut costs.

Many people are surprised when they prepare a budget. They see how much money they spend on things they don't really need. Some people have given up smoking after they discover how much they spend on cigarettes.

Reading a Circle Graph. A *circle graph* is used to compare amounts. Circle graphs are sometimes called *pie charts*. Each section of the graph looks like a slice of a pie. The sections can be compared to one another. They can also be compared to the whole amount. The larger the section, the greater the amount. Often, a circle graph is presented using percents. The whole circle is always 100 percent. Look at the circle graph on page 99. It shows the percent of net income the average family spends on various goods and services. What percent of the average family's income is spent on housing?

Applying Your Skills and Strategies

_____

What are the four greatest expenses the average family has each month?

_____

_____

Consider the Costs

It is important to look at all of the costs involved before deciding on a purchase. The cost of a new pair of shoes is not just the price of the shoes. There is also an opportunity cost. **Opportunity cost** is the cost of choosing one thing over another. For example, buying the shoes may mean having less money for a winter coat. Good money managers know what the results of most of their buying decisions will be.

Once the decision is made to buy the shoes, how much to spend must be determined. A smart shopper makes this choice by asking: What will be gained by buying a better pair of shoes? What will be given up by buying shoes of a lesser quality? A smart shopper is willing to substitute one thing for another. The shopper may choose a less expensive pair of shoes to save money. Or the shopper may substitute the style of the shoe for a better brand that will last longer. Comparing prices of the same pair of shoes at several stores also may save money.

Check your answers on page 219.

Identifying Cause and Effect.   Every event has at least one cause and one effect. The *cause* tells *why* something happened. The *effect* tells *what happened* as a result of the cause. Words like *because, reason,* and *since* suggest a cause. Words or phrases like *as a result, cost,* and *for this reason* focus on effects. Reread the paragraphs under the heading *Consider the Costs.* What would be an effect of not considering opportunity cost when deciding to buy something?

Applying Your Skills and Strategies

Careful Borrowing

People do not always have enough cash on hand to pay for the things they want or need. They may decide to borrow the money now and pay for it later. Borrowing money can be expensive. So people must consider more than the price of the item and the opportunity costs. The cost of borrowing the money must be considered, too.

How much money can a person afford to borrow? Some experts suggest limiting debts to one fifth of the net income. A person with a net income of $15,000 should not borrow more than $3,000. Borrowing includes anything bought on an installment plan or paid for with a credit card. It also includes using charge accounts at local stores and loans from a bank.

Knowing the cost of borrowing helps people get the most for their money. Interest rates can vary greatly. There was a recent study of new-car loans. It showed that some places charged 10 percent more interest than others. Many loans had hidden costs. In some cases, borrowers had to pay a fee just to apply for the loan. In other cases, borrowers had to pay extra money if payments were late. Some people were charged extra for paying off their loan early.

A smart borrower never signs a loan agreement without reading and understanding the contract. If there is a problem later, the borrower is responsible for what is in the contract.

By law, lenders have to tell people what a loan will cost. Borrowers have a right to know the finance charge. The **finance charge** is the cost of the loan. A borrower also needs to know the annual percentage rate. The **annual percentage rate**, or **APR**, is the percent of interest a lender charges each year for every $100 borrowed. By knowing the APR, it is easy for borrowers to compare loans.

People who manage money well take charge of their finances. They know what they spend their money on and how much they spend. They not only take advantage of opportunities, but they also make the most of those opportunities.

Check your answer on page 219.

Thinking About the Article

Fill in the blank with the word or words that best complete each statement.

1. A detailed financial plan is a _____.

2. The money people have left after taxes are taken out is their

   _____.

3. Payments that stay the same every month are

   _____.

4. The cost of a loan is the _____.

5. The rate of interest a bank charges each year for each $100 of a loan

   is the _____.

Write your answers in the space provided.

6. Review the questions you wrote on page 98. Did the article answer your questions? If you said *yes*, write the answers. If your questions were not answered, write three things you learned from this article.

   _____

   _____

   _____

   _____

   _____

7. What are two benefits of following a budget?

   _____

   _____

8. Suppose someone decides to borrow money to buy a used car that costs $4,000. What costs should be considered?

   _____

   _____

   _____

Check your answers on pages 219–220.

9. Which of the following is an example of a flexible expense?

    (1) rent

    (2) car payment

    (3) groceries

    (4) car insurance

    (5) loan payment

10. The graph on page 99 shows the average American family spends

    (1) more on food than anything else.

    (2) almost half of its income on housing and transportation.

    (3) too much on things that are not important.

    (4) more today than it did ten years ago.

    (5) less today than it did ten years ago.

11. Look at the chart of the Riveras' budget on page 99. They spent twice as much on clothing than they budgeted. They were able to do this because

    (1) there was a sale on clothing at the local store.

    (2) their housing and transportation expenses decreased.

    (3) their credit-card payment was less than they budgeted.

    (4) their utility bill was less than they budgeted.

    (5) the Riveras sold their car.

Write your answer in the space provided.

12. People often buy things on the spur of the moment. This means they make the purchase without giving it much thought. Have you ever bought something on the spur of the moment? What is the opportunity cost for this type of purchase? Explain your answer.

    _____

    _____

    _____

    _____

Section 14

Supply and Demand

Setting the Stage

In a free enterprise system, buyers and sellers exchange goods at a certain price in the market. Two things determine the price of goods. One thing is how great the buyers' demand is for those goods. The other is how much the sellers of those goods supply.

Past: What you already know

You may already know something about supply and demand in a free enterprise system. Write two things you already know.

1. _____

2. _____

Present: What you learn by previewing

Write the headings from the article on pages 105–107 below.

It's All in the Cards

3. _____

4. _____

5. _____

What is the title of the table on page 106?

6. _____

Future: Questions to answer

Write three questions you expect this article to answer.

7. _____

8. _____

9. _____

Check your answers on page 220.

It's All in the Cards

As you read each section, circle the words you don't know. Look up the meanings.

People buy many items during the course of their lives. Some items break easily or are used up. Others last a very long time. Some items become more valuable as they get older. For example, some stamps and coins are worth more now than when they were first made. Many people buy certain items and hope the items will increase in value. These people **profit,** or make money, by selling the items at a higher price than the price they paid. People buy items, such as baseball cards, for this purpose.

A Changing Market

Young people have been collecting baseball cards for many years. Baseball cards are sold in packages containing several cards. A photo of a baseball player appears on the front of each card. On the back is information about the player and his career. In the past, young people traded cards with friends to get a favorite player or an entire team. As these young traders grew up, many lost interest in baseball cards. Some threw out or gave away their card collections. A few could not bear to part with their collections. So they stored their cards away in their homes.

Young people are still collecting baseball cards. Some also collect football, basketball, and hockey cards. There are even cards for cartoon characters and rock-music groups. However, collecting cards is no longer just for kids. Today, over half of all collectors are adults. Some of these collectors invest large amounts of money for cards that feature their favorite players. Often these are players the collectors remember from their childhood. A card from Henry Aaron's rookie, or first, season in the major leagues is worth about $1,400. Recently, someone sold Nolan Ryan's rookie card for $1,200. This person paid one cent for the card in 1968!

Predicting Outcomes. *Predicting outcomes* means trying to figure out what will happen next. It is important to make predictions as you read. Try to guess what will happen next based on what you have read so far. Look for details that can be used as clues. Use what you already know and your past experiences to help make predictions. Reread the paragraphs above. Write a prediction about what the rest of the article might be about.

Applying Your Skills and Strategies

_____

_____

Today, many people are searching their closets, basements, and attics for old baseball cards. They hope to see their penny purchases turn into sales worth thousands of dollars, too. Prices of old baseball cards have never been higher. The reason the price is so high is the result of how supply and demand affect each other.

A Matter of Supply and Demand

Supply is the amount of goods and services sellers are willing to offer at certain prices at a given time. More sellers enter a market when prices are high. Sellers usually increase production when prices are high. In fact, that is exactly what is happening in the sports-card business.

Today there are more companies making baseball cards than ever before. Each company is turning out more and more new cards. The supply of new cards is elastic. An **elastic supply** increases or decreases as the price changes. Since the price of the cards is increasing, the supply is increasing. On the other hand, the supply of older cards is inelastic. An **inelastic supply** is limited. It cannot be increased or decreased no matter what happens to the price. For example, a certain number of Nolan Ryan rookie baseball cards were made in 1968. Those cards can never be made again.

Demand is the amount of goods and services consumers are willing to buy at certain prices at a given time. The demand usually goes up as the price goes down. However, prices go up if the demand is greater than the supply. This is why the prices for old baseball cards are rising. Buyers are competing for a limited supply. The table below shows the value of older baseball cards in 1991.

The Honus Wagner baseball card that sold for $451,000

The Nolan Ryan rookie baseball card

Baseball Cards for Investment				
Player	Rookie Card Year	Card Co.	Card No.	August 1991 Price
Musial, Stan	48	Bowman	36 (MVP)	700.00
Williams, Ted	50	Bowman	98 (FBC)	650.00
Mantle, Mickey	51	Bowman	253	5000.00
Mays, Willie	51	Bowman	305 (ROY)	1850.00
Mantle, Mickey	52	Topps	311 (OP FTC)	8500.00
Banks, Ernie	54	Topps	94	680.00
Aaron, Hank	54	Topps	126	1400.00
Koufax, Sandy	55	Topps	123	1100.00
Clemante, Roberto	55	Topps	164	1150.00
Yastrzemski, Carl	60	Topps	148	375.00
Carew, Rod	67	Topps	569 (ROY DP)	500.00
Seaver, Tom	67	Topps	581 (ROY)	1150.00
Koosman, Ryan	68	Topps	177	1250.00
Jackson, Reggie	69	Topps	260	550.00
Schmidt/Cey	73	Topps	615	450.00
Yount, Robin	75	Topps	223	165.00
Brett, George	75	Topps	228	170.00
Henderson, Rickey	80	Topps	482	200.00
Ripken, Cal	82	Topps	21 (ROY)	30.00
Sandberg, Ryne	83	Topps	83	45.00
Boggs, Wade	83	Topps	498	35.00
Strawberry, D.	83	Topps Traded	108T (ROY XRC)	95.00
Clemens, Roger	84	Fleer Update	U27 (XRC)	150.00
McGwire, Mark	85	Topps	401	18.00
Fielder, Cecil	86	Donruss	512	16.00
Clark, Will	87	Fleer	269	26.00
Bonds, Barry	87	Fleer	604	12.00
Griffey Jr., Ken	89	Upper Deck	1	40.00
Maas, Kevin	90	Upper Deck	70	4.00
Justice, Dave	90	Upper Deck	711 (ROY)	7.00
Speculation Cards				
Rose, Pete	63	Topps	537 (ROY)	600.00
Smith, Ozzie	79	Topps	116	50.00
Gwynn, Tony	83	Topps	482	25.00
Williams, Matt	86	Fleer	101	6.00
Jefferies, Gregg	88	Fleer	137	7.00
Sheffield, Gary	89	Upper Deck	13B (COR)	2.00
Martinez, Ramon	89	Upper Deck	18	4.00
Sabo, Chris	89	Upper Deck	180	2.50
Offerman, Jose	90	Upper Deck	46	1.50
McDonald, Ben	90	Upper Deck	54B (COR)	3.00

Reading a Table.   A *table* organizes information in columns and rows. The title tells what kind of information is in the table. Look at the table on page 106. To find the 1991 value of a Willie Mays baseball card, read down the column under the heading *Player*. When you come to *Willie Mays*, read across the row to *August 1991*. The Willie Mays card is valued at $1,850. Write the August 1991 values of the two Mickey Mantle baseball cards made by Bowman and Topps.

Cards featuring Mickey Mantle in his rookie season are scarce. Items become **scarce** when the demand is greater than the supply. The Mickey Mantle rookie baseball card is scarce, and people are willing to pay a lot of money to get it. People are willing to pay even more money for cards that are extremely rare.

Scarcity and Price

Recently a baseball card sold for over $400,000. It featured Honus Wagner. He was a shortstop for the Pittsburgh Pirates in the early 1900s. Why is his card so valuable? In the early 1900s, tobacco companies distributed baseball cards. Wagner was a non-smoker. He objected to any connection with a tobacco product. So the company took his card off the market. Today, only forty Wagner cards are known to exist. Eight of these cards are in excellent condition. It was one of those eight that sold for over $400,000. The value of the Wagner card is due to the fact that it is rare.

A recent example shows how a card can become rare. A 13-year-old boy bought a 1968 Nolan Ryan rookie baseball card for $12 at a store. The card was really worth $1,200, but the store clerk did not read the price correctly. The store has a big sign that reads "All sales final," but the owner took the boy to court.

During the trial, the boy told the judge that he had already traded the Ryan card. He had traded it for two cards that were worth about $2,200. The judge was furious. She ordered that the Nolan Ryan card be brought to court as evidence. The new owner agreed but asked that the court's *Exhibit 1* sticker remain on the card after the case was settled. The card, with the sticker, could be worth as much as $3,000. The trial and the sticker made the card rare, so it increased in value.

Today, many people are buying cards hoping to find a rare one and strike it rich. Some people doubt that anyone will get rich from cards produced in the last few years. They say the supply of new cards is far too great. Others disagree. They believe that baseball cards will never lose value. One trader stated, "As long as there are baseball fans, there will be baseball cards, and those cards will be worth something."

Check your answer on page 220.

Thinking About the Article

Fill in the blank with the word or words that best complete each statement.

1. The amount of goods and services consumers are willing to buy at certain prices at a given time is called the _____.

2. The amount of goods and services sellers are willing to offer at certain prices is called the _____.

3. When production increases or decreases as the price changes, the supply is _____.

4. When the demand for a product is greater than the supply, the product is said to be _____.

Write your answers in the space provided.

5. Review the questions you wrote on page 104. Did the article answer your questions? If you said *yes*, write the answers. If your questions were not answered, write three things you learned from this article.

_____

_____

_____

_____

_____

6. When the demand for a product decreases, what usually happens to the price of that product?

_____

_____

7. When the supply of a product decreases, what usually happens to the price of that product?

_____

_____

Circle the number of the best answer.

8. Which of the following is an example of an inelastic supply?

    (1) clothes for work

    (2) cars made in the 1940s

    (3) chicken at a grocery store

    (4) radios with tape players

    (5) new bedroom furniture

9. Look at the table on page 106. Which of the following best explains why someone would buy a Chris Sabo card?

    (1) Sabo earns a large salary.

    (2) The demand for the Sabo card may increase over time.

    (3) The demand for the Sabo card may decrease over time.

    (4) Sabo may be traded to another team.

    (5) The Sabo card could be involved in a court case.

10. Look at the table on page 106. There are two Mickey Mantle cards listed. Which of the following best explains why the Topps Mickey Mantle card is worth more than the Bowman card?

    (1) The card from Bowman is older than the one from Topps.

    (2) The Topps card was printed in larger quantities.

    (3) The Bowman card was printed in smaller quantities.

    (4) The Topps card is scarcer than the one from Bowman.

    (5) Both cards are scarce.

Write your answer in the space provided.

11. Would you advise someone to invest his or her money in baseball cards? Do you think baseball cards will increase in value? Explain your answer.

    _____

    _____

    _____

    _____

    _____

15

Inflation and Recession

Setting the Stage

Economic activity in a free enterprise system is always changing. There are times when the economy grows very fast. During these years, there are many jobs available and people prosper. There are also times when economic growth is slow. These are times of recession.

Past: What you already know

You may already know something about times of prosperity and times of recession. Write two things you already know.

1. _____

2. _____

Present: What you learn by previewing

Write the headings from the article on pages 111–113 below.

The Business Cycle

3. _____

4. _____

5. _____

6. _____

What is the title of the graph on page 111?

7. _____

Future: Questions to answer

Write three questions you expect this article to answer.

8. _____

9. _____

10. _____

The Business Cycle

As you read each section, circle the words you don't know. Look up the meanings.

Over the past thirty years, the United States economy has grown enormously. But it has not been a steady growth. From time to time, there have been recessions. A **recession** is a time when business activity slows down. Demand for goods decreases. So does the production of these goods. Fewer workers are needed in plants and factories. As a result, unemployment rises. People have less money to spend, so prices begin to fall.

The United States has had five recessions since 1960. After a while, each recession ended and the economy grew again. The shifting of an economy from growth to recession and back to growth is called the **business cycle**. The business cycle affects the way people live and work.

A Different Kind of Recession

In 1981, the United States was in a recession. Many businesses were in trouble. Production and sales were down. The unemployment rate was high. The **unemployment rate** is the percent of workers in the labor force without jobs. Yet to everyone's surprise, prices kept rising. A time when prices are rising is called **inflation**.

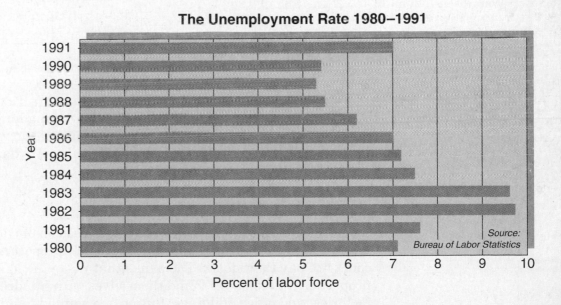

The Unemployment Rate 1980–1991

Source: Bureau of Labor Statistics

The rise in prices was due partly to events in the Middle East. A group of countries there tried to control the price of oil by limiting the oil supply. The group was successful. Between 1973 and 1981, prices rose to more than twice what they had been. As a result, the price of almost every product that used oil went up. Inflation made the recession worse than it might have been.

Recovery and Growth

In 1982, President Ronald Reagan had a plan to help the economy grow again. The plan allowed wealthy people and large companies to pay less taxes. He believed this would encourage these people and companies to spend their money.

By 1983, the economy was growing again. Oil prices dropped because the supply of oil was now greater than the demand. The oil producers of the Middle East discovered they could not control the oil supply for long periods of time. The government was spending more money on planes, rockets, and other military goods. So the defense industry grew. Other parts of the economy were expanding also. For example, the computer industry was growing rapidly.

Reading a Bar Graph. A *bar graph* is often used to make comparisons. The title tells what information is presented in the graph. The labels along the side and bottom of a graph tell how it is organized. Look at the bar graph on page 111. You can compare the amounts by looking at the length of the bars. In what year was unemployment the highest?

Applying Your Skills and Strategies

Was unemployment lower in 1983 or 1984?

As the economy grew, the unemployment rate dropped. Inflation also slowed. Consumers and companies were borrowing large sums of money, and they were spending it. This was the main reason why the economy grew so quickly. In the 1980s, individual consumers, large companies, and the government went deeper into debt.

A Recession Begins

By 1990, the economy was facing a recession once again. Many businesses that borrowed heavily to invest in property during the 1980s could not pay their debts. The banks that made the loans took over the properties. These banks found themselves with hundreds of empty stores, factories, and office buildings. But no one wanted to buy them. So the banks had no way to get their money back. Some banks made too many of these bad loans. These banks failed, meaning they could not stay in business. People worried about their savings and their jobs. So they bought less. Factories, in turn, produced less.

A recession began again. Businesses that had borrowed too much money were at fault. Banks that loaned money without considering the risks were to blame, too. The government was also at fault. Its policies encouraged businesses to borrow too much money.

                                            Check your answers on page 221.

Some economists also blame the recession on world events. By the end of the 1980s, the cold war was ending. The government cut its military spending. As a result, the defense industry was in trouble.

Then in August 1990, Saddam Hussein of Iraq invaded Kuwait. The invasion and the war in the Middle East that followed shook consumer confidence. **Consumer confidence** is the way buyers feel about the economy. Consumers buy about two thirds of all the goods and services that are produced in the United States. If consumers are fearful of the future, they do not buy as many goods.

Drawing Conclusions. A conclusion is an idea that follows logically from the information you have. To be true, conclusions must be supported by facts. You have just read that unemployment and people spending less are two results of recession. You can conclude that consumer confidence would fall if consumers believed a recession was coming. Draw a conclusion about the loss of consumer confidence during the war in the Middle East.

Applying Your Skills and Strategies

Managing the Economy

Are there ways to prevent a recession or stop inflation? Many economists do not think so. Some have been looking for ways to manage the economy since the 1930s. Those were the years of the Great Depression. A **depression** is a severe recession that lasts for a very long time. During the Great Depression, nearly fifteen million Americans were out of work. Many lost their homes. Others lost their savings when thousands of banks failed.

Over the years, the government has passed laws and created agencies to deal with recessions. One of the most important agencies is the Federal Reserve Board, or "The Fed." The Fed is a government agency that manages the country's money supply. It uses interest—the cost of borrowing—to keep inflation and recession under control. When prices rise, the Fed raises interest rates. People are less likely to borrow money when the cost of borrowing is high. When the economy slows, the Fed lowers interest rates. The Fed tries to keep rates high enough to discourage inflation and low enough to encourage businesses to expand.

Why then do we still have recessions? Why is inflation still a problem? The Fed cannot foresee a long labor strike, a crop failure, or a world crisis. Sometimes the Fed makes mistakes. But the agency is still important. A business executive compared the Federal Reserve Board to weather forecasters. "Both are wrong every once in awhile. Yet without them, people would be *flying blind*."

Check your answer on page 221.

Thinking About the Article

Fill in the blank with the word or words that best complete each statement.

1. A time when business activity slows is called a _____.

2. The way the economy shifts from growth to recession to growth is

   called the _____.

3. The percent of workers who are without jobs is the

   _____.

4. A period when most prices are rising is called _____.

Write your answers in the space provided.

5. Review the questions you wrote on page 110. Did the article answer your questions? If you said *yes*, write the answers. If your questions were not answered, write three things you learned from this article.

   _____

   _____

   _____

   _____

   _____

6. Why were people surprised when prices continued to rise during the recession that began in 1981?

   _____

   _____

7. Why did rising prices make it harder for the Fed to control the recession in the early 1980s?

   _____

   _____

   _____

Check your answers on page 221.

8. Name two causes of the recession that began in 1990.

_____

_____

Circle the number of the best answer for each question.

9. When consumers have confidence in the economy, they tend to

    (1) save more than they spend.

    (2) buy more.

    (3) buy less.

    (4) ignore signs of a recession.

    (5) borrow less.

10. Which of the following best explains why inflation occurs?

    (1) Inflation is due to overborrowing.

    (2) Inflation is due to events in other countries.

    (3) Inflation is the fault of governments.

    (4) Inflation is the fault of banks and large corporations.

    (5) Inflation is caused by many different factors.

11. Look at the bar graph on page 111. Which of the following is the best conclusion that can be drawn from the graph?

    (1) The unemployment rate usually stays the same over time.

    (2) The country never recovered from the recession in the early 1980s.

    (3) The defense industry borrowed too much money in 1985.

    (4) The country was recovering from the recession by the mid-1980s.

    (5) Banks tried to create jobs in the early 1980s.

Write your answer in the space provided.

12. A recession affects many people in different ways. Were you or someone you know affected by the last recession? Explain your answer.

_____

_____

_____

Section 16

World Trade

Setting the Stage

Long ago, farms and factories produced goods for local markets. Within the last hundred years, many companies began to sell to a national market. Today, many companies are selling goods to an international, or world, market. As international trade has grown, companies have changed the way they do business. They have also changed the ways they produce goods and services.

Past: What you already know

You may already know something about world trade. Write two things you already know.

1. _____

2. _____

Present: What you learn by previewing

Write the headings from the article on pages 117–119 below.

Going Global

3. _____

4. _____

5. _____

What is the title of the graph on page 117?

6. _____

Future: Questions to answer

Write three questions you expect this article to answer.

7. _____

8. _____

9. _____

Going Global

*As you read each
section, circle the
words you don't
know. Look up the
meanings.*

Today, more than ever before in history, what happens in one country
affects people around the world. Also, the economic systems of countries
around the world are tied together. These ties affect the kinds of goods
people buy and sell. They also affect the jobs people have and who their
employers are.

The Growth of Trade

World trade is growing rapidly. The United States is playing a leading
role in this growth. It is the world's largest exporter. **Exporters** sell their
goods to other countries. About 18 percent of all the goods sold in markets
around the world come from the United States. The United States is also
the world's largest importer. **Importers** buy goods from other countries. In
recent years, Americans have bought even more goods than they have sold.

What kinds of goods do Americans buy from other countries? The
list includes oil, aluminum, and other resources used to build and run
machines. It also includes consumer goods—everything from tea and cocoa
to televisions and cars. What kinds of things do Americans sell? American
exports include computers, airplanes, robots, wheat, beef, corn, and office
machines.

Americans also export services. **Service industries** sell services by
employing people who meet the needs of other people. Education, banking,
and medicine are service industries. Hotels, restaurants, and theme parks
are also service industries. Some Americans export services that teach
people from other countries how to manage a business. The United States
is the world's largest exporter of services. It is also the world's largest
importer of services.

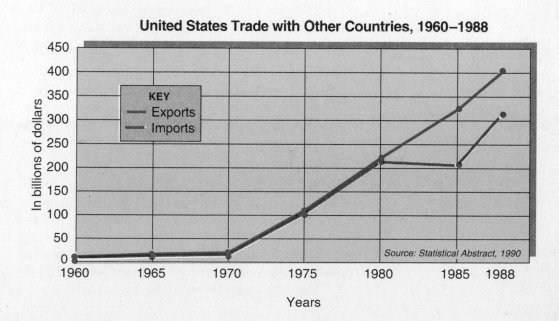

United States Trade with Other Countries, 1960–1988

Source: Statistical Abstract, 1990

KEY
— Exports
— Imports

In billions of dollars

Years

Reading a Line Graph. *Line graphs* are used to compare information and show change over a period of time. The title and the graph key tell you what is being compared. Look at the graph on page 117. Each line is a different color, making it easier to compare the information. What does each line show?

_____

_____

_____

Imports and exports have been rising since 1960. How is this shown on the graph?

_____

_____

Multinational Companies

As world trade has become more important, many companies have changed the way they do business. Some have even changed *where* they do business. The first American companies to sell goods around the world exported or imported raw materials. **Raw materials** are the base materials used to make goods. Oil is an example of a raw material. Later, companies sold finished products to people in other countries. Today, many large companies are **multinational**, with factories worldwide.

As multinational companies have grown, their outlook on the world has changed. The head of one multinational company explained the change by saying, "Once, you dropped an American off in Venezuela or Thailand with a boatload of toothpaste and had him build a business. Now we go into partnership with local business people or the local government."

Hundreds of other American companies are also becoming more international in their outlook. Some bought small companies in countries around the world. Others joined together to form one very large company. Still others work as partners with other companies on special projects. Under these arrangements, a rival in one market might be a partner in another market.

The United States is not the only country with multinational companies. Many of the new companies are European. Some are based in Japan, South Korea, Taiwan, and Singapore. Just as American companies do business around the world, foreign companies have built factories in the United States. They have also bought many American businesses. By 1987, European companies alone had invested over $92 billion in the United States. They employed two million Americans.

As multinational companies grow, it is harder to tell if they are American, Japanese, German, or Swiss. For example, a Swiss company is the world's largest food producer. It manages businesses around the world, including two American companies. Today, over 95 percent of the company's business takes place outside of Switzerland. In fact, very few of the company's employees are Swiss.

Applying Your Skills and Strategies

Supporting Conclusions. You draw a conclusion by reading for the main idea. You also read for details that lead to a conclusion. These details are called *supporting statements*. Reread the last paragraph above. You can conclude that, in time, the Swiss food company will no longer be considered a Swiss company. Write two statements that support this conclusion.

_____

_____

_____

Signs of change can be seen almost everywhere. Workers in Taiwan turn out sneakers for a German company. They are sold in shops throughout North America and Europe. A Japanese company runs a plant in Alabama. The plant makes videotapes for the European market. An American car company designs some of its cars in Germany. The company does the engineering in Ireland. Then the cars are built in South Korea and sold in the United States.

Competing Globally

Today, goods and services travel around the world at great speeds. Technology and ideas spread quickly. Scientists say that many tools and methods are outdated within four years of their invention. Not too long ago, countries tried to keep their advances in technology a secret. They did not want to share ideas. Today, there are few secrets. People have learned that as ideas spread, they are improved for everyone's good. So countries are now working together to develop new tools and methods to do business.

To compete successfully in today's world, a country needs more than the latest technology. It also needs workers who are able to use that technology. The head of an American multinational company says, "The essence of business as we move into the 21st century is going to be tapping the talent of good people. It's not about where you locate plants, it's how you locate the best people and motivate them."

This means that Americans are no longer just competing with other Americans for jobs. They are also competing with people from around the world.

Thinking About the Article

1. An _____ sells goods to other countries.

2. An _____ buys goods from other countries.

3. Companies that produce and sell goods in many different countries

   are _____.

Write your answers in the space provided.

4. Review the questions you wrote on page 116. Did the article answer
   your questions? If you said *yes*, write the answers. If your questions
   were not answered, write three things you learned from this article.

   _____

   _____

   _____

   _____

   _____

5. Why are some companies called multinational?

   _____

   _____

6. What are two examples of service industries?

   _____

   _____

7. Name two ways American companies have changed as world trade has
   become more important to the way they do business.

   _____

   _____

   _____

Circle the number of the best answer.

8. Which of the following <u>best</u> describes the growth of imports and exports, using the graph on page 117?

    (1) sharp increases in imports and decreases in exports

    (2) decreases in imports and increases in exports

    (3) increases in both imports and exports

    (4) increases in both imports and exports but a sharper increase in imports

    (5) decreases in both exports and imports

9. A country's ability to compete in the 1990s will depend on the

    (1) skill of its workers.

    (2) amount of resources it has.

    (3) number of multinational companies it has.

    (4) amount of its imports.

    (5) amount of its exports.

10. Which of the following is the best reason for countries sharing their tools and methods that are needed to do business?

    (1) Countries keep their advances in technology secret.

    (2) Countries want to start multinational companies.

    (3) Education in many countries must be improved.

    (4) Ideas are improved as they spread.

    (5) Large companies are looking to take over smaller ones.

Write your answer in the space provided.

11. The head of a multinational company said, "It's not about where you locate plants, it's how you locate the best people and motivate them." If other business people agree, what localities will have the best job opportunities? Explain your answer.

_____

_____

_____

_____

Check your answers on page 222.

Unit 3 Review:
Economics

Increasing Demand

Producers of goods and services are always looking for ways to increase demand. **Demand** is the amount of goods and services people are willing to buy at a given price. One way to increase demand is to find new uses for products. New uses for a product will attract new customers. Farm products are a good example. In recent years, scientists have found ways to increase the demand for many crops, especially the demand for corn.

For years, corn was considered just a food product. Today, however, corn is used to make everything from paint to diapers. In some cases, corn is a good substitute for oil in making paint. It is being used to make films and coatings for wood and metal. Corn can also be used as a fuel.

Adding a small amount of cornstarch to plastic can help protect the environment. Plastic does not decompose or break down. It lasts forever—unless a small amount of cornstarch is used to make the plastic. Then the plastic will decompose. As a result, cornstarch is being added to plastic products, such as diapers and plastic bags.

No one is sure how many other products can be improved with a little corn. As the demand grows, so does the supply of corn, and farmers have a reason to grow more corn.

Circle the number of the best answer.

1. According to the article, which of the following would be most likely to encourage the new uses of corn?

    (1) people who like to eat corn

    (2) people who use corn as animal feed

    (3) gasoline producers

    (4) wheat farmers

    (5) people who are concerned about the environment

2. Which of the following is the best conclusion that can be drawn from the passage?

    (1) Demand for corn is likely to increase.

    (2) Demand for corn is likely to decrease.

    (3) The supply of corn is likely to stay the same.

    (4) The supply of corn is likely to decrease.

    (5) Supply and demand will stay the same.

The Federal Budget

**The Federal Government Dollar
(Fiscal Year 1991 Estimate)**

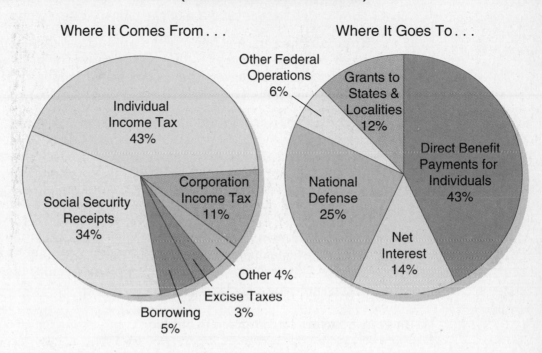

Where It Comes From . . .

Other Federal Operations 6%

Individual Income Tax 43%

Social Security Receipts 34%

Corporation Income Tax 11%

Other 4%

Excise Taxes 3%

Borrowing 5%

Where It Goes To . . .

Grants to States & Localities 12%

National Defense 25%

Direct Benefit Payments for Individuals 43%

Net Interest 14%

Write your answers in the space provided.

3. How does the government get the largest percent of its income?

_____

4. Where is the largest percent of the government's income spent?

_____

Circle the number of the best answer.

5. Which of the following is best supported by the graph entitled *Where It Comes From . . .?*

   (1) More than half of the government's income comes from individual income tax and social security.

   (2) Corporations pay more taxes than individuals.

   (3) The government does not have to borrow to pay its bills.

   (4) Contributions to social security make up over half the government's income.

   (5) Excise taxes make a big difference in the government's income.

Go on to the next page.

Deceptive Selling

Almost everyone has been the victim of deceptive selling methods. Perhaps you paid too much for an item. Maybe the product you bought was not worth as much as you thought it was. Smart shoppers learn to be wary. They watch for one or more of the following selling practices.

Special Pricing. A seller offers a product at a "special low price." The seller tells the customer to buy now because the price will go up soon. However, in many cases, the special price is actually higher than the price of the same item at other stores.

Bait and Switch. An ad offers an item at a very low price. When customers go to buy that item, they are told that the item is an inferior product. The seller then suggests switching to a more expensive model of the same item. The seller may also tell buyers that the advertised item is "out of stock." The customers are then urged to buy the more expensive model that is "in stock."

Chain Referrals. Customers are told that if they buy a product and then refer other customers, they will get a gift or a reduced price. Often the price of the product, even with the gift or discount, is higher than the price of the same item at other stores.

Write your answers in the space provided.

6. An ad offers a great deal on a television set. When the customer goes to buy the item, the seller says it is out of stock. However, the seller points out that a much better, more expensive model is in stock. Which method is the seller using?

7. A seller tells the buyer that the price of compact disc players is expected to double and maybe triple in the next few months. There will never be a better time to buy than now. Which method is the seller using?

Circle the number of the best answer.

8. Which of the following statements is supported by the article?

    (1) All sellers are dishonest.

    (2) Let the buyer beware.

    (3) If a deal sounds good, buy the item.

    (4) Never check prices in other stores.

    (5) Don't buy an item if you don't need it.

Go on to the next page.

Occupations with an Estimated Job Growth of 20% or More, 1988 and 2000

	Employment (thousands)		Percent change
	1988	2000	1988-2000
Registered nurses	1577	2190	39
Waiters and waitresses	1786	2337	31
Nursing aides, orderlies, and attendants	1184	1562	32
Guards	795	1050	32
Computer programmers	519	769	48
Food preparation workers	1027	1260	23
Licensed practical nurses	626	855	37
Computer systems analysts	403	617	53
Accountants and auditors	963	1174	22
Child care workers	670	856	28
Gardeners and groundskeepers, except farm	760	943	24
Lawyers	582	763	31
Electrical and electronics engineers	430	615	40
Food service and lodging managers	560	721	29
Home health aides	236	397	68
Cooks, restaurant	572	728	27
Physicians	535	684	28
Teacher's aides and educational assistants	682	827	21
Electrical and electronic engineering technicians	341	471	38
Dining room and cafeteria attendants and bar helpers	448	578	29
Medical secretaries	207	327	58
Social workers	385	495	29

Write your answers in the space provided.

9. Which occupation is expected to have the greatest growth by 2000?

_____

10. What is the expected percent of increase of guards by 2000?

_____

Circle the number of the best answer.

11. Which of the following cannot be determined from the table?

   (1) number of jobs in each occupation in 1988

   (2) percent of increase of each occupation

   (3) occupations that are declining most rapidly

   (4) occupations that are increasing most rapidly

   (5) number of jobs expected for each occupation by 2000

Check your answers on page 222.

POLITICAL SCIENCE

The Democratic National Convention in Atlanta in 1988

Political scientists study politics and government. In doing so, they focus on three questions: What are the government's aims or goals? Who governs? How is the government organized? In answering these questions, they try to determine how government affects people's lives.

A **constitution** is a plan for government. In the United States, the Constitution answers all three questions. The goals of government are explained at the beginning. It says "the people" want the states to be united into one country. The government must be fair, keep the peace, and guard the freedom of all Americans.

The Constitution goes on to explain who governs and how the government is organized. Power is divided between the states and the federal government. It also divides the power of the federal government. Congress makes the laws. The President enforces those laws. The courts explain the meaning of the laws.

When the Constitution was written, the United States had 13 states and about 4 million people. Most people could not vote. A voter had to own property. He also had to be a white male over the age of 21. Today the United States has fifty states and over 250 million people. Today almost every American citizen over the age of 18 has the right to vote. As a result, more people are participating in politics than ever before.

One person who took advantage of the opportunity to participate in politics was Barbara Jordan. Jordan was a representative in Congress from Texas. When she was growing up in the 1940s, African Americans in Texas could not attend the same schools as white children. Even colleges were segregated. So Jordan attended a college for African-American students. After she graduated with highest honors, she went to law school. She became the first woman and the first African American to enter Boston University Law School.

Barbara Jordan

When Jordan graduated, she returned to Texas and began a law practice. She became involved in politics. In 1966, she became the first African-American woman ever elected to the Texas State Senate. In 1972, she decided to run for a seat in the United States House of Representatives. To the surprise of many people, she won. She became the second African-American woman to serve in the House of Representatives. Shirley Chisholm of New York was the first. In 1978, she left government to become a professor. Today she teaches government at a university.

This unit features articles about government and politics.

■ The article about local government shows how even the most basic services can make a big difference in our lives.

■ The article about state government shows how people can make a difference in getting laws passed.

■ The article about the Bill of Rights explains how a poor man in Florida challenged the government and won.

■ The article about voting shows how candidates run for office and try to persuade people to vote for them.

■ The article about the way Americans debate issues examines the arguments for and against gun-control laws.

Section 17

Local Government

Setting the Stage

Local governments provide the basic services of a city, town, or county. The most basic service provided is picking up the trash. Trash collection is something most people take for granted. Since the 1980s, however, people have been paying closer attention to their trash. Communities across the nation are facing a garbage crisis.

Past: What you already know

You may already know something about local government, or the garbage crisis. Write two things you already know.

1. _____

2. _____

Present: What you learn by previewing

Write the headings from the article on pages 129–131 below.

The Garbage Crisis

3. _____

4. _____

5. _____

What is the title of the cartoon on page 130?

6. _____

Future: Questions to answer

Write three questions you expect this article to answer.

7. _____

8. _____

9. _____

The Garbage Crisis

As you read each section, circle the words you don't know. Look up the meanings.

Cities, towns, and counties make up the different levels of local government. Local government manages the police and fire departments, paves the streets, and collects the garbage. It is the government that most directly affects the quality of our lives. Today, many local governments are facing a garbage crisis.

Mountains of Trash

People use up many products and then throw them away. As a result, Americans produce about 160 million tons of garbage each year! That number does not include waste from factories. It does not even include abandoned cars. Between 1960 and 1985, the amount of trash people produced increased by 80 percent. Experts expect it to rise another 20 percent by the year 2000. Counties and towns **recycle**, or process to use again, about 10 percent of the trash. Another 10 percent is burned. The rest is carted off to landfills. A **landfill** is a place where trash is buried under thin layers of earth.

Finding the Implied Main Idea. The *topic sentence* of a paragraph tells the main idea of the paragraph. Sometimes a paragraph has no topic sentence. So the main idea is not stated, it is *implied*. The reader must determine the main idea from the *details* in the paragraph. Reread the paragraph above. Write the main idea of that paragraph below.

Applying Your Skills and Strategies

By 1996, about half of the country's nearly 6,000 landfills will close. Many landfills are closing because they are full. Others are closing because they are dangerous. As garbage decays, it forms a poison that can seep into the soil. There, it pollutes **groundwater,** which is an underground source of water. It is the water found in wells, springs, ponds, and aquifers. About half of the country's drinking water comes from groundwater. Decaying garbage also forms methane. Methane is a colorless, odorless gas that burns easily.

Many communities need new landfills to replace ones that are closing. Yet they are finding it hard to open a new landfill. Experts call it the first law of garbage: "Everybody wants it picked up, but nobody wants it put down."

Taking Responsibility

Most communities have **ordinances,** or laws, that deal with trash removal. Many of these laws are new. Some of the laws require people to separate hazardous wastes from the rest of their trash. **Hazardous wastes** are those items that harm the environment. They include old batteries, motor oil, and certain kinds of paint. Other laws focus on reducing the amount of trash that gets carted off to a landfill. Over eight hundred communities have set up compost centers. In these centers, yard waste, such as grass clippings and leaves, is turned into rich soil for gardeners.

State governments also have laws that deal with trash removal. Local governments must obey state laws as well as their own ordinances. For example, most communities need a state permit to open a landfill. A **permit** is a document that gives a town, a business, or an individual permission to do something.

Local governments must also enforce state laws that encourage recycling. In some states, people pay extra money as a deposit on soda cans and bottles. When the empty bottles or cans are returned, the money is refunded. Several states require the recycling of paper and aluminum.

Local governments must enforce federal laws. The **Environmental Protection Agency (EPA)** sets guidelines on landfills and other efforts to dispose of trash.

© Wicks/Rothco. Reprinted with permission.

Reading a Political Cartoon. A *political cartoon* expresses an opinion on an issue. The artist uses symbols and exaggerated drawings to express his or her views. The title often provides an important clue to what the cartoonist is trying to say. It is also important to know what the symbols mean. Study the cartoon on page 130. What symbol is used?

_____

What does the symbol represent?

_____

Reduce, Reuse, and Recycle

Communities across the nation are improving trash disposal in a variety of ways. People are being urged to practice the three R's of waste disposal: reduce trash, reuse whenever possible, and recycle more.

Many communities are cleaning up old landfills. Whenever a new landfill is opened, new state and federal guidelines are followed closely. Garbage dumps are no longer built near aquifers or lakes. The new landfills are safer, too. Garbage is no longer dumped into an open pit. The pit is lined with layers of sand, plastic, and clay before the trash is thrown into it. This keeps the garbage from oozing into the ground outside the pit. Pumps are used to drain dangerous liquids from decaying garbage. Some pumps remove and save the methane gas to be used to make electricity. When the landfill is full, it too can be recycled. Airports, hospitals, and parks have been built on landfills.

In every city and town, local governments are taking a closer look at what people throw away. Their goal is to waste less and recycle more. Most people think that landfills are filled with fast-food containers and disposable diapers. Yet diapers and food containers account for less than 2 percent of all garbage. About half of all trash is paper. Grass clippings and food scraps account for another 15 percent.

As a result, many towns no longer pick up yard waste. Paper and other items are being recycled at curbside bins. Some towns are getting people to take part in recycling programs by charging for trash pickup. Usually, households are charged by the can. Those who produce more trash pay more. One citizen said of the charges, "I've been [recycling] for years, but many of my friends and neighbors said they couldn't be bothered. But now they bother because it's hitting them in the pocketbook."

Individuals, as well as the government, must do their part to prevent the garbage crisis from getting worse.

Thinking About the Article

Fill in the blank with the word or words that best complete each statement.

1. A _____ is a place where garbage is buried under thin layers of earth.

2. An underground source of water is known as

   _____.

3. The law of a city or town is called an _____.

4. Wastes that endanger the environment are known as

   _____.

5. A state document that gives a town permission to build a landfill is

   called a _____.

Write your answers in the space provided.

6. Review the questions you wrote on page 128. Did the article answer your questions? If you said *yes*, write the answers. If your questions were not answered, write three things you learned from this article.

   _____

   _____

   _____

   _____

   _____

7. Name three ways local governments are dealing with the garbage crisis.

   _____

   _____

   _____

   _____

Circle the number of the best answer.

8. The cartoon on page 130 is expressing the opinion that

    (1) Americans produce too much garbage.

    (2) Americans should clean up the Statue of Liberty.

    (3) Americans should stop littering.

    (4) The United States needs more landfills.

    (5) Americans should recycle more paper.

9. Some cities now charge people according to how much garbage they produce. The success of these programs supports the opinion that

    (1) only individuals can end the garbage crisis.

    (2) people take basic services for granted.

    (3) people care when it hits their pocketbooks.

    (4) nobody wants his or her trash picked up.

    (5) the garbage crisis is the government's problem.

10. Which of the following is the best conclusion that can be drawn from the article?

    (1) Local governments need to do more to deal with the garbage crisis.

    (2) Individuals and all levels of government must deal with the garbage crisis.

    (3) Recycling is the answer to the garbage crisis.

    (4) Local governments must solve the garbage crisis.

    (5) Safer landfills are the answer to the garbage crisis.

Write your answer in the space provided.

11. Is the garbage crisis an individual or government responsibility? Or is it the responsibility of both? Explain your answer.

_____

_____

_____

_____

_____

Section 18

State Government

Setting the Stage

Every year, about 4000 people die in motorcycle accidents. Another 100,000 are injured. Many deaths and injuries might be prevented if motorcyclists wore helmets. Since the 1960s, some Americans have been pushing for laws that would require motorcyclists to wear helmets. Others believe that wearing a helmet is a personal choice and the government should not interfere.

Past: What you already know

You may already know something about laws requiring motorcyclists to wear helmets. Write two things you already know.

1. _____

2. _____

Present: What you learn by previewing

Write the headings from the article on pages 135–137 below.

The Debate Over Helmets

3. _____

4. _____

What is the title of the diagram on page 136?

5. _____

Future: Questions to answer

Write three questions you expect this article to answer.

6. _____

7. _____

8. _____

Check your answers on page 223.

The Debate Over Helmets

As you read each section, circle the words you don't know. Look up the meanings.

In 1988, Gary Busey, a well-known actor, picked up his motorcycle from a repair shop in Culver City, California. The actor got on his motorcycle and began to ride down the street. As usual, he rode without a helmet. A few seconds later, Busey tried to make an illegal turn around a bus. He skidded and was thrown from the motorcycle. His head slammed against the sidewalk. Busey barely survived.

As the actor slowly recovered, his crash became the center of a debate. On one side was a group of California lawmakers. On the other side were many of the state's motorcyclists, including Busey. The day after Busey's accident, Richard Floyd, a member of the California State Assembly, introduced a bill. A **bill** is a proposal for a law. If Floyd's bill became a law, all motorcyclists would have to wear helmets. It was not the first time lawmakers in California considered such a law. Only a few months earlier, Busey and other well-known motorcyclists helped defeat a similar bill.

Applying Your Skills and Strategies

Distinguishing Fact from Opinion. A *fact* is a statement about something that actually happened or actually exists. A fact can be proved. An *opinion* is a statement that expresses what a person or group of people think or believe about a fact. Reread the first two paragraphs of this article. What is Richard Floyd's opinion about motorcyclists wearing helmets?

The Debate Begins

The debate over laws requiring motorcycle helmets began in the 1960s. People wanted to reduce the number of accidents on the nation's highways. Some people wanted tougher state laws. Others urged Congress to pass helmet laws for the whole country.

In 1966, Congress took action by passing the Highway Safety Act. It allowed the United States government to hold back money for highways from any state that did not pass a helmet law. Why didn't Congress just pass a helmet law for the entire country? Congress does not have the power to pass this kind of law. The United States has a federal system of government. In a **federal system**, governing is divided between the state government and the government of the entire country. One of the state government's responsibilities is to build and fix the highways in that state. The states are also responsible for highway safety.

Good highways benefit the entire country. So the federal government gives the states a lot of the money needed to build and fix their highways. From time to time, the federal government insisted that the states pass certain laws or the money would be cut off. Among those laws was a helmet law. By 1970, forty-seven states had a helmet law. In these states, the number of deaths from motorcycle accidents dropped sharply.

From the start, many motorcyclists were against helmet laws. They lobbied against helmet laws in state legislatures and in Congress. To **lobby** is to try to get lawmakers to see an issue a certain way. In 1976, the motorcyclists convinced Congress to change the Highway Safety Act. In the years that followed, motorcyclists lobbied state legislatures. By 1980, twenty-nine states had removed or weakened their helmet laws. As expected, the number of deaths and serious injuries from motorcycle accidents increased. In one state that weakened its helmet law, injuries rose to almost twice what they were.

How a Bill Becomes a Law

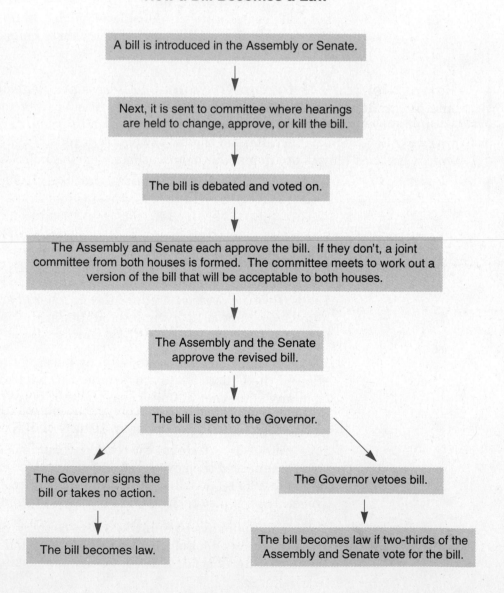

A bill is introduced in the Assembly or Senate.

Next, it is sent to committee where hearings are held to change, approve, or kill the bill.

The bill is debated and voted on.

The Assembly and Senate each approve the bill. If they don't, a joint committee from both houses is formed. The committee meets to work out a version of the bill that will be acceptable to both houses.

The Assembly and the Senate approve the revised bill.

The bill is sent to the Governor.

The Governor signs the bill or takes no action.

The Governor vetoes bill.

The bill becomes law.

The bill becomes law if two-thirds of the Assembly and Senate vote for the bill.

California had a helmet law only for motorcyclists under the age of $15\frac{1}{2}$. Some lawmakers tried again and again to pass a law that would apply to all motorcyclists. Each time their efforts failed. Floyd saw Busey's crash as a chance to try one more time. Like every state except Nebraska, the California legislature is divided into two houses. The houses are the **State Assembly** and the **Senate**. A bill must be passed by both houses. Floyd is a member of the State Assembly. So he introduced his bill there. The diagram on page 136 shows what happened to his bill as it made its way through the legislature. The process took almost a year.

Reading a Diagram. A *diagram* is a drawing that often shows steps in a process. The title tells what the diagram is about. Arrows are used to show how one step leads to the next. Study the diagram on page 136. Read each step in the process for how a bill becomes a law. Where is the bill sent after the assembly and the senate pass the same revised version of the bill?

Applying Your Skills and Strategies

_____

_____

In 1990, after the senate and assembly passed the same revised version of Floyd's bill, it was sent to the governor of California. The **governor** is the chief executive of a state. The governor is part of the process for passing new laws. In this case, the governor did not want the bill to pass. So he vetoed it. To **veto** a bill means that the governor refused to sign it into law. The governor agreed with the motorcyclists. He thought that the decision to wear a helmet was a personal choice. In his opinion, the state should require only children to wear helmets, not adults.

Look at the diagram on page 136. When the governor vetoes a bill it goes back to the legislature. It becomes law only if two thirds of both houses vote for the bill. In this case, the bill did not get the two-thirds vote.

The Struggle Continues

Floyd still insisted that the state should require motorcyclists to wear helmets. He argued that motorcycle accidents cost the people of California $100 million each year. He used a study of 105 people injured in motorcycle accidents in another state to support his view. The people of that state paid for over 60 percent of the total medical bills for the injured motorcyclists.

Floyd and others who supported the bill refused to give up. In 1991, California finally passed a helmet law. By then, the state had a new governor with a different point of view on the issue. The new governor signed the bill into law. In other states, however, the fight for and against helmet laws continues.

Thinking About the Article

Fill in the blank with the word or words that best complete each statement.

1. A proposed law is called a _____.

2. In a _____ system, responsibility is divided between state government and a national government.

3. When motorcyclists try to persuade lawmakers to do away with

   helmet laws, they _____ against the law.

4. The _____ is the chief executive of a state government.

5. A governor can _____, or refuse to sign, a proposed law.

Write your answers in the space provided.

6. Review the questions you wrote on page 134. Did the article answer your questions? If you said *yes*, write the answers. If your questions were not answered, write three things you learned from this article.

   _____

   _____

   _____

   _____

   _____

7. What were two effects of the Highway Safety Act of 1966?

   _____

   _____

   _____

8. In 1976, Congress changed the Highway Safety Act. What was the major outcome of this change?

   _____

   _____

                          Check your answers on page 223.

9. The diagram on page 136 shows that

    (1) the governor decides if a bill becomes law.

    (2) the state legislature always has the final say on whether a bill becomes law.

    (3) the state legislature has the final say only if two thirds of its members support the bill.

    (4) the governor must sign a bill to make it a law.

    (5) the state assembly and senate have the final say, as long as they both pass the same revised version of the bill.

10. Which of the following is a statement of fact?

    (1) To wear or not wear a helmet is a personal matter.

    (2) The decision to wear a helmet is a matter for the states to decide.

    (3) The decision to wear a helmet is a matter for the federal government to decide.

    (4) Motorcyclists lobbied against helmet laws in Congress and state legislatures.

    (5) Motorcyclists like to feel the wind through their hair.

11. According to the article, which of the following is most likely to support a law requiring that all drivers wear seat belts?

    (1) the governor of California in 1989

    (2) lawmakers who supported the 1966 Highway Safety Act

    (3) Gary Busey

    (4) motorcyclists

    (5) lawmakers who supported the 1976 Highway Safety Act

Write your answer in the space provided.

12. Do you believe there should be a helmet law? Explain your answer. Do you think people who ride bicycles should also be required to wear helmets? Explain your answer.

_____

_____

_____

_____

Section 19

The Constitution

Setting the Stage

The United States Constitution is the plan for our government. It states what the government can and cannot do. A section of the Constitution is called the Bill of Rights. The Bill of Rights protects the rights of American citizens.

Past: What you already know

You may already know something about the Constitution and the Bill of Rights. Write two things you already know.

1. _____

2. _____

Present: What you learn by previewing

Write the headings from the article on pages 141–143 below.

Guarding Our Rights

3. _____

4. _____

5. _____

What is the title of the diagram on page 142?

6. _____

Future: Questions to answer

Write three questions you expect this article to answer.

7. _____

8. _____

9. _____

Guarding Our Rights

As you read each section, circle the words you don't know. Look up the meanings.

The first ten amendments to the Constitution are called the Bill of Rights. An **amendment** is an addition or change. When the Constitution was first written in 1787, several states refused to approve it. These states wanted the Constitution to include a list of rights for individuals. The Bill of Rights was written and, in 1791, it became part of the Constitution. The Bill of Rights insures many rights for individuals. Below is a summary of the four amendments that protect the rights of people accused of a crime.

Fifth Amendment. A person cannot be tried for a crime unless **indicted**, or formally charged with a crime. The accused cannot be tried twice for the same crime. People cannot be forced to testify against themselves. The government cannot take a person's life, freedom, or property without **due process.** That means everyone has the right to a fair trial.

Sixth Amendment. Those accused of a crime have a right to a speedy and public trial. They must be told what the charges are. They are entitled to a lawyer. They also have the right to question anyone who testifies against them and to call witnesses in their own defense.

Seventh Amendment. A person is entitled to a trial by jury.

Eighth Amendment. Bails and fines cannot be unusually large. Punishments cannot be cruel or unusual.

The Gideon Case

In June 1961, Clarence Gideon was charged with "breaking and entering" in Bar Harbor, Florida. Later that summer, he was tried and found guilty. He could not afford a lawyer, and the state would not provide one for him. In Florida at that time, the state supplied free legal help only to those accused of a crime that called for the death penalty. The charges against Gideon were not that serious. So he had to act as his own lawyer. Gideon believed that he did not get a fair trial. He believed his trial went against the Constitution, especially the Bill of Rights.

Applying an Idea to a New Context. When Gideon read the Constitution, he *applied* what he read to his own situation. He thought about each idea in terms of how it might affect his case. Reread the four amendments described above. What rights did Gideon think the state failed to protect?

Applying Your Skills and Strategies

_____

_____

Check your answer on page 224.

The Courts and the Constitution

Gideon firmly believed that the Bill of Rights applied to his case. But the judge in the Florida trial court did not think it was wrong for Gideon to act as his own lawyer. Gideon disagreed. In time, his case reached the highest court in this country, the United States Supreme Court. The Supreme Court interprets the Constitution. The judges decide how the law of the Constitution applies to a particular case.

How Cases Reach the Supreme Court

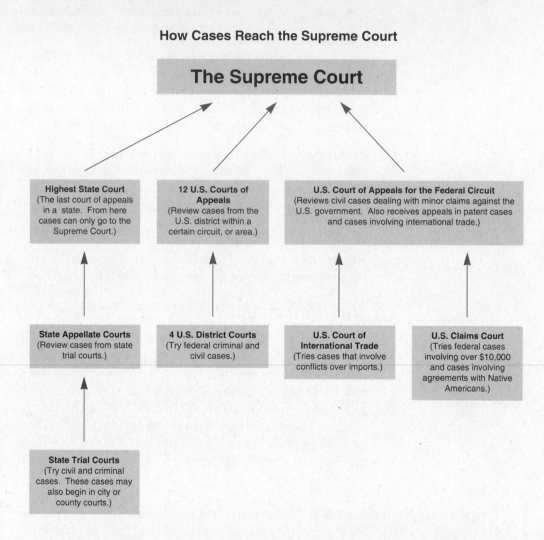

The chart shows how cases reach the Supreme Court. Hundreds of cases go through this process. The Supreme Court, however, can hear only a few of those cases. Still, Gideon felt he had nothing to lose by trying. He sent the Supreme Court justices a handwritten letter on prison stationery. In his letter, he asked the Court to release him from prison because the Florida law went against the Constitution. Gideon stated that the state court had to provide him with a lawyer because he could not afford one. Since this did not happen, he did not receive a fair trial.

Making Inferences from a Diagram. A diagram shows steps in a process. Making an *inference* means figuring out something based on the information given. Look at the diagram on page 142. Use the diagram and what you know about Gideon's case. What steps did his case take to get to the Supreme Court?

_____

_____

_____

_____

_____

The first page of Clarence Gideon's letter to the Supreme Court

The Supreme Court agreed to hear Gideon's case. The Court felt that his case was a clear constitutional issue. Many states had strong feelings about the matter. Twenty-two states asked the justices to rule in Gideon's favor. A **justice** is a judge who serves on the Supreme Court. Three states, including Florida, asked that the Court rule against Gideon.

A Landmark Decision

The nine justices disagreed among themselves on how to decide Gideon's case. There was a great deal of discussion. Then, on March 18, 1963, the Supreme Court ruled in Gideon's favor. The Court stated that the right to a lawyer may not be essential for a fair trial in some countries, but it is in the United States. To show why, they quoted from a case the Court heard in 1932. "(The accused) requires the guiding hand of counsel (lawyer) at every step in the proceedings against him. Without it, though he be not guilty (even though he is not guilty), he faces the danger of conviction because he does not know how to establish his innocence."

The Gideon case is considered a landmark decision. It is important to all Americans. It changed the way cases are tried. Today anyone accused of a crime has the right to a lawyer. If the person cannot afford a lawyer, the court will appoint one without charge.

Check your answer on page 224.

Thinking About the Article

Fill in the blank with the word or words that best complete each statement.

1. A list of individual rights is known as a _____.

2. An _____ is a change or addition to a constitution.

3. The plan for our government is called the

   _____.

4. The highest court in our country is the _____.

5. A person's right to a fair trial is _____.

Write your answers in the space provided.

6. Review the questions you wrote on page 140. Did the article answer your questions? If you said *yes*, write the answers. If your questions were not answered, write three things you learned from this article.

   _____

   _____

   _____

   _____

   _____

7. How does the Supreme Court protect the rights identified in the first ten amendments to the Constitution?

   _____

   _____

   _____

8. Look at the diagram on page 142. What court had to rule on Gideon's case before it reached the Supreme Court? Where was this court?

   _____

   _____

Circle the number of the best answer.

9. The Bill of Rights protects the rights of

   (1) local governments.

   (2) state governments.

   (3) all people.

   (4) the federal government.

   (5) just poor people.

10. Which statement is true based on the diagram on page 142?

    (1) Every criminal case goes to the Supreme Court.

    (2) All cases begin in the state trial courts.

    (3) The Supreme Court must hear all the cases from the U.S. Court of Appeals.

    (4) All cases must be heard in at least two courts before going to the Supreme Court.

    (5) The President appoints Supreme Court justices.

11. Which of the following best explains why the Gideon case was so important?

    (1) Only poor people accused of a serious crime have the right to a lawyer supplied by the court at no charge.

    (2) The Supreme Court will read handwritten appeals.

    (3) People accused of any crime have the right to a lawyer supplied by the court if they cannot afford one.

    (4) All appeals made to the Supreme Court must be made by a lawyer.

    (5) People accused of any crime have the right to a lawyer supplied by the court if they pay part of the cost.

Write your answer in the space provided.

12. What do you think would have happened in this country if the Supreme Court did not rule in Gideon's favor? How would it have affected the rights of poor people? Explain your answer.

    _____

    _____

    _____

Elections and the American People

Setting the Stage

Elections are a part of American life. On Election Day, people vote for men and women to lead their community, state, or nation. The right to vote is one of the most important rights of an American citizen. Voting gives people a voice in who runs the government and how it is run.

Past: What you already know

You may already know something about elections in the United States. Write two things you already know.

1. _____

2. _____

Present: What you learn by previewing

Write the headings from the article on pages 147–149 below.

On the Campaign Trail

3. _____

4. _____

5. _____

What does the picture on page 148 show?

6. _____

_____

Future: Questions to answer

Write three questions you expect this article to answer.

7. _____

8. _____

9. _____

Check your answers on page 224.

On the Campaign Trail

As you read each section, circle the words you don't know. Look up the meanings.

Every November there is an election somewhere in the United States. Every four years the people elect the president of the United States. Members of the House of Representatives are elected every two years. United States senators are elected every six years. In addition, Americans choose governors, mayors, state and local officials, judges, sheriffs, and many other government leaders. People also vote on other matters on Election Day. They may vote to approve the local school budget. Or they may vote on changes to the state constitution. By voting, people decide on important issues and choose who represents them in government.

The Role of Political Parties

Before most elections, there is a series of events called a campaign. A **campaign** is designed to get people to vote a certain way. Some campaigns are used to persuade people to vote for a certain candidate. A **candidate** is a person who is running for political office. The campaign requires large sums of money and the hard work of many people. So most candidates have the support of a political party. A **political party** is a group of people who have similar ideas about public issues. Members of each party work together in an effort to put their ideas into effect. To do this, each party **nominates**, or chooses, its own candidates for election. If the candidate wins the election, the party knows its goals are supported.

Supporting Conclusions.   Draw a *conclusion* based on *facts*. First identify the main idea and supporting details of a paragraph as you read. Then make sure this information supports your conclusion.

Applying Your Skills and Strategies

Reread the first paragraph under the heading *The Role of Political Parties*. One conclusion you can draw is: When candidates are elected they will act according to the wishes of their political party. Write the main idea and two details that support this conclusion.

_____

_____

_____

_____

The Democratic and Republican parties are the two major political parties in the United States. Just about every election has candidates from one or both of these parties. There are also many smaller political parties. These parties do not have enough support to run candidates for every political office.

Persuading the Voters

Many Americans learn about the candidates and the issues from the media. The **media** include radio, television, newspapers, and magazines. Reporters use the media to present news stories and information about a campaign. Most reporters try to tell the facts and not take sides with any candidate. However, people who run a campaign also use the media. They often run ads to convince people to vote a certain way. The name of the person or group who paid for the ad is often stated. This tells people that the ad is not the point of view of the media or the reporters.

Care for Kids

Vote Yes ✓ Issue 22
Lorain City Schools

"The Number 22 means a lot to me. ISSUE 22, the income tax for schools, means a lot to kids in Lorain. Education is one of the most important things we can give our kids.

That's why ISSUE 22 is so important.

So, on Sundays, remember Number 22, Felix Wright of the Cleveland Browns.

But on Election Day Remember ISSUE 22 for kids.

Show you Care for Kids."

-Felix Wright, Number 22
The Cleveland Browns

Paid for by Care For Kids Committee, 3259 Amhurst Ave., Lorain, Ohio 44052, Terri Houle, Treasurer.

...let them know they can depend on you.

Political ads use the same methods to win votes that are used to sell a product. For example, in the ad on page 148, a well-known football player is used to **endorse**, or support, Issue 22.

Many people are concerned about the use of such ads in political campaigns. In recent years, there have been many political ads that use emotions to present the issues. Some experts who study political campaigns say candidates use these types of ads because they work. Other experts disagree. They say these types of ads are irritating the voters. As a result, people are staying home rather than voting.

Identifying Faulty Logic in Political Ads. Political ads often appeal to the strong emotions of voters. The people that supported Issue 22 ran the political ad that appears on page 148. Some political ads try to get people to use logic. In *logic*, the truth of one statement depends on the truth of an earlier statement. Reread the ad. The argument in the ad is, if you vote *yes* on Issue 22, then you care about kids. This argument uses logic that is *faulty*, or not correct, to suggest something about people who vote *no* on Issue 22. What logically faulty suggestion does the ad make?

Applying Your Skills and Strategies

Campaigns are very expensive. When George Washington ran for president 200 years ago, he did not spend any money. Today, millions of dollars are spent on campaigns to elect a president. Running a television ad just once can cost hundreds of thousands of dollars.

The Rising Cost of Campaigns

In 1976, it cost a candidate about $600,000 to win a seat in the United States Senate. By 1990, the cost was over $4 million. Raising money has become an important task of political parties. Some of the money comes from individuals. However, most of it comes from **political action committees** (PAC's). Special interest groups, such as the National Rifle Association, set up PAC's. The PAC's give money to candidates with interests similar to those of the special interest groups.

PAC's often have a major effect on an election, especially in a close race. Is it the money that makes the difference? Or is it that many PAC's do a good job of getting members to vote? The experts are not sure. They do know that PAC's can help candidates win. PAC's can also help defeat candidates who oppose their views.

Some people are concerned about the high cost of running for office. They say that the system favors wealthy candidates over poorer ones. They also note that as the cost of running for office has gone up, fewer voters show up at the polls. It has been said that "bad officials are elected by good citizens who do not vote."

Check your answer on page 225.

Thinking About the Article

Fill in the blank with the word or words that best complete each statement.

1. A series of events designed to win votes is called a _____.

2. A person who runs for office is a _____.

3. People with similar ideas on public issues who work to elect

   candidates to public office belong to a _____.

4. Special interest groups set up _____

   _____ to give money to candidates who support their
   point of view.

5. If a well-known person publicly supports a point of view, he or she

   _____ that point of view.

Write your answers in the space provided.

6. Review the questions you wrote on page 146. Did the article answer
   your questions? If you said *yes*, write the answers. If your questions
   were not answered, write three things you learned from this article.

   _____

   _____

   _____

   _____

   _____

7. Look at the ad on page 148. Write the statement that tells that the ad
   does not express the point of view of the newspaper in which it was
   printed.

   _____

8. What information would the ad on page 148 contain if it presented
   just the issues?

   _____

   _____

Circle the number of the best answer.

9. Which is an example of taking sides in a political campaign?

    (1) A newspaper story discusses campaign issues.

    (2) A debate between two candidates is on television.

    (3) A radio announcer points out errors in political ads.

    (4) A magazine publishes stories about one candidate only.

    (5) A newspaper runs political ads paid for by others.

10. If Joe Hall runs for the state assembly, he could win. If he wins, he will vote against a motorcycle helmet law. If he votes against the helmet law, then the number of deaths due to motorcycle accidents will increase.

    What is the faulty logic?

    (1) If Joe Hall runs for the state assembly, he could win.

    (2) If he wins, he will vote against a motorcycle helmet law.

    (3) If he votes against the helmet law, the number of deaths due to motorcycle accidents will increase.

    (4) Joe Hall is not the only one voting.

    (5) The number of deaths due to motorcycle accidents has nothing to do with whether people wear helmets.

11. Which of the following is the best reason for a special interest group to form a political action committee?

    (1) giving money to the candidates who need it the most

    (2) supporting a candidate with the same views on key issues

    (3) running political ads that present only the issues

    (4) making sure people stay home and don't vote

    (5) supporting all of the candidates running for office

Write your answer in the space provided.

12. What does the saying "bad officials are elected by good citizens who do not vote" mean? Do you agree with it? Explain your answer.

    _____

    _____

    _____

    _____

Debating an Issue

Setting the Stage

Each year, guns are involved in the death or injury of about 30,000 Americans. Most of these people are shot by someone they know. Many people think it is time to pass a tough law that will control the sale of guns. However, others believe the Constitution protects a citizen's right to own a gun.

Past: What you already know

You may already know something about the dispute over strict gun-control laws. Write two things you already know.

1. _____

2. _____

Present: What you learn by previewing

Write the headings from the article on pages 153–155 below.

The Fight to Limit Guns

3. _____

4. _____

5. _____

What do the political cartoons on pages 154 and 155 show?

6. _____

_____

Future: Questions to answer

Write three questions you expect this article to answer.

7. _____

8. _____

9. _____

The Fight to Limit Guns

As you read each section, circle the words you don't know. Look up the meanings.

In the 1980s, nearly 225,000 Americans were killed by handguns. Countless other Americans were injured by gunfire. Among them were President Ronald Reagan and James Brady, his press secretary. The two men were shot in 1981. The President made a full recovery. Although Brady has made great progress, he was not as lucky. He is still unable to speak clearly or walk.

Americans were outraged when the President was shot. Many were shocked to find out the number of homicides involving guns. In the 1980s, homicide was the leading cause of death among African-American men. Guns were the weapons most often used in homicides in this country.

By the late 1980s, some people were even using guns made for the armed forces. These guns are designed to be used in battle during a war. A man arrested for murder in California used a military weapon. He bought his rifle in Oregon. Oregon had a law that controlled the sale of guns, but it did not apply to military weapons. The law was passed before these guns were available.

Gun Control—Yes or No?

Gun-control laws put limits on the sale of guns to the public. In 1989, there were over 23,000 gun-control laws in the United States. Some laws, like the one in Oregon, were state laws. Others were city ordinances. Yet with all these laws, no one law applied to everyone in the United States. Many Americans believed that only a tough federal gun-control law could deal with the problem. A **federal** law applies to the whole country.

The lawmakers in Congress pass federal laws. Some of these laws control business and trade that cross state lines. Many guns are shipped across state lines or boundaries. Some guns are imported from other countries. Congress also passes laws to control trade, or business, between the United States and other countries. Congress could pass a law that would ban the shipment of certain guns across state or international lines. The law would also limit the sale of certain guns. Most people agree that Congress has the right to pass a federal gun-control law. However, not everyone agrees that Congress should pass this law.

Distinguishing Fact from Opinion. In the paragraphs above, there are many facts about guns. Nothing can change these *facts*. But people have different thoughts, or *opinions*, about the facts. Write two opinions people have about Congress passing gun-control laws.

Applying Your Skills and Strategies

_____

_____

The Argument Against Gun Control

For a long time, the National Rifle Association (NRA) has led the fight against gun-control laws. The group was founded in 1871 to teach safety and marksmanship to gun owners. Since the 1970s, however, the group has worked to protect the right of every American to own a gun.

YOU CAN'T SHOOT ME... THIS STATE OUTLAWS HANDGUNS.

BAN HANDGUNS FOR EVER!

BOB DIX union leader

Bob Dix, *Manchester Union Leader*. Reprinted with permission.

The NRA believes the American people have a right to own guns and other weapons. It points out that this right is protected by the Second Amendment to the Constitution. It contends that the right to own guns protects the freedom of all Americans. It wants to insure that this right not be limited in any way.

The NRA states that people need guns for self-defense. **Self-defense** is a person's right to protect himself or herself. People who support the NRA contend that they have a right to defend themselves and not be victims. It is their belief that they should have the freedom to choose the most effective means available for their self-defense.

The NRA shows that most gun owners are law-abiding people. The owners are safe, sane, and courteous in their use of guns. They have never been, nor will they ever be, a threat to law and order. Why, then, the NRA asks, "should an honest citizen be deprived of a firearm for sport or self-defense when, for a gangster, obtaining a gun is just a matter of showing up on the right street corner with enough money?"

The NRA agrees that crime is a problem in the United States. But it does not believe that the answer is to have laws controlling guns. The NRA thinks that lawmakers should pass tougher laws to punish criminals. The NRA argues that gun control laws do not stop crime. Violent crime has risen in some cities even after strict gun-control laws were passed locally. Senator Orrin Hatch stated, "Blaming guns for a criminal's violence makes no more sense than blaming automobiles for drunk driving."

The Argument for Gun Control

James Brady and his wife, Sarah, disagree with the NRA. They speak for a group known as Handgun Control, Inc. This group is working to get Congress to pass a federal gun-control law. The Bradys and others who favor gun control use several arguments to support their cause.

Gun-control supporters say the issue is not whether the Second Amendment allows citizens to own guns. They show how there are limits on many rights protected by the Constitution. The First Amendment gives Americans the right to hold public meetings, rallies, and parades. Yet most

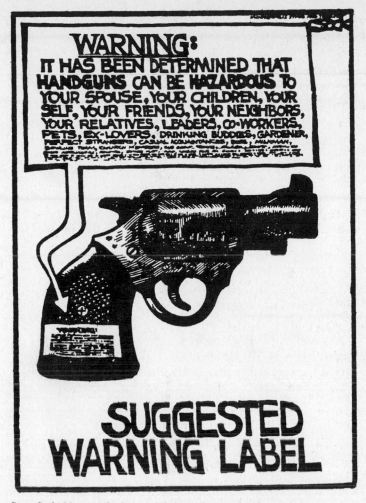

WARNING:
IT HAS BEEN DETERMINED THAT HANDGUNS CAN BE HAZARDOUS TO YOUR SPOUSE, YOUR CHILDREN, YOURSELF, YOUR FRIENDS, YOUR NEIGHBORS, YOUR RELATIVES, LEADERS, CO-WORKERS, PETS, EX-LOVERS, DRINKING BUDDIES, GARDENER, PERFECT STRANGERS, CASUAL ACQUAINTANCES...

SUGGESTED WARNING LABEL

Steve Sack, *Minneapolis Star and Tribune*. Reprinted with permission.

cities require people to get a permit before holding a rally in a public place. Why should the right to own guns be treated any differently? They say the Constitution also protects the public safety. So it is irresponsible to allow people to own a deadly weapon without a permit.

Those who favor gun control point out guns are not useful for self-defense. They say that most break-ins take place when no one is at home. Burglars are just as likely to steal guns as anything else they find. In fact, burglars can get more for selling a gun than they can for selling a TV or stereo. Gun-control supporters also point to research on guns. Research shows that a gun kept for protection is six times more likely to kill someone the gun owner knows than it is to kill a thief. A 1968 study showed that for every burglar stopped by a gun, four gun owners or their family members were killed.

Handgun Control, Inc. agrees that most gun owners are law-abiding citizens. In testifying before Congress, Jim Brady said, "I don't question the rights of responsible gun owners. That's not the issue. The issue is whether the John Hinckleys (the man who shot Brady) of the world should be able to walk into gun stores and purchase handguns instantly."

People in favor of gun-control laws do not think the laws will stop crime. They believe, however, that these laws will reduce violence. The head of a police officers' union says, "No one claims gun control will stop all gun-related crime. But a survey found that 28 percent of prison inmates said they had bought firearms over the counter. Stopping 28 percent of crime should be significant."

Reading Political Cartoons. A political cartoon expresses an opinion of the person who drew the cartoon. The cartoons on pages 154 and 155 express opposing views about gun control. How does the cartoon on page 154 agree with the point of view of the NRA?

Applying Your Skills and Strategies

Thinking About the Article

Fill in the blank with the word or words that best complete each statement.

1. A law passed by Congress that applies to everyone in the United

    States is called a _____ law.

2. Laws that put limits on the sale and shipment of guns are called

    _____ laws.

3. When people protect themselves from an attacker, it is an act of

    _____ .

Write your answers in the space provided.

4. Review the questions you wrote on page 152. Did the article answer your questions? If you said *yes*, write the answers. If your questions were not answered, write three things you learned from this article.

    _____

    _____

    _____

    _____

5. The groups for and against gun control agree on some issues and disagree on others. What are two issues on which the two groups agree?

    _____

    _____

    _____

6. What are two issues on which the groups do not agree?

    _____

    _____

    _____

Circle the number of the best answer.

7. Which of the following is a statement of <u>fact</u> about guns?

   (1) Owning weapons is a freedom that should not be limited.

   (2) Blaming guns for a criminal's violence makes no more sense than blaming automobiles for drunk driving.

   (3) The right to own guns should be limited.

   (4) Anyone should be able to purchase handguns instantly.

   (5) Each year, guns are involved in the death or injury of about 30,000 Americans.

8. Which of the following statements expresses the point of view of the cartoon on page 154?

   (1) Tough gun-control laws will not reduce violence.

   (2) Gun-control laws do not stop criminals.

   (3) A gun kept for protection is more likely to kill someone the gun owner knows than an attacker.

   (4) When criminals know that someone can handle a gun, they are less likely to attack.

   (5) Guns don't kill people, people kill people.

9. Which of the following statements expresses the point of view of the cartoon on page 155?

   (1) Tough gun-control laws will not reduce violence.

   (2) Gun-control laws do not stop criminals.

   (3) A gun kept for protection is more likely to kill someone the gun owner knows than an attacker.

   (4) Criminals avoid someone who can handle a gun.

   (5) Guns don't kill people, people kill people.

Write your answer in the space provided.

10. Based on the arguments presented in this article, are you for or against gun control? Give reasons to support your opinion.

   _____

   _____

   _____

   _____

Unit 4 Review:
Political Science

The Miranda Decision

In March 1963, a young girl was kidnaped and raped. Ten days later, the police arrested Ernesto Miranda. After two hours of questioning, he confessed to the crime. That confession was used as evidence against Miranda at his trial. He was found guilty. In 1966, the Supreme Court overturned Miranda's conviction. They believed that the police had violated Miranda's constitutional rights. This is called the Miranda Decision.

As a result of the court's decision, the police now have to follow three rules, known as Miranda rights, when making an arrest. First, people must be informed of their right to remain silent. Second, anything they choose to say can and will be used against them in court. Third, they have the right to have a lawyer present while they are questioned. If they cannot afford a lawyer, one will be appointed to represent them.

In 1986, a new case reached the Supreme Court. The New York City police chased a man suspected of rape into a store. When the police officers checked to see if the man had a weapon, they found an empty holster. When the police asked where the gun was, the suspect told them. *After* the police found the gun, they read the man his Miranda rights. Could the gun and the man's statement still be used as evidence against him? "Yes," said the Supreme Court. "The need for answers to questions in a situation posing a threat to public safety outweighs the need for the rule protecting the Fifth Amendment's privilege against self-incrimination."

Write your answer in the space provided.

1. Name three ways the two cases described in the article are alike.

_____

_____

_____

Circle the number of the best answer.

2. Which conclusion can be drawn from the article?

   (1) The Supreme Court can reverse decisions.

   (2) When public safety is threatened, our rights may be limited.

   (3) The Supreme Court does not always side with criminals.

   (4) Miranda rights make it harder for the police to make arrests.

   (5) The Miranda rules no longer exist.

Checks and Balances in the Federal Government

Powers

Congress:

Passes laws
Can pass a law over
    president's veto
    if two thirds of
    Congress approves it
Can propose amendments
    to the Constitution
Appointment of federal
    court judges approved
    by Senate

President:

Can approve or veto
    laws passed by Congress
Appoints federal court judges
Negotiates foreign treaties
Can pardon federal offenders

Supreme Court:

Judges the meaning
    of laws
May rule that laws
    passed by Congress
    are unconstitutional
May rule that actions
    by president are
    unconstitutional

Checks on Powers

By President:
Can veto a law passed
    by Congress

By the Supreme Court:
Can rule that a law
    passed by Congress
    is unconstitutional

By Congress:
Can pass laws over
    president's veto by a
    two-thirds vote
May impeach or remove
    president for high
    crimes or misdemeanors
Appropriates money

By Senate:
Approves treaties
Approves president's
    appointments to
    federal courts

By Congress:
May propose an amendment
    to the Constitution if Supreme
    Court rules that a law is
    unconstitutional
May impeach or remove a
    federal judge

By President:
May pardon federal offenders
Appoints federal court judges

By Senate:
Approves federal court judges

Circle the number of the best answer.

3. Which of the following statements is supported by the diagram?

   (1) Congress is the most powerful branch.

   (2) Each branch of government can check, or control, the power of the other branches.

   (3) The President is more powerful than the other two branches.

   (4) The Supreme Court is the most powerful branch.

   (5) Each branch works separately from the other two branches.

4. The diagram best supports the conclusion that the system of checks and balances

   (1) is how the Constitution limits the power of the federal government.

   (2) is how Congress controls the power of the President.

   (3) is how the courts control the President and Congress.

   (4) keeps the federal government from becoming more powerful than the states.

   (5) keeps each branch of government separate from the others.

Voting Makes a Difference

Just before elections, the ads appear. "Don't forget to vote!" "Every vote counts." "Make your vote count!" Most registered voters do go to the polls. However, many people who are eligible to vote fail to register. Almost every American citizen who is at least 18 years of age is eligible to vote. To **register** means to complete a form that tells the voter's name, address, place of birth, and date of birth.

Registered voters go to an assigned polling place to vote on Election Day. There, workers check the voting list to make sure the person is registered to vote. This keeps people from voting in the wrong place and from voting more than once. In some polling places, voters step into a voting booth where they pull levers on a machine. In other places, votes are made by punching holes in computer cards or by marking a paper ballot. Do the votes make a difference? Studies show they do. Many elections are decided by a handful of votes. Even in presidential elections, changes in a small number of votes have made a big difference.

Experts say that there has never been a president elected by a majority of the voting-age population. Abraham Lincoln received 55 percent of the vote when he ran for president in 1864. But that was only 13.4 percent of the voting-age population. About 51 percent of the voters backed Ronald Reagan in 1980. But he had the votes of only 26.9 percent of the voting-age population. Would the election results have been different if everyone who was eligible to vote had voted? No one will ever know.

Write your answers in the space provided.

5. To _____ to vote, a person must complete a form.

6. Why is a person's date of birth important on the voter's registration form?

_____

Circle the number of the best answer.

7. Which of the following statements is supported by the article?

   (1) If you pay taxes, you must register to vote.

   (2) Registering is a way of keeping people from voting.

   (3) Most people are registered to vote.

   (4) More people would vote if they registered.

   (5) Every vote can make a difference.

Go on to the next page.

Reprinted with permission of
The Minneapolis Star and Roy Justus.

Authoritarianism and the Spirit of Freedom

Write your answers in the space provided.

8. What does the person with the club represent?

_____

_____

9. How is the Spirit of Freedom represented?

_____

_____

Circle the number of the best answer.

10. Based on the cartoon, authoritarianism is a government
    (1) that does not allow freedom.
    (2) of the people, for the people, and by the people.
    (3) that is run by a strong leader.
    (4) that is a world power.
    (5) that enjoys freedom.

Check your answers on page 226.

Unit

5

BEHAVIORAL SCIENCE

Individuals belong to many different groups. These groups help shape how individuals act and behave.

People throughout the world live in some form of a group. The first group that a child learns to live with is its family. The group might consist of parents, brothers, and sisters. Some families might include other relatives and even friends. As children grow up, they become members of other groups. They may belong to school, work, religious, and social groups. Each of these groups is a part of a society. A **society** is linked by political, social, and economic ties. People in a society share a **culture**, or way of life.

The **behavioral sciences** look at the individuals and groups in many different ways. The behavioral sciences include sociology, psychology, and anthropology. These sciences focus on people and the way people act. Yet each is concerned with a different set of questions. **Sociologists** are concerned with group behavior. They ask the questions: To what groups do individuals belong? How are those groups organized? How do they affect the way individuals behave?

Psychologists are more concerned with individuals than with groups. They want to know why individuals act the way they do. So they ask: How do physical factors affect the way people behave? What difference does personality make? How was a person raised? What events shaped the person's life? What is normal behavior? What is not normal behavior?

Anthropologists study the culture a society creates. They believe that culture provides important clues to human behavior. The questions anthropologists ask stress comparisons and contrasts. They try to discover how all cultures are alike. They also want to know what makes each culture different. They consider the ways different cultures influence one another.

Margaret Mead

Margaret Mead was one of the first American anthropologists. She studied the culture of the Samoans and other Pacific Islanders in the 1920s and 1930s. She wrote a number of books based on her work. She also taught anthropology to college and graduate students. Toward the end of her life, Mead wrote articles for popular magazines. She wanted everyone to understand how culture affects a person's life. Margaret Mead's concerns are the concerns of all behavioral scientists. They try to find out more about people in order to help us understand ourselves.

This unit features articles about human behavior and culture.

- The article about body language tells how people communicate and send messages without saying a word.

- The article about male and female roles shows how many of the things people think of as natural behavior are actually learned.

- The article about friendship explores how relationships affect the way and how well people live.

- The article about the United States as a multicultural nation focuses on how people of various cultures live together.

- The article about jazz shows how jazz evolved from other cultures and how it influenced music in other cultures.

Body Language

Setting the Stage

People communicate with more than just words. The way a person stands sends a message. The look on a person's face can say a great deal, too. Even the distance that two people are standing apart can tell a story. A person can say many things with body language without uttering a word.

Past: What you already know

You may already know something about body language. Write two things you already know.

1. _____

2. _____

Present: What you learn by previewing

Write the headings from the article on pages 165–167 below.

Speaking Without Words

3. _____

4. _____

5. _____

What does the photo on page 165 show?

6. _____

_____

Future: Questions to answer

Write three questions you expect this article to answer.

7. _____

8. _____

9. _____

Speaking Without Words

As you read each section, circle the words you don't know. Look up the meanings.

Humans signal one another with words or movements. Some signals, such as a smile, are innate. When something is **innate**, a person is born with it. These innate signals mean the same thing to all people. However, most signals are learned as part of a person's culture. **Culture** is a way of life. Words and the way they are expressed are a part of a person's culture.

Research of human behavior suggests that words do not matter as much as the *way* those words are stated. The tone of voice and body language can reveal many things. **Body language** is unspoken communication. Nods, smiles, and hand motions, used as words are spoken, are body language. How far apart and the way people sit or stand are also body language.

Posture and orientation usually show who is in charge.

Posture Counts

Posture, the way people stand or sit, can show how people feel about each other. If people like the person they are talking to, they pay attention. They may also imitate the way that person sits or stands. They do not copy the other person's posture on purpose. It usually happens naturally. When it happens, it is a sign of friendliness and respect. Posture can also show who is in charge. When a leader speaks, people pay more attention. The leader sets the tone. The group responds to the leader.

Orientation is the direction in which people turn their body, especially the head. It is a mark of respect. A person who faces the leader is showing respect. Someone who is unhappy with a leader is likely to have a **closed posture**. This person will sit back with crossed legs and folded arms. A person who supports the leader has an **open posture**. Leaning forward to listen is an example of an open posture.

Where people sit or stand is as much a part of body language as the way they sit or stand. A person who stands too close to someone else can seem "pushy." A person who stays too far away may seem unfriendly. How close is too close? How far is too far? The answer depends on the situation and the people involved. Experts say most people interact within four distance zones: intimate, personal, social, and public.

Too Close for Comfort

The first zone, **intimate distance**, ranges from actual contact to about eighteen inches apart. A parent and a child or a couple in love interact at intimate distances. If a stranger sits that close, most people will move away.

If they cannot move away, they will do other things to keep the stranger at a distance. For example, on a crowded elevator people stare straight ahead. They tend to hold their bodies stiffly. They also avoid touching one another.

Applying an Idea to a New Context. Ideas are often presented and learned in one particular situation or context. For example, the idea of an intimate zone was presented in the context of people in a crowded elevator. This idea can be applied to another situation or context. Reread the paragraph above. Apply the idea to the following situation: Two strangers are sitting next to each other in a crowded bus. What body language are these people likely to use?

Applying Your Skills and Strategies

_____

_____

The second zone is **personal distance**. The range of this zone is about eighteen inches to four feet. When people are at a personal distance they are close enough to shake hands. They are also close enough to talk privately. Most conversations at parties or on the street are within this zone.

Social distance is the third zone. The range of this zone is from about four to twelve feet. Four feet is the distance between a customer and a clerk in a store. Often, it is the distance between a boss and an employee. Twelve feet is the distance a judge sits from the accused during a trial.

Public distance is the fourth zone. This zone is any distance over twelve feet. Public distance is the distance between the teacher and students in many classrooms. It is also the distance between a speaker and the audience at a large rally. At that distance, people have trouble seeing. Therefore, body language is often exaggerated to stress a point or underscore an emotion.

                              Check your answer on page 226.

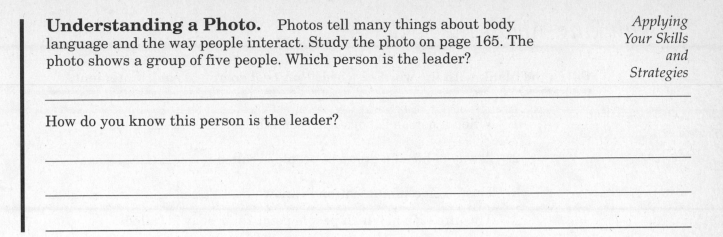

Understanding a Photo. Photos tell many things about body language and the way people interact. Study the photo on page 165. The photo shows a group of five people. Which person is the leader?

_____

How do you know this person is the leader?

_____

_____

_____

Some people use distance to enhance their position. A boss may move from social distance to personal distance to check an employee's work. In doing so, the boss is letting the employee know who is in charge. The police sometimes use distance in a similar way when questioning a suspect.

Meaningful Gestures

Gestures are also a part of body language. **Gestures** are body movements, such as hand and eye movements. Look at the photo on page 165. The speaker is using hand movements as he speaks. These gestures may be used to emphasize what the speaker is saying. It might help to clarify or explain what is being said. However, gestures can also signal nervousness. They can even show signs of worry or panic. For example, a nervous speaker may constantly shuffle papers. Someone in a panic may wring his or her hands while speaking.

Some gestures are innate. Smiles are innate. So are the gestures people use to show sadness, anger, disgust, surprise, and fear. Other gestures are learned as part of a person's culture. These gestures do not have the same meaning to all people.

For example, people in the culture of the United States believe it's important to "look someone in the eye." It shows honesty. This is not the case in Latin America and some other parts of the world. In these cultures it is disrespectful to look directly at a powerful person. It is more respectful to look away when speaking.

Body language has a strong influence on conversations and meetings between people. Body language tells about how culture affects a person's interaction with others. It also grows from a person's feelings about himself or herself as well as others. A confident person has different body language from someone who is shy or hesitant. Understanding body language helps you to understand how one person views another and how people view you.

Thinking About the Article

Fill in the blank with the word or words that best complete each statement.

1. When a person is born with something it is _____.

2. A way of life of a group of people is called its _____.

3. Unspoken communication is known as _____.

4. The direction in which people point their body is called

   _____.

5. Pointing a finger is a hand movement, or _____.

Write your answers in the space provided.

6. Review the questions you wrote on page 164. Did the article answer your questions? If you said *yes*, write the answers. If your questions were not answered, write three things you learned from this article.

   _____

   _____

   _____

   _____

   _____

7. How can a person use body language to show agreement with a speaker?

   _____

   _____

   _____

8. Two people from different countries meet for the first time. One person smiles while speaking. Do you think the other person will understand this gesture? Explain your answer.

   _____

   _____

Circle the number of the best answer.

9. Which of the following signals honesty and respect in the United States?

    (1) looking a person in the eye

    (2) lowering the eyes

    (3) looking serious

    (4) leaning the head toward the speaker

    (5) bowing toward the speaker

10. Two friends are arguing. Yet their posture and gestures are similar. What is their body language saying?

    (1) This argument may destroy our friendship.

    (2) This argument is not important.

    (3) We may argue, but we are still friends.

    (4) Arguments are fun.

    (5) We argue in different ways.

11. As the police question a suspect, they move closer to the suspect. Which statement best describes their message to the suspect?

    (1) Relax! Feel comfortable.

    (2) We are in charge.

    (3) Show us disrespect.

    (4) We are your friends.

    (5) We would like your cooperation.

Write your answer in the space provided.

12. Think about your body language. How does it affect your communication with other people? Do you think they understand your messages? Explain your answer.

    _____

    _____

    _____

    _____

    _____

Section 23

Male and Female Roles

Setting the Stage

Why are little boys drawn to toys such as cars and guns? Why do little girls prefer dolls? Are boys and girls *born* with different talents and interests? Or is it *culture* that makes the difference? Psychologists and sociologists have been exploring such questions for over one hundred years.

Past: What you already know

You may already know something about how male-female roles are established in young children. Write two things you already know.

1. _____

2. _____

Present: What you learn by previewing

Write the headings from the article on pages 171–173 below.

How Children Learn Roles

3. _____

4. _____

5. _____

What is the cartoon on page 172 about?

6. _____

_____

Future: Questions to answer

Write three questions you expect this article to answer.

7. _____

8. _____

9. _____

How Children Learn Roles

As you read each section, circle the words you don't know. Look up the meanings.

Newborn babies look very much alike. They also act alike. If it were not for the pink and blue blankets in hospital nurseries, it would be difficult to tell boys from girls. Yet from the start, many parents see differences. Some parents say that their baby girl, like all little girls, is very sociable. Others are convinced that their baby boys are always tougher and stronger than little girls. Some people think that there are natural differences in the ways boys and girls behave. Others believe differences are a result of the way the children are raised.

Identifying Faulty Logic. A statement with faulty logic may seem reasonable and logical at first glance. It is only when you look more closely that the statement makes no sense. Often such statements contain a hasty generalization. A *hasty generalization* is a broad statement based on little or no evidence. Words such as *all*, *none*, *never*, and *always* signal hasty generalizations. Reread the paragraph above. Write one statement from the paragraph that contains a hasty generalization.

Applying Your Skills and Strategies

_____

_____

_____

What Comes Naturally?

In recent years, people have changed their ideas about what is natural behavior and what is learned. Things that people once thought were instinctive may, in fact, be learned. **Instincts** are innate. Eating and sleeping are instincts. They do not have to be taught. Social scientists now say that there are very few innate differences between the sexes. They believe that males and females are more alike than they are different. There is a wider range of differences within each sex than there is between the sexes.

For years, many people believed that girls had innately better language skills than boys. They believed girls learned to speak earlier. They also thought it was easier for girls to learn to read. People believed that boys were innately better at math. However, new studies show that boys and girls are about equal in their natural ability to use language. Boys do have a slight edge in math, but not enough to account for differences in math test scores in school.

Some people think that boys are more active and more competitive than girls. Research does suggest that there may be innate differences in how active the two sexes are. There is some evidence that boys are more active even before birth. But are boys more competitive?

The evidence is not as clear on whether boys are more competitive than girls. However, males are somewhat more likely to be violent than females. In other aggressive behavior, males and females are the same.

Are girls born with a mothering instinct? Apart from the fact that women give birth and care for children, there is little evidence that caring for others is an instinct. However, studies have shown that newborn girls are more likely than boys to cry in response to the cry of another infant. Studies also show that young girls are more likely than boys to comfort or help their mother when she is upset. In general, however, the research does not show that females are born with the ability to care for others. It is something that is learned.

"Okay...Heads, *I* hunt animals and you raise the kids. Tails..."

© 1991; Reprinted courtesy of Bunny Hoest and Parade Magazine.

Learning the Rules

Most of what we think of as male or female behavior is cultural behavior. **Cultural behavior** is learned from the way of life into which children are born. Learning begins at birth. By the time children are ready for school, they have learned how society distinguishes between male and female roles.

A psychiatrist explains why this is important. "One of the things that is very helpful to children is to learn what their identity is. There are rules about being feminine and there are rules about being masculine. You can argue until the cows come home about whether those are good or bad societal influences, but when you look at the children, they love to know the differences. It solidifies who they are."

Young children learn the "rules" of being masculine and feminine much the way they learn how to walk and talk. It is a part of a long process called socialization. **Socialization** is the process by which people learn to fit into their culture. Socialization is molding a person to fit into a group.

Gender Stereotypes

Any person or group who shapes a child's values, beliefs, or behavior is a **socializing agent.** Parents are not the only socializing agents, yet they are the most important. Studies suggest that many parents begin socializing their children at birth. In one study, fathers were asked to describe their newborns. They saw their sons as firm, well-coordinated, alert, and strong. Daughters were seen as soft, awkward, weak, and delicate. Fathers saw their babies in terms of a gender stereotype. A **stereotype** is a general idea about how all people within a group or culture behave. A **gender stereotype** is a stereotype about males and females.

Interpreting a Cartoon. Cartoons express the artist's point of view on a certain subject. Often cartoons are humorous. They may even poke fun at somebody or something. Look at the cartoon on page 172. What does the cartoon say about gender stereotypes?

Applying Your Skills and Strategies

_____

_____

_____

Children learn stereotypes by watching and listening. Then they imitate what they have seen and heard. They can also learn by being told what is right or wrong. Children apply what they learn to different situations. Children also learn through experiences. For example, how parents react to babies when the babies cry carries a clear and distinct message.

The learning children experience helps to shape the kind of people they become. Children may not become the kind of people the parents hoped they would be. However, they will fit into their culture.

People who work with young children can see the effects of learning. A toy company in New York has a nursery where local children come to play and learn. Staff members watch the children. The children cannot see them watching. The children are observed so the company can find out what kinds of toys children like. What the staff discovered is that children will play with any toy up until the age of three or four. Beyond this age, children play with toys according to gender stereotypes.

Many people believe that stereotypes limit opportunity and freedom. A well-known writer argues that people do not think or act as members of a category or group. They act as individuals. This writer argues that it is "unreasonable and irritating to assume that *all* one's tastes and preferences have to be conditioned by the class to which one belongs."

Check your answer on page 227.

Thinking About the Article

Fill in the blank with the word or words that best complete each statement.

1. Sleeping and eating are examples of _____.

2. The process of learning how to fit into a culture is called

   _____.

3. The people who teach a child values, beliefs, and behavior are

   _____.

4. Ideas about how all men or women should behave are

   _____.

5. Learned behavior is _____.

Write your answers in the space provided.

6. Review the questions you wrote on page 170. Did the article answer your questions? If you said *yes*, write the answers. If your questions were not answered, write three things you learned from this article.

   _____

   _____

   _____

   _____

   _____

7. According to the research described in the article, what are three innate differences between males and females?

   _____

   _____

   _____

8. What are two male-female differences that are learned?

   _____

   _____

Circle the number of the best answer.

9. Which of the following statements is <u>not</u> a gender stereotype?

    (1) Boys will be boys.

    (2) Taking care of children is women's work.

    (3) Boys tend to be better at math than girls.

    (4) Boys are always more competitive than girls.

    (5) Girls are born mothers.

10. Which of the following is an example of cultural behavior?

    (1) eating

    (2) eating with a spoon

    (3) sleeping

    (4) crying

    (5) breathing

11. Which of the following is the <u>best</u> conclusion you can draw from the article?

    (1) Innate differences between men and women determine the roles each plays in society.

    (2) Some boys have trouble learning to read.

    (3) Some girls have trouble learning math.

    (4) Girls are treated better than boys.

    (5) Most of what we think of as male or female behavior is the result of socialization.

Write your answer in the space provided.

12. Have gender stereotypes ever been applied to you? If so, how have they been applied? Explain your answer.

    _____

    _____

    _____

    _____

    _____

Relationships

Setting the Stage

People having meaningful relationships with others is a vital part of being human. The relationship can be in the form of a strong family tie. Or it can be an intimate relationship with a partner. People are discovering the value of strong relationships with friends outside the family.

Past: What you already know

You may already know something about relationships. Write two things you already know.

1. _____

2. _____

Present: What you learn by previewing

Write the headings from the article on pages 177–179 below.

The Power of Friendship

3. _____

4. _____

5. _____

What does the picture on page 178 show?

6. _____

Future: Questions to answer

Write three questions you expect this article to answer.

7. _____

8. _____

9. _____

The Power of Friendship

As you read each section, circle the words you don't know. Look up the meanings.

Many people live great distances from their family members. In some cases, families members see one another only once or twice a year. Some families do not even get together that often. In addition, a significant percentage of marriages are breaking up. More and more people are seeking out friends for the comfort and support families once provided. Good friends can make the world a more comfortable place in which to live. Doctors are also finding that friends contribute to good health.

Friends for Health

The California Department of Mental Health has a program called "Friends Can Be Good Medicine." A doctor who helped set up the program says that "people who are connected to other people, either friends or family, tend to have longer lives and less incidence of a variety of diseases—not just depression but unexpected things like heart disease, certain forms of cancer, and strokes."

Doctors in other states agree. A psychologist in Pennsylvania says, "We're less interested in the number of friends people have than in whether they feel accepted, loved, supported, and emotionally in tune with those around them." What is the reason for this interest in how people relate to their friends? People who cut themselves off from others are about three times more likely to die young. This is true even if they don't smoke. It is true even if they exercise regularly. Studies have been made of pregnant women who are under stress. Those without close friends have three times as many complications as those with strong social support.

Recognizing Values. *Values* are influenced by culture. They are the things people feel are important, beautiful, or worthwhile. Values can be determined by how people act. Values can also be inferred from what people say. Reread what the Pennsylvania psychologist says about friendship. What is her view of how people value friends and friendship?

Applying Your Skills and Strategies

_____

_____

_____

The impact of friendship on health is important. Yet the value of friendship goes beyond good health. To many people, the world would be a frightening place without the help and support of friends. It would also be a lonely place without friends to share the good times and the bad.

Friends for Life

Close friends are people we trust. They are the people we can count on in times of trouble. Close friendships are very demanding. Therefore, it is not surprising that most people do not have many close friends. They do, however, have many casual friends.

Casual friends are the people we call to play ball or see a movie. They are our coworkers—the ones we join for coffee or lunch. Many casual relationships are limited to particular times and settings. Two people may help and support each other at work but know nothing about the other's private life. A group may get together once a week to play basketball but never see one another away from the basketball court. Yet the time they spend together may be very important to everyone involved. Casual friendships can be long lasting. They provide a sense of belonging and companionship.

Close friends and casual friends are a part of a **social network**. A social network helps people cope with daily life. However, many people do not have as large a social network as they need. So they turn to groups for help and support. Local newspapers often have calendars like the one on this page. It shows the kinds of support groups found in many communities.

CALENDAR OF EVENTS

TODAY
Garfield-Perry Toastmaster's Club will meet for lunch 12:10-1:10 p.m. at Diamond's Restaurant, Richmond Mall, Richmond Heights. Group provides its members communication and leadership development programs. Information: 555-2426 or 555-3737.

The Adult Literacy Program will meet 7:15 p.m. in Room 17, St. Clare's School, 5659 Mayfield Road, Lyndhurst. Information: 555-8457.

FRIDAY
Selrec Heritage Club will hold a picnic 1-7 p.m. at Lyndhurst Park Pavilion. Bring your own picnic basket.

SATURDAY
Meridia Heart Institute/ Severance Town Center will co-sponsor a National Heart Attack Risk Study 9 a.m. to 4 p.m. at Severance Town Center, Mayfield and Taylor roads, Cleveland Heights. For appointments: 1-800-555-0004.

SUNDAY
North Eastern Ohio Folk Dancing Club will meet at noon at North Chagrin Auditorium. Members $4, non-members $6. Information: 555-3255.

MONDAY
AARP/East Suburban Cuyahoga County Chapter 371 will meet 1 p.m. at Mayfield Heights Community Center, 6306 Marsol Road, Mayfield Heights. Program: Baritone Mark D. Walter will entertain. Guests welcome; refreshments following meeting. Information: 555-2934.
East Side Non-Smoking Singles will meet 7 p.m. at CH-UH Public Library, 13866 Cedar Road; University Heights. Program: Free classic movie "Band Wagon" will be shown starring Fred Astaire and Cyd Charisse. Information: 555-1632.

TUESDAY
National Society to Prevent Blindness will sponsor free glaucoma screening tests 10 a.m. to 6 p.m. at Maygate Plaza, 6371 Mayfield Road, Mayfield Heights. Information: 555-6466.

WEDNESDAY
Coin Collectors will meet 7 p.m. (every Wednesday) at Noble Road Presbyterian Church, 2780 Noble Road, Cleveland Heights. Information: 555-9227.

Single Parents Support Group will meet 1:15 p.m. at Beachwood Public Library, 25501 Shaker Blvd. Free and open to families and friends. Information: 555-8457.

Recovery Inc. free self-help group that demonstrates how to deal with anxiety, depression, nervous fears and panics will meet 1:30 p.m. at 4050 Monticello Blvd., Cleveland Heights. Open to the public. Information: 555-4442.

NEXT THURSDAY
Futures Unlimited support group for cancer survivors will meet 7-8:30 p.m. (second and fourth Thursday each month) in the Bolwell Health Center, University Hospitals, 2078 Abington Road. Parking free. Information: 555-7387.

A doctor noted, "It's strange that people who go to bed lonely every night might be living next door to each other but have no way to meet." Groups provide a way for people with common interests to meet.

Drawing Conclusions from a Table. To draw a conclusion, a reader must identify the important details. Then a judgment or decision can be made based on those details. Look at the calendar on page 178. It is a calendar of the meetings various groups will have during a week. Similar calendars appear in local newspapers throughout the country. Read the names of the groups. What conclusion can you draw about the people in this community?

Applying Your Skills and Strategies

Forming meaningful friendships is a skill children learn just as they learn to read and write. Friendship means nothing to infants. Yet by the time babies become teenagers, they will have formed close friendships. Some of them will last a lifetime.

Making Friends

A very young child defines a friend simply as a playmate. By the time the child is ready for school, a friend is someone who is helpful. The idea that friends can be helpful and loyal to one another develops more slowly. Most school-age children believe that a friend should be loyal. However, children are less certain that they must return that loyalty. By the age of nine, many children are able to see things from a friend's point of view. Friends now share secrets and make sacrifices for each other. By the age of twelve, many children have an adult understanding of friendship.

Teen-agers seem to have a greater need for friends than any other age group. **Adolescence,** the teen-age years, is a time of rapid physical and emotional growth. So teen-agers have a strong need to share experiences and try new identities. That is why most teen-agers are part of a group. A group allows members to talk freely. The group offers support as teen-agers try to separate themselves from their family and establish their own identity. As teen-agers become more confident, groups break up. Members may remain friends, but they begin to form friendships outside the group.

Over the years, a person may meet from five hundred to twenty-five hundred people. From all of these people comes a handful of friends. Friends tend to be peers. A **peer** is an equal. Peers usually have the same **status,** or level, in society. Friends also share values. They have the same ideas about what is right, important, or worthwhile, as well as having common interests.

Check your answer on page 228.

Thinking About the Article

1. A person's close and casual friends are part of that person's

   _____.

2. The teen-age years are known as _____.

3. A person's friends tend to be equals, or _____.

4. A person's _____ is his or her level in a society.

5. A person's beliefs about what is right or worthwhile are known as his

   or her _____.

Write your answers in the space provided.

6. Review the questions you wrote on page 176. Did the article answer your questions? If you said *yes*, write the answers. If your questions were not answered, write three things you learned from this article.

   _____

   _____

   _____

   _____

   _____

7. Why do young children have difficulty understanding the saying, "To have a friend, you must be one"?

   _____

   _____

8. Name three ways friendship enhances a person's life.

   _____

   _____

   _____

Circle the number of the best answer.

9. Which of the following conclusions does the calendar on page 178 support?

    (1) People do not value friendship.

    (2) Too many families live far apart.

    (3) People need more help than their social networks can provide.

    (4) Too many people are lonely.

    (5) Too many people have emotional problems.

10. For the past twenty years, a group of men have been getting together once a week to play cards. They do not see one another the rest of the week. Which value about friendship are they <u>most</u> likely to share?

    (1) Casual relationships can be satisfying.

    (2) Friendships lead to good health.

    (3) You can always count on your best friends.

    (4) You can confide in people who are friends.

    (5) Casual friendships do not last.

11. Which of the following sayings best summarizes the article?

    (1) Tell me who your friends are and I will tell you who you are.

    (2) New friends are silver; old friends are gold.

    (3) A friend in need is a friend indeed.

    (4) The rich man has as many flatterers as friends.

    (5) To have a friend, you must be one.

Write your answer in the space provided.

12. Think about two or three of your friends. Do you feel they are casual friends or close friends? Explain your answer.

_____

_____

_____

_____

A Multicultural Nation

Setting the Stage

The United States has always been home to people of many different cultures. When the nation was founded, most Americans traced their roots to northern Europe or Africa. By the early 1900s, the nation was also home to people with roots in southern and eastern Europe. Today many people have roots in Asia and Latin America.

Past: What you already know

You may already know something about the many different cultural groups that live in the United States. Write two things you already know.

1. _____

2. _____

Present: What you learn by previewing

Write the headings from the article on pages 183–185 below.

Cultural Diversity

3. _____

4. _____

What do the maps on page 184 show?

5. _____

_____

Future: Questions to answer

Write three questions you expect this article to answer.

6. _____

7. _____

8. _____

Cultural Diversity

As you read each section, circle the words you don't know. Look up the meanings.

Americans belong to many different ethnic groups. An **ethnic group** is a group of people linked by race, language, religion, or culture. Many ethnic groups are in the minority population of the United States. A **minority** is an amount that is less than half of the total. Americans who trace their roots back to Europe are in the majority. A **majority** is more than half of the total. How do we find out this information about the population? This information comes from taking a census.

Counting Heads

A **census** is a counting of all the people in a country. Every ten years, the United States takes a census. In 1980, about 80 percent of all Americans traced their roots to Europe. They were in the majority. By 1990, European Americans made up about 75 percent of the population. In fact, in a few states, they are just barely in the majority. For example, only 57 percent of all the people in California are European Americans.

Throughout the country, the minority population is growing. Today, about 12 percent of the nation is African American. Hispanics represent 9 percent of the population. Asian Americans make up 2.9 percent. A little less than 1 percent is Native American.

Getting Meaning from Context. As you read, you may not understand what every word means. One way to find out the meaning of an unknown word is to look it up in the glossary or dictionary. Another way is to figure out the meaning using clues from other words in the sentence or paragraph. For example, the word *roots* in the first paragraph does not have anything to do with trees. Instead, it is used to describe what countries people in United States came from originally. Look at the title of the article. Then reread the paragraphs above. What does *cultural diversity* mean?

Applying Your Skills and Strategies

_____

_____

_____

The census tells us how many people live in the United States. It also tells us where people in the various ethnic groups live. In addition, the census indicates which areas of the country have the greatest growth in ethnic population. The two maps on the next page are based on the census taken in 1990.

Check your answer on page 228.

States with the Highest Concentration of Minority Populations, 1990

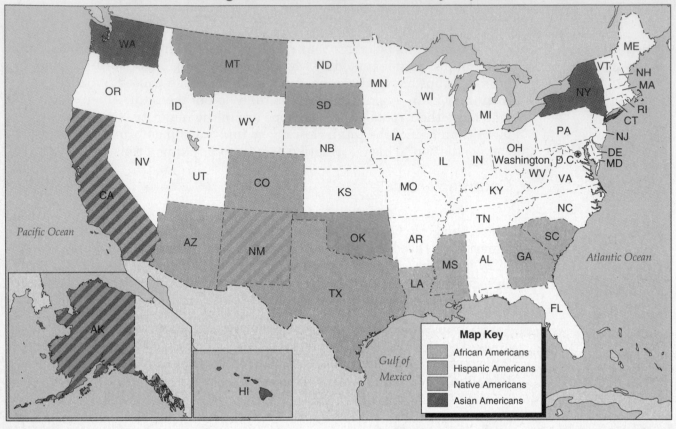

States with the Greatest Increase In Minority Populations, 1990

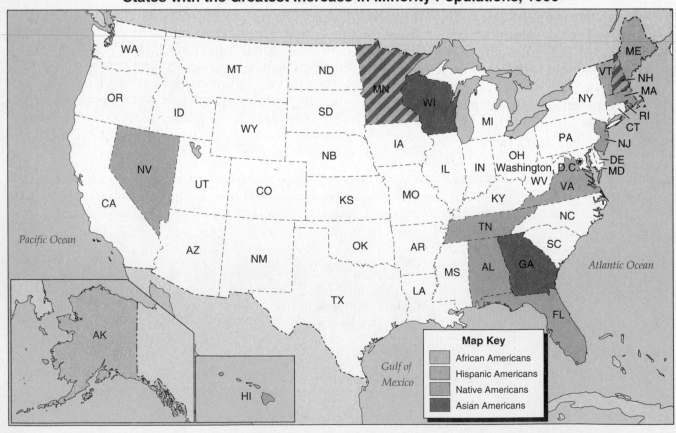

Reading Population Maps. A *population map* shows where people live. Look at the maps on page 184. The top map shows where the ethnic population is concentrated. That means it shows where most members of ethnic groups live. The bottom map shows the states that had the largest increase in minority populations between 1980 and 1990. The map keys tell how each group is shown on the maps. States with different colors have more than one ethnic group. Which states have the highest concentration of Hispanics?

New Hampshire (NH) had large increases of which three minority groups?

The census shows how many Americans belong to a certain ethnic group. It also tells where most people within this group live. However, there are things the census does not tell us. For example, the census does not tell what it is like to have values and beliefs that may differ from those of the majority. In addition, within a very large ethnic group there are many different, smaller ethnic groups. For example, Hispanics with Mexican roots have cultural differences from Hispanics with their roots in Puerto Rico. The same is true of African Americans, Asian Americans, Native Americans, and European Americans. The smaller ethnic groups within each larger group have their own values and beliefs.

Similarities and Differences

People learn the culture of the society in which they live over a long period of time. It is not surprising, then, that many people come to believe that their way of life is the natural and right way to live. This belief is called ethnocentrism. **Ethnocentrism** helps hold an ethnic group together since members share many of the same values. However, this belief leads some people to think other ways of living are wrong. This can cause a misunderstanding that leads to prejudice and discrimination.

People once thought that to be united, everyone in a country had to share the same culture. Newcomers had to assimilate. **Assimilate** means to give up one's culture to be like the majority. Today many people think that there is value in diversity. Antonia Hernandez, the head of the Mexican-American Legal and Educational Defense Fund, writes, "Unity is the completed puzzle, diversity the pieces of the puzzle. And until we recognize every piece, we cannot have true unity. That's the debate that's going on today, or that is where the debate should be aimed. By acknowledging the contributions made to our country by Native Americans, and by Hispanics and blacks and Asians, we're really strengthening our unity."

Thinking About the Article

Fill in the blank with the word or words that best complete each statement.

1. European Americans account for more than half of the population.

   They are in the _____ .

2. A counting of all the people in a country is a _____ .

3. An _____ shares a common culture, language, religion, or race.

4. The belief that one's own way of life is the only right way to live is

   called _____ .

Write your answers in the space provided.

5. Review the questions you wrote on page 182. Did the article answer your questions? If you said *yes*, write the answers. If your questions were not answered, write three things you learned from this article.

   _____

   _____

   _____

   _____

   _____

6. Why could ethnocentrism lead to prejudice and discrimination?

   _____

   _____

   _____

7. Look at the maps on page 184. What do you notice about the states with the highest concentration of minorities and the states with the largest increases in minorities?

   _____

   _____

                          Check your answers on page 228.

Circle the number of the best answer.

8. Which of the following is the <u>best</u> conclusion you can draw from the two maps on page 184?

    (1) Minority groups tend to stay where they are.

    (2) Minority groups are spreading throughout the country.

    (3) Minority groups live only in the large cities.

    (4) There was no increase in the population of minority groups in most states.

    (5) Every state had an increase in the population of minority groups.

9. Which of the following statements is <u>not</u> an example of ethnocentrism?

    (1) <u>They</u> care only about making money; *we* value family.

    (2) It is better to eat with a fork than with chopsticks.

    (3) Only Native Americans care for the environment.

    (4) The United States is home to many different ethnic groups.

    (5) To be beautiful you must be thin, blond, and rich.

10. People who value diversity are most likely to believe that

    (1) newcomers must become assimilated as quickly as possible.

    (2) people should learn not only about themselves but also about the contributions of other groups.

    (3) to be united, people must be more alike than different.

    (4) we should stress our similarities, not our differences.

    (5) ethnic differences divide a nation.

Write your answer in the space provided.

11. Have you ever felt it necessary to go against your values or beliefs in order to assimilate into a larger group? Explain your answer.

    _____

    _____

    _____

    _____

Section 26

Culture Change

Setting the Stage

Music is an important part of a culture. It reflects cultural values, feelings, and emotions. Yet people from one culture can enjoy the music of another culture. In time, music from one culture may even become a part of another. Much of today's mainstream music has its roots in other cultures.

Past: What you already know

You may already know something about music and the way it spreads from culture to culture. Write two things you already know.

1. _____

2. _____

Present: What you learn by previewing

Write the headings from the article on pages 189–191 below.

A World of Music

3. _____

4. _____

5. _____

What do the photos on pages 190 and 191 show?

6. _____

Future: Questions to answer

Write three questions you expect this article to answer.

7. _____

8. _____

9. _____

Check your answers on page 229.

A World of Music

As you read each section, circle the words you don't know. Look up the meanings.

Music is a **cultural trait**. That means it is a part of a culture. Like other cultural traits, music does not stay the same over the years. Styles of music change. Music today is very different from the music of past generations. In some cases, the change is slow and gradual so no one notices. In other cases, the change happens quickly.

Some changes are the result of technology. **Technology** is the use of tools and scientific knowledge. For example, new inventions like synthesizers are changing the sounds musicians can make. Other changes are due to changes in cultural traits. This can occur when people of one culture come in contact with people of another culture. Every culture borrows music and a variety of ideas from other cultures. The spread of cultural traits is called **diffusion**.

Whenever people borrow something from another culture, they adapt it to their own way of life. **Adapt** means to change something to fit one's culture. Music is a good example of the way cultural traits are diffused and adapted. Many pieces of American music today are based on African and African-American traditions. A **tradition** is a cultural trait passed from one generation to the next.

Comparing and Contrasting. Good readers compare and contrast ideas as they read. To *compare* ideas is to show how they are alike. To *contrast* ideas is to point out how they are different. What are two reasons why music today is different from the music of many years ago?

Applying Your Skills and Strategies

_____

_____

_____

How Music Grows and Changes

From the 1600s to the early 1800s, millions of people were taken from Africa against their will. They were brought to America in chains. Although the Africans lost their freedom, they tried to keep their culture alive. For the most part, they succeeded. The Africans passed many of the traditions of their culture down through the generations. Yet as time went by, their culture began to change. One thing that changed was the music.

In Africa, music was part of everyday life. It was closely tied to the daily routine. People moved to rhythm. They marked that rhythm by singing, clapping their hands, ringing bells, and beating drums. Often there were many different rhythms going at once. Yet they all were connected into a single sound.

In the United States, that musical tradition could be heard in the songs the African Americans sang. Yet, within a few years, those songs were no longer African songs. The language was different. The content of the music reflected the African-Americans' life in a new land. The spirituals, or religious songs, African Americans sang in church were not quite the same as African religious music. The rhythms were often the same, as were some of the melodies. But the words were different.

African Americans became acculturated. **Acculturation** means to borrow and adapt cultural traits from other cultures. African Americans borrowed cultural traits from the European-American culture. They adapted those traits to their own way of life. Acculturation takes place when contacts between cultures are deep and long lasting. However, it is never one-sided. European Americans also borrowed from the African-American culture. At first it was limited. In the early 1800s, people knew very little about those who lived in other parts of the country. Few people traveled far from home. So most people had little or no contact with other cultures.

Diffusion of African-American Music

However, by the late 1800s, contacts became more frequent, especially musical contacts. Many musicians traveled from town to town. Wherever they went, they put on minstrel shows. A **minstrel** is someone who sings, dances, and tells jokes. The minstrels were both African Americans and European Americans. They all used African-American rhythms and melodies in their shows. These shows helped African-American music become part of the culture of all Americans.

Manu Dibango

New inventions, such as the phonograph and the radio, introduced people to African-American music. These inventions came at a time when African Americans were developing jazz. **Jazz** is a *way* of playing music. One feature of jazz is **syncopation**. What would normally be the weak beat is stressed instead of the strong beat. It often means playing one rhythm against another. Another feature of jazz is **improvisation**. This means that a tune is rarely played the same way twice. If the musicians are feeling happy, they make the music sound happy. If they are feeling sad, the music sounds sad or blue. The **blues** are a part of jazz. Jazz is African in its rhythms. Yet many of the songs the musicians played were European. Jazz has its roots in the South.

Jazz and Other Cultures

Between 1910 and 1920, jazz spread north. Many jazz musicians were moving to large northern cities. There they played in nightclubs, churches, and dance halls. They also made records. Before long, European-American musicians were also playing jazz.

Dizzy Gillespie

Records brought jazz to other countries. Many people heard their first jazz record on the radio. Among them was the musician Manu Dibango. He liked jazz so much that he began to blend it with traditional African music. Musicians in other places also began to adapt jazz to their music. Cubans, Puerto Ricans, and Brazilians developed their own kind of jazz. It used drums and other instruments to create amazing rhythms. American jazz musicians, like Dizzy Gillespie, added these instruments to their music. When people borrow, each change leads to other changes.

Today jazz is not as popular as it once was. Other styles of music have become more popular. These other styles have resulted from borrowing and adapting. They are also a result of **collaborations**. That means musicians of other cultures play together. Language differences do not seem to matter.

Understanding a Photo. Often, photos and pictures contain as much information as words. The musician in the photo on page 190 is Manu Dibango. He was born in Cameroon, a country in West Africa. The musician in the photo on this page is Dizzy Gillespie. He is an African American born in the United States. Look at the clothes each musician is wearing. What do their clothes say about cultural borrowing?

Applying Your Skills and Strategies

_____

_____

_____

Youssou N'Dour, a popular singer from Senegal, explained, "Music has no language—it has no frontiers. It's a message that people receive directly. And they get the message of African music through the rhythm, the groove."

Thinking About the Article

Fill in the blank with the word or words that best complete each statement.

1. A part of a culture, such as music or art, is called a

   _____.

2. The spread of an idea from one culture to another is

   _____.

3. When people borrow a trait from one culture and change it to fit

   another culture, they are _____ it.

4. Cultural traits passed down through the generations are called

   _____.

5. When cultures borrow and adapt traits from other cultures they

   become _____.

Write your answers in the space provided.

6. Review the questions you wrote on page 188. Did the article answer your questions? If you said *yes*, write the answers. If your questions were not answered, write three things you learned from this article.

   _____

   _____

   _____

   _____

   _____

7. How are the African-American spirituals an example of acculturation?

   _____

   _____

   _____

   _____

8. Which is the <u>best</u> example of how the people of one culture adapt what they borrow from another culture?

    (1) Restaurants in the United States serve Italian pizza.

    (2) American restaurants create new French-bread pizzas and bagel pizzas.

    (3) Pizza is served in American public school cafeterias.

    (4) Magazines provide recipes for Italian pizza.

    (5) Americans list pizza as one of their favorite foods.

9. Which of the following is the <u>best</u> example of tradition?

    (1) African Americans create jazz.

    (2) Dizzy Gillespie wears African-style clothing.

    (3) Manu Dibango wears American-style clothing.

    (4) African Americans blend African music with jazz.

    (5) Musicians from several cultures collaborate.

10. Which of the following elements of jazz is most important in the creation of the blues?

    (1) improvisation

    (2) syncopation

    (3) strong rhythms

    (4) melodies

    (5) words

Write your answer in the space provided.

11. Think about the kind of music you like. How is it different from the music people listened to many years ago? How is it similar? Explain your answer.

    _____

    _____

    _____

    _____

    _____

Unit 5 Review:
Behavioral Science

Native Americans

The Bureau of Indian Affairs (BIA) is part of the United States government. In the early 1900s, the BIA believed Native Americans should be **assimilated** into the society of the United States. That means the BIA wanted Native Americans to give up their own cultural values and become more like the majority of the people in the United States.

Rebecca Grant is a Cherokee who lives in North Carolina. She was among the children who were forced to attend schools run by the BIA. "I was in boarding school when I was six years old. . . . They tried to assimilate us, make us white people—destroy our tradition, our customs. They punished us if we talked our language in school. But you always know who you are, from the day you're born to the day you die." Today Grant teaches college and advises people on Native-American crafts and herbal medicines.

Betty Mae Jumper is a Seminole who grew up in the Florida Everglades. Like Grant, she also attended a BIA boarding school. She fought assimilation, too. Jumper became the Seminoles' first woman tribal chairperson. Jumper is also a storyteller. Storytelling is an important part of Seminole culture and keeps the Seminole customs and traditions alive.

Write your answers in the space provided.

1. What statement by Rebecca Grant tells you that she did <u>not</u> assimilate into the culture of the majority?

    _____

2. How does Betty Mae Jumper keep the Seminole traditions alive?

    _____

Circle the number of the best answer.

3. Which of the following is the <u>best</u> conclusion that can be drawn from the article?

    (1) Native Americans cannot succeed in the United States.

    (2) Efforts to assimilate may fail, but Native Americans have succeeded in the United States.

    (3) The Cherokee are more traditional than the Seminole.

    (4) Native-American cultures do not change.

    (5) The Seminole are more traditional than the Cherokee.

Cultural Values

Drawing by C. E. Martin; © 1961, 1989 The New Yorker Magazine, Inc.

Write your answers in the space provided.

4. How does the child performing see herself?

_____

5. Which classmate comes closest to seeing the child's performance the way she does?

_____

Circle the number of the best answer.

6. The conclusion that can be drawn from the cartoon is that

   (1) people who belong to the same culture do not always see things in the same way.

   (2) people from different cultures see others in different ways.

   (3) everyone reads body language in similar ways.

   (4) children have to be taught to interpret body language.

   (5) the child does not know how to communicate.

Go on to the next page.

Male-Female Roles

Many people consider certain jobs as "men's work." They also regard other jobs as "women's work." Fighting fires is thought to be a man's job. Being a mechanic or an airplane pilot is considered men's work, too. On the other hand, teaching very young children is considered women's work. Nursing and secretarial work are also thought of as women's jobs. In recent years, many women have challenged such notions. There are now women firefighters and pilots. There are women who work as mechanics and engineers, too. They are proving that women can handle jobs traditionally thought of as men's work.

A number of men are also beginning to challenge traditional ideas about work. They are doing jobs that were once thought to be women's work. Some men teach nursery school. Other men work as secretaries and receptionists. Still other men are nurses. All are learning that it is never easy to change traditional ideas but, in time, attitudes do change.

First, a man has to overcome his own attitudes before he can become a nurse. Then, he still has to face the attitudes of his coworkers and his patients. A woman who has worked with two male nurses says that the first was "what I would've expected of a male nurse. He was rough, never really talked to patients, never really took care of them emotionally. Bill's the exact opposite. He's been a big surprise." Her comments are typical. As people encounter male nurses, their opinions slowly change. As one man put it, "Once they know you have the ability to do the job, you're accepted."

Circle the number of the best answer.

7.   Which of the following conclusions is supported by the article?

   (1)   Men should always do men's work.

   (2)   Women should always do women's work.

   (3)   Attitudes about work are changing for men and women.

   (4)   Attitudes about work are changing only for men.

   (5)   Attitudes about work are changing only for women.

8.   Which of the following beliefs is reflected in the views of the woman who has worked with two male nurses?

   (1)   Women are gentler and more caring than men.

   (2)   Men have an easier time overcoming stereotypes.

   (3)   Men always make great nurses.

   (4)   Men should stick to men's work.

   (5)   Women are not as prejudiced as men.

Body Language

The President of the United States addressing Congress

9. Who is the leader of this group?

_____

10. How do you know this person is the leader?

_____

_____

Circle the number of the best answer.

11. The group shows its respect for the speaker by

    (1) standing and applauding.

    (2) dressing in formal clothes.

    (3) moving closer to the speaker.

    (4) moving away from the speaker.

    (5) smiling and nodding.

The Nile River

The Nile is the longest river in the world. It is more than 4,100 miles long. The river begins in the mountains of central Africa and flows north through Egypt to the Mediterranean Sea. Each spring, heavy rains fall in the highlands of central Africa. The rainwater swells the river. By late summer, the swollen river used to flood Egypt. The water would spread across the river valley until it reached the desert just beyond the river.

Early Egyptian farmers learned how to live beside a river that flooded each year. They dug **channels** to carry the floodwaters to their fields. The farmers let the water stand in the fields for weeks until the soil was soaked. Then the water was drained. The river also left fresh, rich, black soil on the land. The fields could be used every year without wearing out the soil. By early fall, the farmers were ready to plant their crops.

Since the Nile River flooded only once a year, the farmers could plant only one crop a year. The rest of the year, the land was too dry for farming. Then in 1970, the Egyptians completed one of the biggest building projects in the world. It was a huge dam at Aswan in southern Egypt. It stopped the flooding and trapped the water in a manmade lake 300 miles long. Today farmers have water whenever they need it. However, since the Nile River no longer floods, Egypt's soil is not as rich as it used to be.

Write your answers in the space provided.

1. Farmers dug _____ to carry the floodwaters to their fields.
2. What caused the annual flooding of the Nile River?

_____

Circle the number of the best answer.

3. Since ancient times, people have said that Egypt is a gift of the Nile. That means
   (1) without the river, the whole country would be a desert.
   (2) the river brought farmers rich, black soil year after year.
   (3) the river flooded each year.
   (4) the river allows farmers to irrigate.
   (5) without the river, the country would not be united.

Go on to the next page.

World Climates

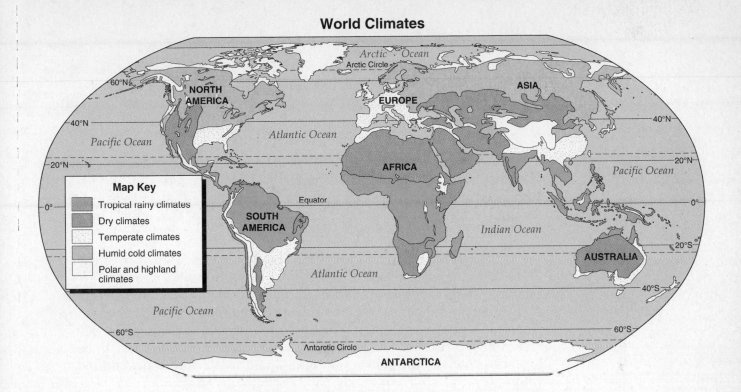

Map Key
- Tropical rainy climates
- Dry climates
- Temperate climates
- Humid cold climates
- Polar and highland climates

Write your answer in the space provided.

4. Tropical climates are hot and very rainy. Between what latitudes are most of the world's tropical climates found?

Circle the number of the best answer.

5. The northern half of Africa is mostly a

(1) tropical rainy climate.

(2) dry climate.

(3) temperate climate.

(4) humid cold climate.

(5) polar and highland climate.

Women in War

Women played an important role in the Gulf War in 1991. During the war, women flew transport planes and helped refuel tankers. Others trained combat pilots. Still others took troops, fuel, and ammunition into enemy territory. Yet women were not allowed to go into combat. Many people wonder if women should be allowed to go to battle.

Throughout history, a handful of women have been in battle. Perhaps the most famous was Mary Ludwig Hays McCauley, better known as Molly Pitcher. During the American Revolution, she carried water to the gunners during the battle of Monmouth, New Jersey, in 1778. When her husband was killed in the fighting, she took his place.

Deborah Sampson also fought in the Revolution. However, she disguised herself as a man and joined a Massachusetts regiment. Sampson fought in several battles and was seriously wounded. When a doctor discovered her secret, he told her commander, who then told General George Washington. Washington ordered that Sampson be honorably discharged on October 23, 1783. After Sampson's death, her husband received the pension normally paid to the wife of a wounded veteran.

The first woman to lead soldiers into battle was Harriet Tubman. Tubman, an African American, worked as a spy for the Union army during the Civil War. She also led scouting raids. A Boston newspaper described one of her raids. "Colonel Montgomery and his gallant band of 300 black soldiers, under the guidance of a black woman, dashed into the enemy's country, . . . brought off near 800 slaves and thousands of dollars' worth of property, without losing a man or receiving a scratch."

Write your answer in the space provided.

6. What do Molly Pitcher, Deborah Sampson, and Harriet Tubman have in common?

Circle the number of the best answer.

7. It can be concluded from the article that

   (1) women never wanted to take part in battles.

   (2) some women have already proved themselves in combat.

   (3) women shouldn't be allowed to take part in combat.

   (4) women have fought in every war in American history.

   (5) all women soldiers wanted to fight in the Gulf War.

Go on to the next page.

Labor Reform

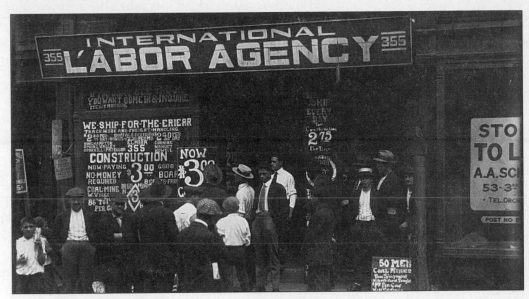

Men in front of a labor agency in New York City in 1910

Write your answer in the space provided.

8. Why were so many men and boys gathered around the building?

_____

Circle the number of the best answer.

9. The photograph was taken in New York City. It can be inferred from the photograph that

    (1) few New Yorkers were willing to work.

    (2) many jobs were available in New York City.

    (3) many jobs were available in other parts of the country.

    (4) most jobs required special skills.

    (5) most jobs were open only to adult men.

10. Who might be most attracted to the kinds of jobs advertised?

    (1) married men with young children

    (2) 12-year-old boys

    (3) young, single men with no family responsibilities

    (4) men in their early sixties

    (5) people from other countries

Go on to the next page.

The Language of Sales

Sale advertising has a language all its own. For example, an item *on sale* is different from a *clearance sale* item. There are also *promotional sale* items.

The price of an item *on sale* is lower than the price before the sale began. The store hopes to attract people into the store by putting certain items on sale. When the sale is over, the item will be sold at the original, higher price. Items on sale are available at lower prices for a short period of time.

During a *clearance sale* a store is trying to sell all of a certain item. The prices are greatly reduced for different reasons. Perhaps the item has not been selling well at a higher price. The item may be seasonal. For example, there is often a clearance sale on winter coats in March.

A *promotional sale* item does not come from the store's regular stock. It is brought into the store especially for the sale. Often, promotional sale items are not as inexpensive as the same items bought at a clearance sale.

Consumer experts say that the best way to make sure that you are paying the best price is to check several stores before buying. A good sale offers discounts of about 40 to 50 percent off the original price.

Write your answers in the space provided.

11. During the fall of one year a store has swimsuits left over from the summer. The price is reduced to sell the remaining stock. This is an

    example of a _____ sale.

12. An item is _____ if the price is lowered for a short time to attract new customers.

Circle the number of the best answer.

13. Which of the following is an example of a promotional sale?

    (1) A store lowers the price of shoes to attract new customers.

    (2) A new brand of shoes is brought in and sold at a low price.

    (3) In the spring, a store lowers the price of winter shoes.

    (4) A store sells shoes at the original price.

    (5) The price of shoes is reduced by 50 percent.

Go on to the next page.

Sales of Microcomputers

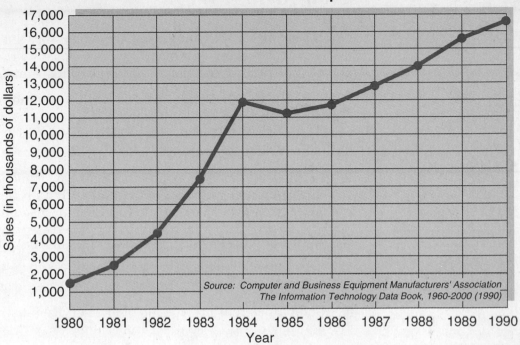

Source: Computer and Business Equipment Manufacturers' Association
The Information Technology Data Book, 1960-2000 (1990)

Write your answers in the space provided.

14. A decade is a ten-year period. In which part of the decade shown on the graph did sales of personal computers grow the fastest?

15. What happened the year after personal computer manufacturers experienced the largest growth?

Circle the number of the best answer.

16. A conclusion that could be drawn from the graph is that

   (1) the market for personal computers peaked in 1985.

   (2) the market for personal computers boomed in the early 1980s.

   (3) the market for personal computers dropped in the late 1980s.

   (4) the market for personal computers peaked in 1989.

   (5) there was no market for personal computers before 1980.

Go on to the next page.

Civil Rights

About 43 million Americans have disabilities. Many of them face discrimination every day. Many jobs are closed to them. Those who have physical disabilities cannot enter many schools and stores.

In July 1990, Congress passed a bill. It defines disability as a physical or mental condition that "substantially limits" a major life activity, such as walking or seeing. The bill covers people with the disease AIDS and alcoholics and drug users who are in treatment programs. The bill states:

■ Employers, including state and local governments, may not discriminate against an individual with a disability in hiring or promotion if the person is qualified to do the job.

■ Trains and buses must be accessible to people with disabilities.

■ Restaurants, hotels, and retail stores must remove any physical barriers to access and provide help for those who cannot hear or see.

■ Companies that provide telephone service must make available special equipment for those who cannot hear.

On July 26, 1990, President Bush signed the bill into law. The law will be enforced in stages to give businesses and governments time to remodel or order special equipment. If a small business can show it would face hardships in obeying the law, it does not have to comply.

Circle the number of the best answer.

17. Which of the following is discriminatory under the new law?

   (1) An alcoholic is fired for drinking on the job.

   (2) A deaf woman is turned down for a job because she lacks job skills.

   (3) A man in a wheelchair cannot get to work because he cannot get into the subway station.

   (4) A blind woman is fired for missing too many days of work.

   (5) A company refuses to hire a man because it proved it cannot afford the equipment he would need to do his job.

18. How does the law address the concerns of a business that would have a great hardship providing access?

   (1) Obeying the law is voluntary.

   (2) The law does not address any concerns.

   (3) If a business proves hardship, it does not have to obey the law.

   (4) If a business proves hardship, it still must obey the law.

   (5) All businesses must hire people with disabilities.

Go on to the next page.

How City Governments Spend Their Money

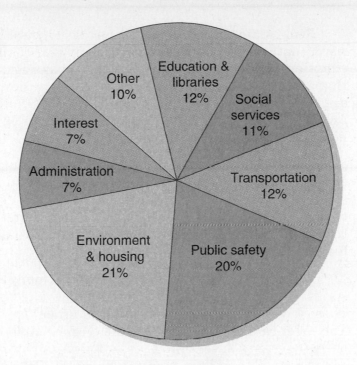

Write your answer in the space provided.

19. In what two areas do cities spend most of their money?

Circle the number of the best answer.

20. Based on the graph, which of the following is a function of city government?

    (1) installing a traffic light at a busy intersection

    (2) building schools in the community

    (3) paying the bill for repairs on the local hospital

    (4) making a heavily-traveled local road wider

    (5) all of the above

21. A city needs new buses. From which part of the budget will the money come?

    (1) administration

    (2) environment and housing

    (3) public safety

    (4) social services

    (5) transportation

Go on to the next page.

Cross-Cultural Communication

Real-estate agents are people who sell or rent houses and apartments. As the nation's population changes, many real-estate agents are learning **cross-cultural communication**. This means agents try to understand that all cultures have their own sense of what they like or don't like. This sense may be different from the culture of the real-estate agent. For example, many Chinese look for a sense of order or harmony in their homes. They prefer curved lines to straight ones.

How people go about buying or selling a home is cultural. Real-estate agents are also learning how to establish trust. Cultural differences can sometimes get in the way of a sale. For example, many Asians are not used to the process of getting a loan in the United States. Some are offended by requests for financial information. Bank officials, on the other hand, may feel that the person is trying to hide something.

Bargaining can also lead to distrust. In many Asian cultures, people start the bargaining process with a very low bid. Sometimes these offers are so low that the seller is offended. At other times, the price is fixed. The seller cannot or will not bargain. For example, there is usually no bargaining for a lower rent. Cross-cultural communication helps real-estate agents avoid losing the sale or rental. They try to help both sides understand each other.

Write your answers in the space provided.

22. Understanding what people from other cultures like or don't like is

    called _____.

23. What does a real-estate agent try to establish during the bargaining process?

    _____

Circle the number of the best answer.

24. Which of the following is <u>best</u> supported by the article?

    (1) The way houses are sold is changing as the population changes.

    (2) Cultural differences do not matter.

    (3) People from other cultures do not buy homes.

    (4) Real-estate agents are more sensitive to cultural differences than other business people.

    (5) People from other cultures are victims of discrimination.

Go on to the next page.

Male-Female Roles

"Occupation?"
"Woman."

Drawing by Chon Day; © 1940, 1968 The New Yorker Magazine, Inc.

Write your answers in the space provided.

25. The man is asking the woman about her job, or

_____ .

26. What is the job of the woman in the cartoon?

_____

Circle the number of the best answer.

27. With which of the following statements would the cartoonist <u>most</u> likely agree?

(1) All women should get a job.

(2) All women should not get a job.

(3) A woman can do anything a man can do.

(4) Being a woman, homemaker, and mother is a full-time job.

(5) Men should be more sensitive to the concerns of women.

28. The woman in the cartoon probably believes

(1) in equality for men and women.

(2) that women are more capable than men.

(3) that a woman's place is in the home.

(4) that a man's place is in the home.

(5) that women in our society are overworked.

Check your answers on pages 230–231.

POSTTEST
Correlation Chart

Social Studies

The chart below will help you determine your strengths and weaknesses in the five content areas of social studies.

Directions

Circle the number of each item that you answered correctly on the Posttest. Count the number of items you answered correctly in each row. Write the amount in the Total Correct space in each row. (For example, in the Geography row, write the number correct in the blank before *out of 5*). Complete this process for the remaining rows. Then add the 5 totals to get your Total Correct for the whole 28-item Posttest.

Content Areas	Items	Total Correct	Pages
Geography (Pages 12–41)	1, 2, 3 4, 5	_____ out of 5	Pages 32–37 Pages 20–25
History (Pages 42–89)	6, 7 8, 9, 10	_____ out of 5	Pages 56–61 Pages 62–67
Economics (Pages 90–125)	11, 12, 13 14, 15, 16	_____ out of 6	Pages 92–97 Pages 116–121
Political Science (Pages 126–161)	17, 18 19, 20, 21	_____ out of 5	Pages 140–145 Pages 128–133
Behavioral Science (Pages 162–197)	22, 23, 24 25, 26, 27, 28	_____ out of 7	Pages 182–187 Pages 170–175
TOTAL CORRECT FOR INVENTORY _____ out of 28			

If you answered fewer than 25 items correctly, determine in which areas you need further practice. Go back and review the content in those areas. Page numbers for specific instruction in those areas of social studies are given in the right-hand column above.

ANSWERS AND EXPLANATIONS

INVENTORY

PAGE 1

1. The elevation of the Coastal Plains is below 1,000 feet.
2. The elevation of the Great Plains is 1,000 feet to 8,999 feet.

PAGE 2

3. All deserts are dry.
4. Some deserts are hot, others are cold.
5. **(2) People have developed ways to survive in any environment.** According to the article, animals and people can live in all deserts so options 1, 4, and 5 are incorrect. Option 3 is a detail stated in the article, not a conclusion.

PAGE 3

6. Slave owners feared the African Americans would use their guns to try to end slavery.
7. Patriot leaders allowed free African Americans to join their army.
8. **(3) the loss of so many soldiers at Valley Forge** Options 1, 4, and 5 had no bearing on the feelings of Patriot leaders about African Americans. Option 2 resulted in Patriot leaders allowing free African Americans to join, but not slaves.

PAGE 4

9. North Korea started the war by invading South Korea.
10. **(1) North Korea moved into the South and retook South Korea's capital.** According to the timeline, option 2 took place almost two years after China entered the war. Options 3–5 took place before China entered the war.
11. **(3) By 1951, the two sides were deadlocked, and the deadlock was not broken until truce talks began in June 1952.** Options 1, 2, and 4 summarize one part of the timeline, but they do not reflect the entire timeline. Option 5 is true but it is not a summary of the timeline.

PAGE 5

12. It is a buyers' market.
13. It is a sellers' market.
14. **(2) goes down.** According to the article, the demand for recycled paper is low and the supply of old newspapers is high. So many sellers do not have buyers. This causes the price to drop, so the other options are incorrect.

PAGE 6

15. In 1950 the rank of the three auto producers was the United States, Europe, and Japan.
16. In 1970 the rank of the three auto producers was Europe, the United States, and Japan.
17. In 1990 the rank of the three auto producers was Europe, Japan, and the United States.
18. **(2) European auto producers may be a more serious threat to the United States auto industry than the Japanese.** Option 1 may be true, but since the Europeans have been the leaders since the 1960s, option 2 is the best conclusion. Option 3 is incorrect since the opposite is true. There is no evidence in the graph to support options 4 and 5.

PAGE 7

19. segregated
20. Americans marched on Washington to demand that Congress pass a civil-rights bill.
21. **(2) live up to the nation's values and beliefs.** In his speech, King reminds Americans of the values and beliefs on which the United States was built. He was not asking Americans to change their values or ignore their heritage, so options 1 and 5 are incorrect. Americans were already marching on Washington, D.C. so option 3 is incorrect. Option 4 was the goal of the march but not the main point of King's speech.

22. **(3) electors** According to the diagram, the voters elect the electors. The electors, in turn, choose the president and vice president so options 1 and 5 are incorrect. Options 2 and 4 are not supported by the diagram.

23. **(1) by winning by a large margin in states with few electors and losing by a narrow margin in states with many electors** The candidate who has the most votes in a state wins all of the state's electoral votes. So option 2 is incorrect. Support from the electors is necessary to win, so option 3 is incorrect. Candidates without options 4 and 5 could not run in an election as a Democrat or a Republican.

PAGE 9

24. anxiety reaction
25. Doctors believe shyness can be overcome because it is a learned behavior.
26. **(2) tend to have low self-esteem.** According to the article, most of the techniques for overcoming shyness focus on building self-esteem and a positive self-image. Therefore, the other options are incorrect.

PAGE 10

27. The restaurants' signs indicate foods from different cultures.
28. **(2) The man may enjoy foods from other cultures but sometimes prefers food from his own culture.** Since the man is saying he wants ham and eggs, option 1 is incorrect. The cartoon does not support options 3 and 4. The man is not saying that American food is superior or that food from other cultures is inferior. He is stating a preference for ham and eggs. If option 5 were true, there would not be any restaurants with foods from other cultures.

UNIT 1: GEOGRAPHY

SECTION 1

PAGE 14

1–2. Answers should be things you knew before reading the article.
3. Culture: Hunters on the Plains
4. Economics: Ranchers on the Plains
5. Economics: Farmers on the Plains
6. The map shows average annual rainfall in the United States.
7–8. Questions should be things you expected the article to answer.

PAGE 15

The Great Plains generally receives 10–20 inches of rain each year.

PAGE 16

You should have underlined the following sentence: *Native Americans were the first people to live on the Great Plains.*

PAGES 18–19

1. region
2. steppe
3. conserve
4. climate
5. aquifer
6. You should have written the answers to the questions you wrote on page 14 or two things you learned from the article.
7. The Great Plains receive only 10–20 inches of rain each year, which is not enough for trees to grow.
8. The three tools that made farming easier were plows with steel blades, giant power drills, and windmills.
9. Answers should include two of the following: Farmers planted rows of trees to hold the soil in place. Farmers made good use of what little rain they got. Farmers plowed their fields in ways that protected the soil. Farmers could tap water from a huge aquifer.

10. **(2) The invention of new tools and machines helped people live on the Great Plains.** According to the article, people have always lived on the Great Plains so options 1 and 4 are incorrect. Option 3 is incorrect because the opposite is true. Farmers were not helped by the aquifer until new machines were invented in the 1940s, so option 5 is incorrect.

11–12. There are many possible answers. Sample answer for 11: The Spanish explorers brought horses and cattle to the Americas.

SECTION 2

PAGE 20

1–2. Answers should be things you knew before reading the article.
3. Water and Wind
4. Mountains and Climate
5. The map shows latitude and climate.
6–7. Questions should be things you expected the article to answer.

PAGE 21

Places near the North and South poles are the farthest from the equator. They get very little sunlight.

PAGE 23

Denver is close to 40° N. Quito is close to 0°. Bowen is close to 20° S. Oslo is close to 60° N.

PAGES 24–25

1. equator
2. current
3. latitude
4. marine
5. continental
6. elevation
7. You should have written the answers to the questions you wrote on page 20 or three things you learned from the article.
8. There are many possible answers. Sample answer: Differences in climate are a result of latitude, nearness to large bodies of water, winds, and the effects of mountain ranges.
9. There are many possible answers. Sample answer: When the moist ocean winds reach the mountains, the winds are forced to rise. As air rises it cools. Since cold air cannot hold much moisture, it begins to rain. By the time the winds reach the other side of the mountain, they are dry.

10. **(5) direct rays from the sun** According to the article, direct rays from the sun produce warm temperatures in the tropics. Options 1 and 3 explain why the polar regions are cold. Option 2 explains why a place might get more rainfall. Option 4 helps to explain why southern Alaska has a mild climate.

11. **(2) marine climate** According to the article, the climate in southern Alaska is shaped by the ocean. It is a marine climate. Option 1 does not explain why southern Alaska is milder than Montana. Option 3 describes Montana's climate. It does not describe the climate of southern Alaska. Options 4 and 5 do not explain the differences in climate.

12. There are many possible answers.

SECTION 3

PAGE 26

1–2. Answers should be things you knew before reading the article.
3. Disaster in Prince William Sound
4. The Cleanup
5. The Effects of the Oil Spill
6. The map shows the oil spill in Prince William Sound.
7–9. Questions should be things you expected the article to answer.

PAGE 27

You may have circled many words. Here are the boldfaced words you should have circled along with their definitions.

Environment: the living and nonliving things that make a place

Glaciers: huge masses of ice that flow slowly over land

Iceberg: a huge block of ice that has broken off from a glacier

Crude oil: untreated oil

PAGE 29

Kodiak Island is about 300 miles from Prince William Sound. The distance is two markings, or 2 x 150 = 300 miles.

PAGES 30–31

1. environment
2. Icebergs
3. crude oil
4. glacier
5. You should have written the answers to the questions you wrote on page 26 or three things you learned from the article.
6. Prince William Sound was home to a wide variety of birds, fish, mammals, and other wildlife.
7. Answers should include two of the following: The storm spread the oil further. The storm carried oil to the beaches. The storm made it impossible to use chemicals to stop the spread of the oil.
8. Spraying hot water killed wildlife and forced the oil deeper into gravel beaches.
9. As a result of the oil spill, over 1,100 miles of coastline were polluted. It was a serious threat to the coastal environment.
10. **(4) Workers pushed the oil onto the beaches.** According to the article, options 1, 2, 3, and 5 were all used as part of the cleanup effort at Prince William Sound.
11. **(1) The oil-thick water killed many types of wildlife.** According to the article, options 2 and 3 describe the environment of Prince William Sound both before and after the oil spill. Options 4 and 5 describe the way people use that environment.
12. There are many possible answers.

SECTION 4

PAGE 32

1–2. Answers should be things you knew before reading the article.
3. Water: A Scarce Resource
4. Black Gold in the Desert
5. Resources and National Borders

6. The map shows mineral resources in the Middle East.
7–9. Questions should be things you expected the article to answer.

PAGE 33

There are many possible answers. Sample: Something that is scarce is in short supply.

PAGE 34

Coal, iron, phosphates, and natural gas are also found in the Middle East.

PAGES 36–37

1. resource
2. nonrenewable
3. oasis
4. desalination plants
5. You should have written the answers to the questions you wrote on page 32 or three things you learned from the article.
6. There are many possible answers. Sample: The machines that use oil as a fuel had not yet been invented or were not widely used. People had also not yet discovered all of the products that they could make from oil.
7. There are many possible answers. Sample: People throughout the region live near water. They settle near the coasts or along rivers.
8. The Aswan High Dam has stopped the yearly flooding of the Nile. It allows farmers to plant crops throughout the year and provides electricity for Egyptian factories.
9. **(2) trenches direct rainwater to terraces** The article does not mention anything about options 1 and 5. Option 3 is a method using water but is not run-off agriculture. Option 4 is a direct result of building a dam.
10. **(4) The Middle East has over sixty percent of all the world's known oil reserves.** According to the article, option 1 is an effect of the oil industry on the Middle East. Options 2 and 3 are facts about resources. Option 5 tells about the history of oil as a resource in the Middle East. It is not a reason for the region's wealth.

11. **(1) building pipelines from rivers to dry areas** According to the article, options 2, 3, 4, and 5 have all been used as methods for using water wisely in the Middle East.
12. There are many possible answers.

UNIT 1 REVIEW

PAGE 38

1. **(3) Earth Day makes people more aware of their environment.** According to the article, environmentalists are always concerned about the environment so options 1 and 4 are incorrect. There is nothing in the article to support option 2. Option 5 is true but does not best summarize the article.
2. **(5) Solving environmental problems requires people to change their attitudes and behavior.** According to the article, the experiences of the 1980s showed that options 1 and 4 were not complete solutions. Laws, if enforced, are important to solving environmental problems so option 2 is incorrect. If option 3 were true, Earth Day 90 would not have been organized.

PAGE 39

3. Peary's final trip began at Cape Columbia.
4. 85°N
5. 87°N
6. **(2) knowing his location in terms of latitude** If Peary could figure out the latitude of his location, he would always know where he was and how far he had to go. The other options may have been important to Peary but not in terms of direction.

PAGE 40

7. **(4) to get water for their crops and animals.** According to the article, irrigation is used to create a water supply, so options 1–3 are incorrect. There is no evidence in the article to support option 5.
8. **(4) Texas is large with many resources throughout the state.** The other options are true, but only option 4 provides the most complete reason.

PAGE 41

9. An oil derrick is used to show oil-producing states.
10. A cow is used to show cattle-producing states.
11. **(3) how much oil is produced in the top oil-producing states** The map does not show how much oil and cattle are produced. The map does show the number and location of top cattle-ranching and oil-producing states, so the other options are incorrect.

UNIT 2: HISTORY

SECTION 5

PAGE 44

1–3. Answers should be things you knew before reading the article.
4. A Colony in Virginia
5. A Colony in Massachusetts
6. More Colonies
7. The map shows English voyages to North America.
8–10. Questions should be things you expected the article to answer.

PAGE 45

Answers should include two of the following: *Beginning in the 1500s* is a clue phrase. *The first* is a clue phrase. *By 1600* is a clue phrase.

PAGE 47

The map shows the first colonists' voyage to Jamestown and the Pilgrims' journey to Plymouth.

PAGES 48–49

1. colony
2. peninsula
3. pilgrims
4. cash crop
5. You should have written the answers to the questions you wrote on page 44 or three things you learned from the article.

6. There are many possible answers. Sample answers: The colonists could make money by selling tobacco in Europe. Europeans were willing to pay high prices for tobacco. It was not a crop that Europeans already grew.

7. The first winter in Plymouth, like the first winter in Jamestown, was a time of hunger. People in neither colony had enough food for the winter. Many people died.

8. **(4) after the London Company got the approval of King James.** According to the article, options 1 and 3 happened before 1607. Options 2 and 5 happened much later.

9. **(3) Tobacco grown in Virginia could be sold in Europe.** According to the article, option 1 was a reason the colony survived its first winter. Option 2 tells why the colony was in danger. Options 4 and 5 are reasons Jamestown was founded. They are not reasons for its success.

10. **(2) The colony was abandoned a year after it was founded.** According to the article, options 1, 3, 4, and 5 are all true statements about the colony in Massachusetts.

11. There are many possible answers.

SECTION 6

PAGE 50

1–2. Answers should be things you knew before reading the article.
3. Growing Disagreements
4. A Tea Party in Boston
5. The Battles of Lexington and Concord
6. The timeline shows events leading to the American Revolution.
7–9. Questions should be things you expected the article to answer.

PAGE 51

One cause of England's debt was the war with France. One effect of England's debt was that Parliament demanded the colonies pay more taxes.

PAGE 53

The timeline covers 1763–1776.

PAGES 54–55

1. Parliament
2. repealed
3. boycott
4. Minutemen
5. You should have written the answers to the questions you wrote on page 50 or three things you learned from the article.
6. There are many possible answers. Sample answer: Angry colonists forced tax collectors out of town.
7. Parliament would not repeal the tea tax.
8. **(2) signing of the Declaration of Independence** According to the article, it was signed after the war began. Options 1, 3, 4, and 5 were all causes of the American Revolution.
9. **(5) beginning of the American Revolution** According to the article, all of the other options were causes leading up to the battles.
10. **(4) approve the Declaration of Independence.** There is no evidence in the article to support options 1 and 3. Option 2 happened as a result of the First Continental Congress. Neither Continental Congress ever approved the Stamp Act, so option 5 is incorrect.
11. There are many possible answers. Sample answer: The shot marked the beginning of the American Revolution. As a result of that war, the American colonies won their independence from England.

SECTION 7

PAGE 56

1–2. Answers should be things you knew before reading the article.
3. Lincoln's View
4. The Emancipation Proclamation
5. The Fight for Freedom
6. A Proud Record
7. The photograph shows a painting of Union soldiers fighting Confederate soldiers.
8–9. Answers should be things you expected the article to answer.

PAGE 57

You should have underlined the following sentence: My paramount object in this struggle [the Civil War] is to save the Union, and is <u>not</u> either to save or destroy slavery.

Lincoln's most important point was that he would do anything to save the Union.

PAGE 59

There are many possible answers. Sample answer: The artist seems to side with the Union because the United States flag is at the center of the picture. African-American soldiers appear to be winning.

PAGES 60–61

1. civil war
2. discrimination
3. border states
4. You should have written the answers to the questions you wrote on page 56 or three things you learned from the article.
5. Lincoln feared that allowing African Americans to join the army would upset the border states, causing them to side with the South.
6. Answers should include two of the following: African Americans were not allowed to be officers. They were paid only half as much as white soldiers. They were not allowed to fight with white soldiers even though they had white officers.
7. **(1) African Americans fought bravely for the Union.** According to the article, option 2 is true, but it is not an idea expressed in the painting. Options 3–5 are details that support the main idea.
8. **(5) Lincoln decides to free the slaves in those states that were fighting against the United States.** According to the article, option 1 happened after the Battle of Antietam. Option 2 happened after Lincoln decided to free the slaves. Options 3 and 4 took place after Lincoln issued the Emancipation Proclamation.
9. **(4) Slaves in the South were freed by Lincoln.** According to the article, option 1 was not accomplished even by the end of the war. Options 2 and 3 took place before the Emancipation Proclamation, so they could not be results. There was no stated connection between option 5 and the Emancipation Proclamation.
10. There are many possible answers.

SECTION 8
PAGE 62

1–2. Answers should be things you knew before reading the article.
3. Learning a Trade
4. The Growth of Factories
5. The Push for Reform
6. New Laws
7. The photograph shows children working in a cannery.
8–10. Questions should be things you expected the article to answer.

PAGE 63

The paragraph contrasts opportunities for boys and girls. The phrase *on the other hand* gives a clue that this is a contrast.

PAGE 65

There are many possible answers. Sample answer: The children are very young. Many have bare feet. The factory is crowded and dirty.

PAGES 66–67

1. child labor
2. apprentice
3. reformers
4. You should have written the answers to the questions you wrote on page 62 or three things you learned from the article.
5. Some parents didn't earn enough money.
6. Answers should include one of the following: The owners said children could do some jobs better than adults. Children were paid less.
7. There are many possible answers. Sample answers: The factory owners did not want him to see the conditions under which children were working. The owners did not want any child labor laws to be passed.
8. **(5) teach reading and writing** The article does not say the master was responsible for teaching the apprentice how to read and write. Options 1–4 were all responsibilities of the master.

9. **(1) He became one of America's most important leaders.** According to the article, options 2 and 3 are incorrect because he was a printer's apprentice. Option 4 is incorrect because the article states that he was 17 when he finished his apprenticeship. Option 5 is incorrect because he went to Philadelphia after completing his apprenticeship.

10. **(5) creating a minimum wage for children** There is no evidence in the article to support a minimum wage for children. In fact, reformers worked to sharply limit children working. The other options were goals of the reformers.

11. There are many possible answers.

SECTION 9

PAGE 68

1–2. Answers should be things you knew before reading the article.
3. The Doors Open
4. Soldiers Without Guns
5. A Changing Labor Force
6. The graph shows women in the labor force from 1940–1950.
7–9. Questions should be things you expected the article to answer.

PAGE 69

There are many possible answers. Sample answer: Because of the war, African Americans were hired to work in the defense industry. Factory owners were forced to end discrimination if they wanted defense contracts.

PAGE 71

The number of women in the labor force increased. The line is higher at 1950 than it was in 1940. If the line graph were extended to 1951, the line would probably rise. The level rose steadily from 1946 to 1950.

PAGES 72–73

1. allies
2. defense industry
3. labor force
4. civil rights
5. You should have written the answers to the questions you wrote on page 68 or three things you learned from the article.

6. There are many possible answers. Sample answer: For the first time, jobs in the defense industry were opened to African Americans and women.

7. Answers should include two of the following: There was a presidential order to end discrimination in companies with national defense contracts. There was a shortage of workers created by men serving in the military. There was an increased need for production of military equipment.

8. **(5) It ended discrimination in companies with national defense contracts.** According to the article, option 1 is incorrect because the order did not end all discrimination. Option 2 is incorrect because the order applied only to companies in the defense industry. The article does not discuss option 3. The article does state that women and African Americans earned more than they had before the war. However, it does not say this was an effect of the presidential order. Therefore option 4 is incorrect.

9. **(4) We are working to help win the war.** According to the article, options 1 and 2 are incorrect because women did all kinds of jobs, even those that were previously done only by men. Option 3 is incorrect because women were an essential part of the labor force since many men were serving in the armed forces. Option 5 is not supported by the article.

10. **(4) women working in the defense industry** According to the article, Rosie the Riveter symbolized women in the entire defense industry. Therefore, options 1 and 3 are incorrect. Rosie the Riveter appeared in the movies and on the cover of a magazine, symbolizing women in the defense industry. So options 2 and 5 are incorrect.

11. There are many possible answers. Sample answers: I would have joined the armed forces. I would have worked in the defense industry.

SECTION 10

PAGE 74

1–2. Answers should be things you knew before reading the article.
3. The Iron Curtain
4. Two Germanys
5. The Berlin Wall
6. The map shows countries controlled by the Soviet Union, countries that were neutral, and countries that were allies of the United States during the cold war.
7–9. Questions should be things you expected the article to answer.

PAGE 76

The Soviets controlled East Germany, Poland, Czechoslovakia, Hungary, Romania, Albania, and Bulgaria.

PAGE 77

There are many possible answers. Sample answer: People in East Germany had very little freedom. Life was difficult there. East Germans saw little or no hope that things would get better any time soon.

PAGES 78–79

1. cold war
2. zones
3. neutral
4. You should have written the answers to the questions you wrote on page 74 or three things you learned from the article.
5. According to Churchill, the spread of Soviet power caused the iron curtain to fall. The effect was the separation of Soviet-controlled countries in Eastern Europe from democratic countries in Western Europe.
6. Seven countries were controlled by the Soviet Union.
7. They used airplanes to bring food, clothing, fuel, and medicine to West Berlin.
8. **(1) The West believed that a rich Germany was the best protection against another war.** According to the article, option 2 was the Soviet view.

There is no evidence in the article to support options 3 and 5. Option 4 is true, but it's not the reason for combining the zones.
9. **(3) stopping the escape of East Germans to West Berlin** According to the article, option 1 took place 12 years before the wall was built. East and West Germany were created 14 years before the wall was built, so options 2 and 5 are incorrect. Option 4 is incorrect because West Berliners were not interested in crossing over into East Berlin. It was just the opposite.
10. **(1) Walls cannot keep people from seeking freedom.** According to the article, recent events proved that options 2 and 3 are incorrect. Option 4 is incorrect because the people of Germany were united only after the wall was destroyed. Option 5 is incorrect because many East Germans tried to leave their country.
11. There are many possible answers. Sample answer: Both Germany and Berlin were divided in much the way the countries of the world were divided by their support of the United States or the Soviet Union.
12. There are many possible answers.

SECTION 11

PAGE 80

1–2. Answers should be things you knew before reading the article.
3. Schwarzkopf at CentCom
4. From Plan to Action
5. Operation Desert Storm
6. The map shows the ground war against Iraq on February 24–28, 1991.
7–9. Questions should be things you expected the article to answer.

PAGE 81

The words that show the special unit's point of view are "threaten Free World interests."

PAGE 83

Attacks came from all directions, but mainly from the west.

1. deter
2. dictator
3. sanctions
4. coalition
5. You should have written the answers to the questions you wrote on page 80 or three things you learned from the article.
6. Schwarzkopf had told reporters that he felt Iraq was a threat to peace in the Middle East.
7. Answers should include two of the following: The United States formed a coalition. It prepared for war. It took part in economic sanctions.
8. Iraq thought that they could break up the coalition by drawing Israel into the war.
9. **(2) it is a good way to prepare for a possible war.** According to the article, Iraq did not invade Kuwait until August, so option 1 is incorrect. Although options 3–5 may be true, they are not the major reasons for the war games.
10. **(2) The Iraqis continued to occupy Kuwait.** Options 1, 3, and 5 are responses to events other than the sanctions. The article gives no evidence to support option 4.
11. **(3) Troops from many countries made it a team effort.** Options 1, 2, 4, and 5 are incorrect because Schwarzkopf made it clear that many countries and branches of the service were responsible for the victory.
12. There are many possible answers.

UNIT 2 REVIEW

PAGE 86

1. **(1) keep the English and French out and to protect Spanish ships.** According to the article, the king wanted to protect the ships and keep out the English and the French so options 2 and 4 are incorrect. There is no evidence in the article to support options 3 or 5.
2. **(4) to drive out the French colonists** According to the article, the king of Spain wanted the French driven out so option 3 is incorrect. Ponce de León searched for the Fountain of Youth, so option 1 is incorrect.

The guarding of the Spanish ships occurred after the French were driven out so option 2 is incorrect. There is no evidence in the article to support option 5.

PAGE 87

3. South Carolina
4. Tennessee
5. Eleven states left the Union.
6. **(4) separated the Union states from the Confederate states.** According to the map, none of the border states lies along the coast or the northern or southern borders, so options 1, 2, and 5 are incorrect. They did not separate the states from the territories so option 3 is incorrect.

PAGE 88

7. **(3) of the fear that Japanese Americans might be spies for Japan.** According to the article, options 1 and 2 were not direct causes of the internment. Option 4 was one effect of the fear about Japanese Americans. There is no evidence to support option 5.
8. **(2) the internment of Japanese Americans was an injustice.** According to the article, the United States government apologized many years later, thus admitting the injustice. Options 3 and 4 are true but they are details stated in the article, not conclusions. Option 1 is incorrect because the opposite was true. There is no evidence to support option 5.

PAGE 89

9. Union membership kept increasing until 1945.
10. Union membership decreased by 1960.
11. Union membership decreased by 1950.
12. **(1) Union membership was greater in 1989 than in 1930.** According to the graph, union membership was about 16 percent in 1989 and only about 11 percent in 1930. The graph does not support the information contained in the other options.

UNIT 3: ECONOMICS

SECTION 12

PAGE 92

1–2. Answers should be things you knew before reading the article.
3. Farming for a Market
4. The Effects of Competition
5. Responding to Change
6. The graphs show the number of farms and the average size of a farm in the United States for 1975–1989.
7–9. Questions should be things you expected the article to answer.

PAGE 93

When the price is low, more people are able to buy the goods. When the price is high, fewer people are able to buy the goods.

PAGE 95

The number of farms decreased from 1975–1989.
The size of the farms increased from 1975–1989.

PAGES 96–97

1. free enterprise system
2. consumers
3. market
4. technology
5. You should have written the answers to the questions you wrote on page 92 or three things you learned from the article.
6. Better tools and new methods allow farmers to increase the amount of goods produced so they can make more money on their crop without increasing the price.
7. Consumers benefit from competition with low prices and many choices.
8. **(3) fewer farms, but they will be larger.** Options 1, 2, 4, and 5 are not supported by the two graphs.
9. **(5) Producers must be more efficient when producing goods.** According to the article, options 1, 2, and 4 are all characteristics of a competitive market, not an effect. Option 3 is incorrect because the opposite is true.
10. **(2) increasing the demand for pork** According to the article, options 1 and 5 are true but not the reason for advertising. Option 3 may be an effect of an increase in demand. There is no evidence to support option 4.
11. There are many possible answers. Sample answer: Competition will cause prices to be lower. A choice of service could be based on the lowest price. If there was less competition, the prices would probably be higher. A choice of service might have to be based on something other than price.

SECTION 13

PAGE 98

1–2. Answers should be things you knew before reading the article.
3. Follow a Plan
4. Consider the Costs
5. Careful Borrowing
6. The chart shows a budget for the Rivera family. The circle graph shows how the average American family spends its income.
7–9. Questions should be things you expected the article to answer.

PAGE 100

The average family spends about 25 percent of its income on housing.
The four greatest expenses are housing, transportation, food, and credit cards.

PAGE 101

Not considering opportunity cost could leave people without money for something they really need.

PAGES 102–103

1. budget
2. net income
3. fixed expenses
4. finance charge
5. annual percentage rate (APR)
6. You should have written the answers to the questions you wrote on page 98 or three things you learned from the article.

7. Answers should include two of the following: Following a budget helps people know how much money they have to spend; it helps them know what they are spending their money on each month. It helps them know what the opportunity costs of a purchase will be. It helps them identify where money can be saved.

8. The person should consider the opportunity costs and the costs of borrowing.

9. **(3) groceries** According to the article, flexible payments vary from month to month. So groceries would be a flexible payment. Options 1, 2, 4, and 5 are examples of fixed payments because they stay the same.

10. **(2) almost half of its income on housing and transportation.** Option 1 is not supported by the graph. It shows that the average family spends only 17 percent of its income on food. Options 3–5 cannot be determined from this circle graph.

11. **(3) their credit-card payment was less than they budgeted.** There is no evidence in the chart to support options 1 and 5. The expenses in option 2 are fixed expenses, so they remained the same. Option 4 is incorrect since their utility bill went up, not down.

12. There are many possible answers. Sample answer: When I bought a TV on the spur of the moment, I did not have enough money to pay for the repairs my car needed when it broke down.

SECTION 14

PAGE 104

1–2. Answers should be things you knew before reading the article.

3. A Changing Market

4. A Matter of Supply and Demand

5. Scarcity and Price

6. The title of the table is "Baseball Cards for Investment."

7–9. Questions should be things you expected the article to answer.

PAGE 105

There are many possible answers. Sample answer: The rest of the article might be about the demand for and increased value of baseball cards.

PAGE 107

The Bowman card is worth $5,000. The Topps card is worth $8,500.

PAGES 108–109

1. demand

2. supply

3. elastic

4. scarce

5. You should have written the answers to the questions you wrote on page 104 or three things you learned from the article.

6. When the demand for a product decreases, the price usually goes down.

7. When the supply of a product decreases, the price usually goes up.

8. **(2) cars made in the 1940s** According to the article, an inelastic supply does not change. Options 1, 3, 4, and 5 are all things whose quantities change at different times. However, there were only a certain number of cars made in the 1940s. They can never be made again.

9. **(2) The demand for the Sabo card may increase over time.** According to the article, there is no evidence to support options 1 and 4. Option 3 is a reason why someone should not buy the card. Option 5 could happen but is not the best reason for buying the card.

10. **(4) The Topps card is scarcer than the one from Bowman.** Option 1 is true, but it has a lower value. If options 2 and 3 were true, the Bowman card would have a higher value. Option 5 is true but does not explain why one card has a higher value than the other.

11. There are many possible answers. Sample answer: I would advise someone not to invest in baseball cards. There are many baseball cards being made by several companies. The price of the cards may not rise that much in the future.

SECTION 15

PAGE 110

1–2. Answers should be things you knew before reading the article.
3. A Different Kind of Recession
4. Recovery and Growth
5. A Recession Begins
6. Managing the Economy
7. The title of the graph is "The Unemployment Rate, 1980–1991."
8–10. Questions should be things you expected the article to answer.

PAGE 112

Unemployment was the highest in 1982. Unemployment was lower in 1984.

PAGE 113

Consumers buy two thirds of all goods and services. A loss of consumer confidence during the war could cause a recession.

PAGES 114–115

1. recession
2. business cycle
3. unemployment rate
4. inflation
5. You should have written the answers to the questions you wrote on page 110 or three things you learned from the article.
6. Prices usually fall during a recession.
7. Rising prices were increasing inflation. The Fed could not lower interest rates without adding to inflation. On the other hand, raising interest rates would increase the effects of the recession.
8. The answer should include two of the following: A cause of the 1990 recession was too much borrowing by consumers, government, and large companies. The war in the Middle East shook consumer confidence. The end of the cold war meant a cut in military spending which hurt the defense industry. Banks failed because they made bad loans.
9. **(2) buy more.** Options 1, 3, and 5 are what consumers do when they lack confidence in the economy. Option 4 is incorrect because consumers cannot afford to ignore signs of a recession.
10. **(5) Inflation is caused by many different factors.** There is no one cause of inflation. Options 1–4 may contribute to inflation, but no one factor is solely responsible.
11. **(4) The country was recovering from the recession by the mid-1980s.** By the mid-1980s, the unemployment rate began to fall, which signaled that the recession was ending. The unemployment rate changes over time so option 1 is incorrect. Option 2 is incorrect because the opposite is true. There is no evidence in the graph or in the article to support options 3 and 5.
12. There are many possible answers.

SECTION 16

PAGE 116

1–2. Answers should be things you knew before reading the article.
3. The Growth of Trade
4. Multinational Companies
5. Competing Globally
6. The title of the graph is "United States Trade with Other Countries, 1960–1988."
7–9. Questions should be things you expected the article to answer.

PAGE 118

One line shows the amount of exports in billions of dollars. The other line shows the amount of imports in billions of dollars. The lines slope upward.

PAGE 119

Answers should include two of the following: The Swiss company manages businesses around the world. Over 95 percent of the Swiss company's business takes place outside of Switzerland. Very few employees are Swiss.

PAGES 120–121

1. exporter
2. importer
3. multinational
4. You should have written the answers to the questions you wrote on page 116 or three things you learned from the article.

5. There are many possible answers. Sample answer: A large portion of the sales comes from outside the home country and a large percentage of the workers are outside the home country.

6. Answers should include two of the following: Education, banking, medicine, hotels, restaurants, and theme parks are examples of service industries.

7. Answers should include two of the following: They have more plants overseas. There is more of a need for sales in foreign markets. There are more partnerships with foreign companies.

8. **(4) increases in both imports and exports but a sharper increase in imports** According to the article, options 1, 2, and 5 fail to describe the upward slope of the lines for both imports and exports. Option 3 does not address the fact that imports have been growing faster than exports.

9. **(1) skill of its workers.** Option 2 is incorrect because the article does not mention anything about resources. Option 3 is incorrect because multinationals do business around the world, not in one particular country. Options 4 and 5 depend on the skill of workers.

10. **(4) Ideas are improved as they spread.** According to the article, more countries are sharing ideas so option 1 is incorrect. Options 2, 3, and 5 may be true, but they are not the reason that countries are sharing their tools and methods.

11. There are many possible answers. Sample: Businesses will locate in countries that they feel have the best people. These countries will have the best job opportunities.

UNIT 3 REVIEW

PAGE 122

1. **(5) people who are concerned about the environment** According to the article, cornstarch helps plastic decompose, which helps the environment. Corn has always been considered a food so options 1 and 2 are incorrect. Options 3 and 4 are incorrect

because these groups could possibly be hurt by the new uses of corn.

2. **(1) Demand for corn is likely to increase.** According to the article, the new products will increase the demand for corn so options 2 and 5 are incorrect. The supply is likely to increase also, so options 3 and 4 are incorrect.

PAGE 123

3. The largest percent of income comes from individual income tax.

4. The largest percent of the government's income is spent on direct benefit payments for individuals.

5. **(1) More than half of the government's income comes from individual income tax and social security.** According to the graph, corporations pay less tax than individuals so option 2 is incorrect. Borrowing is five percent of the income so option 3 is incorrect. Social security is less than fifty percent of the income so option 4 is incorrect. The size of the section for excise taxes indicates that option 5 is incorrect.

PAGE 124

6. The seller is using bait-and-switch advertising.

7. The seller is using the special-pricing method.

8. **(2) Let the buyer beware.** According to the article, buyers should be wary of selling methods used by some sellers. The article does not state that all sellers are dishonest so option 1 is incorrect. Options 3 and 4 are incorrect because the opposite is true. Option 5 may be true but it is not supported by the article.

PAGE 125

9. The home-health-aide occupation is expected to have the greatest growth by 2000.

10. The expected percent of increase in jobs for guards is 32 percent.

11. **(3) occupations that are declining most rapidly** The table shows occupations that are growing and the number of jobs in each occupation. The other options are supported by the table, so they are incorrect.

UNIT 4: POLITICAL SCIENCE

SECTION 17

PAGE 128

1–2. Answers should be things you knew before reading the article.
3. Mountains of Trash
4. Taking Responsibility
5. Reduce, Reuse, Recycle
6. The Throw Away Society is the title of the cartoon.
7–9. Questions should be things you expected the article to answer.

PAGE 129

Too much trash is produced and that amount will continue to rise.

PAGE 131

The symbol is the Statue of Liberty.
The symbol represents the United States.

PAGES 132–133

1. landfill
2. groundwater
3. ordinance
4. hazardous wastes
5. permit
6. You should have written the answers to the questions you wrote on page 128 or three things you learned from the article.
7. Local governments are dealing with the garbage crisis by building safer landfills, passing laws that encourage recycling, and charging people fees according to how much garbage they produce.
8. **(1) Americans produce too much garbage.** Option 2 does not take into account the fact that the Statue of Liberty is a symbol. The cartoonist is likely to agree with options 3 and 5, but they are not the subject of the cartoon. Option 4 is a way the cartoon might be interpreted, but it is not supported by the cartoon's title.
9. **(3) people care when it hits their pocketbooks.** This is the only option that is supported by the fact that people produce less trash when they have to pay

according to how much trash they produce. Options 1, 2, 4, and 5 do not relate to the success of these programs.
10. **(2) Individuals and all levels of government must deal with the garbage crisis.** The article supports the other options but each is only part of the solution.
11. There are many possible answers.

SECTION 18

PAGE 134

1–2. Answers should be things you knew before reading the article.
3. The Debate Begins
4. The Struggle Continues
5. The title of the diagram is "How a Bill Becomes a Law."
6–8. Questions should be things you expected the article to answer.

PAGE 135

Richard Floyd believes all motorcyclists should wear helmets.

PAGE 137

The bill is sent to the governor.

PAGES 138–139

1. bill
2. federal
3. lobby
4. governor
5. veto
6. You should have written the answers to the questions you wrote on page 134 or three things you learned from the article.
7. Answers should include two of the following: Forty-seven states passed helmet laws. There was a decrease in motorcycle deaths and injuries. There was an increase in lobbying efforts by motorcyclists.
8. The major outcome of this change was a sharp increase in deaths and injuries from motorcycle accidents.
9. **(3) the state legislature has the final say only if two thirds of its members support the bill.** Options 1 and 2 are true only in some cases. Option 4 is not true. Option 5 is a part of the way a bill

becomes a law, but it does not relate to who has the final say.

10. **(4) Motorcyclists lobbied against helmet laws in Congress and state legislatures.** This is the only option that can be proved. The other options are things people think or believe, so they are opinions, not facts.

11. **(2) lawmakers who supported the 1966 Highway Safety Act** Some of the same arguments used against helmet laws could be applied to seatbelt laws. So those who are against helmet laws are also likely to be against seatbelt laws. The other options mention people who are against helmet laws.

12. There are many possible answers.

SECTION 19

PAGE 140

1–2. Answers should be things you knew before reading the article.
3. The Gideon Case
4. The Courts and the Constitution
5. A Landmark Decision
6. The title of the diagram is "How Cases Reach the Supreme Court."
7–9. Questions should be things you expected the article to answer.

PAGE 141

The state failed to protect Gideon's right to a fair trial (Fifth Amendment) and his right to a lawyer at no charge (Sixth Amendment).

PAGE 143

Gideon's case went through the state trial courts, the state appellate courts, and the highest state court in Florida.

PAGES 144–145

1. bill of rights
2. amendment
3. Constitution
4. Supreme Court
5. due process
6. You should have written the answers to the questions you wrote on page 140 or three things you learned from the article.

7. The Supreme Court decides whether a law is in keeping with the laws of the Constitution.

8. The highest court in the state of Florida had to rule on Gideon's case before it reached the Supreme Court.

9. **(3) all people.** According to the article, the Bill of Rights protects the rights of individuals, so options 1, 2, and 4 are incorrect. Option 5 is not correct because no one group is singled out.

10. **(4) All cases must be heard in at least two courts before going to the Supreme Court.** According to the diagram, there are at least two courts in each of the three routes to the Supreme Court. Therefore, option 1 is incorrect. Cases can start in any one of four courts so option 2 is incorrect. The diagram does not indicate which cases the Court will hear so option 4 is incorrect. There is nothing in the diagram about option 5.

11. **(3) People accused of any crime have the right to a lawyer supplied by the court at no charge if they cannot afford one.** According to the article, option 1 was the original law that was struck down. Option 2 did happen, but it is not the reason the case was so important. There is no evidence in the article to support options 4 and 5.

12. There are many possible answers.

SECTION 20

PAGE 146

1–2. Answers should be things you knew before reading the article.
3. The Role of Political Parties
4. Persuading the Voters
5. The Rising Cost of Campaigns
6. The picture shows a political ad in support of Issue 22.
7–9. Questions should be things you expected the article to answer.

PAGE 147

People in a political party have similar ideas about public issues. Each party chooses its own candidates for election. Each party wants the elected candidate to support the party's goals.

PAGE 149

If you vote against Issue 22, then you don't care about kids.

PAGES 150–151

1. campaign
2. candidate
3. political party
4. political action committees
5. endorses
6. You should have written the answers to the questions you wrote on page 146 or three things you learned from the article.
7. "Paid for by Care For Kids Committee" is the statement.
8. There are many possible answers. Sample answer: The ad would contain facts about the income tax for schools, such as the amount of tax and how it will be spent.
9. **(4) A magazine publishes stories about one candidate only.** Options 1–3 are ways that the media try to present a balanced picture of a campaign. Option 5 would be taking sides only if the newspaper paid for the ad and publicly supported a candidate.
10. **(3) If he votes against the law, the number of deaths due to motorcycle accidents will increase.** The state does not have a helmet law now. Failure to pass one will not increase the number of deaths. Options 1 and 2 are logical. Options 4 and 5 have nothing to do with the situation.
11. **(2) supporting a candidate with the same views on key issues** According to the article, the special interest groups want to elect people who have the same or similar views. So options 1 and 5 are incorrect. There is no evidence to support options 3 and 4.
12. There are many possible answers.

SECTION 21

PAGE 152

1–2. Answers should be things you knew before reading the article.
3. Gun Control—Yes or No?
4. The Argument Against Gun Control
5. The Argument for Gun Control

6. Both political cartoons deal with the issue of gun control.
7–9. Questions should be things you expected the article to answer.

PAGE 153

Some people feel Congress should pass a tough gun-control law. Others feel Congress should not pass any gun-control laws.

PAGE 155

The cartoon suggests that gun-control laws do not stop criminals.

PAGES 156–157

1. federal
2. gun-control
3. self-defense
4. You should have written the answers to the questions you wrote on page 152 or three things you learned from the article.
5. Answers should include two of the following: Groups for and against gun control agree that violent crime is increasing. Most gun owners are law-abiding citizens. Gun-control laws do not stop crime.
6. Answers should include two of the following: Groups for and against do not agree that guns are useful for self-defense. The right to own guns should never be limited. Gun control-laws reduce violence.
7. **(5) Each year, guns are involved in the death or injury of about 30,000 Americans.** Options 1–4 are all opinions. They cannot be proved true or false. Each is a thought or belief that individuals or groups have about the facts.
8. **(2) Gun-control laws do not stop criminals.** Although the cartoon suggests that option 1 is correct, it is not the main point of the cartoon. Options 3, 4, and 5 are not directly addressed by the cartoon.
9. **(3) A gun kept for protection is more likely to kill someone the gun owner knows than an attacker.** There is no evidence in the cartoon to support options 1, 2, 4, or 5.
10. There are many possible answers.

PAGE 158

1. The two cases are alike because they both involve rape, both men were questioned before their rights were read, neither man had a lawyer present.
2. **(2) When public safety is threatened, our rights may be limited.** According to the article, option 1 is true but is not the best conclusion. There is nothing in the article to support options 3 and 4. Option 5 is not true.

PAGE 159

3. **(2) Each branch of government can check or control the power of the other branches.** According to the diagram, the powers of each branch of government are limited. The branches also work together. Options 1, 3, and 4 are incorrect because no one branch is more powerful than the others. The branches work together so option 5 is incorrect.
4. **(1) is how the Constitution limits the power of the federal government.** Options 2 and 3 are true, but they focus only on part of the diagram. Option 4 is not covered in the diagram. Option 5 is incorrect because the opposite is true.

PAGE 160

5. register
6. A person must be at least 18 years of age to vote.
7. **(5) Every vote can make a difference.** According to the article, the outcome of past elections might have been different if more people voted. Option 1 is incorrect because paying taxes is not one of the requirements for being eligible to vote. Registration is a way of checking if a person is eligible to vote. It is not a way of keeping people from voting, so option 2 is incorrect. Option 3 is incorrect, because the opposite is true. There is no evidence in the article to support option 4.

PAGE 161

8. The person with the club represents authoritarianism.

9. The Spirit of Freedom is represented by a cloud.
10. **(1) that does not allow freedom.** The cartoon suggests that authoritarianism is the opposite of freedom, so options 2 and 5 are incorrect. There is no evidence to support options 3 and 4.

UNIT 5: BEHAVIORAL SCIENCE

SECTION 22

PAGE 164

1–2. Answers should be things you knew before reading the article.
3. Posture Counts
4. Too Close for Comfort
5. Meaningful Gestures
6. The photo shows five people in a meeting or classroom.
7–9. Questions should be things you expected the article to answer.

PAGE 166

The strangers may sit stiffly, avoid touching each other, and not look at each other.

PAGE 167

The man talking is the leader. He is the only one gesturing. The others in the group have oriented their heads and bodies toward him.

PAGES 168–169

1. innate
2. culture
3. body language
4. orientation
5. gesture
6. You should have written the answers to the questions you wrote on page 164 or three things you learned from the article.
7. The person can lean forward, pay close attention, imitate the posture of the speaker, or nod in agreement.
8. The other person will understand the gesture. Smiles are innate and understood by all people.

9. **(1) looking a person in the eye**
According to the article, option 2 does not show honesty and respect in the United States. There is nothing in the article that supports options 3 and 5. Option 4 may or may not be a sign of respect.

10. **(3) We may argue, but we are still friends.** Their body language shows the friends still like each other. It does not suggest that the argument is unimportant or fun. So options 2 and 4 are incorrect. There is nothing to support options 1 and 5.

11. **(2) We are in charge.** According to the article, when someone in authority enters someone's personal zone, it is to show who is in charge. The other options are incorrect because they do not say anything about who is in charge.

12. There are many possible answers.

SECTION 23

PAGE 170

1–2. Answers should be things you knew before reading the article.
3. What Comes Naturally?
4. Learning the Rules
5. Gender Stereotypes
6. The cartoon is about male and female roles.
7–9. Questions should be things you expected the article to answer.

PAGE 171

Answer should be one of the following: Some parents say that their baby girl, like all little girls, is very sociable. Others are convinced that their baby boys are always tougher and stronger than little girls.

PAGE 173

The cartoon says that certain male-female roles may not be innate after all.

PAGES 174–175

1. instincts
2. socialization
3. socializing agents
4. gender stereotypes

5. cultural
6. You should have written the answers to the questions you wrote on page 170 or three things you learned from the article.
7. Three innate differences between boys and girls are that boys have a slight advantage in math, girls are less active, and boys are somewhat more likely to be violent.
8. Answers should include two of the following: Girls are raised to care for others. Boys are raised to be more competitive and more aggressive. Girls are more likely to prefer dolls while boys favor cars.

9. **(3) Boys tend to be better at math than girls.** It is the only option that does not make the hasty generalization that all boys or all girls are alike in any way.

10. **(2) eating with a spoon** All of the other options are incorrect because those behaviors are instinctive, or innate.

11. **(5) Most of what we think of as male or female behavior is the result of socialization.** According to the article, there are not that many innate differences so option 1 is incorrect. Options 2 and 3 may be a result of socialization but they are not the best conclusion. There is no evidence to support option 4.

12. There are many possible answers.

SECTION 24

PAGE 176

1–2. Answers should be things you knew before reading the article.
3. Friends for Health
4. Friends for Life
5. Making Friends
6. The picture shows a calendar of events from a newspaper.
7–9. Questions should be things you expected the article to answer.

PAGE 177

The number of friends a person has does not matter. What is important are friends who are accepting and supportive.

There are many people in the community with a wide range of interests who want to expand their social network.

PAGES 180–181

1. social network
2. adolescence
3. peers
4. status
5. values
6. You should have written the answers to the questions you wrote on page 176 or three things you learned from the article.
7. Young children tend to focus only on what friends can do for them.
8. Answers should include three of the following: Friendships improve health. They provide a source of emotional support. They help people cope with daily life. They provide security and companionship.
9. **(3) People need more help than their social networks can provide.** Options 4 and 5 might explain the reason for some, but not all, of the groups. The opposite is true of option 1. Option 2 may be true but it is not a conclusion that can be supported by the calendar.
10. **(1) Casual relationships can be satisfying.** According to the article, casual friendships provide a sense of belonging and companionship. Some of the group may support options 2, 3, and 4, but there is no evidence that the entire group would agree. The fact that the group has been meeting for twenty years suggests option 5 is incorrect.
11. **(3) A friend in need is a friend indeed.** The other options support one or two ideas expressed in the article but do not reflect the entire article.
12. There are many possible answers.

SECTION 25

PAGE 182

1–2. Answers should be things you knew before reading the article.
3. Counting Heads
4. Similarities and Differences
5. One map shows where minorities are concentrated. The other shows the states that had the largest increases in minority population.
6–8. Questions should be things that you expected the article to answer.

PAGE 183

Cultural diversity is having many different ethnic groups or minorities living in the same country.

PAGE 185

New Mexico, California, Texas, Arizona, and Colorado have the highest concentration of Hispanics.

New Hampshire had large increases of Asian Americans, African Americans, and Hispanics.

PAGES 186–187

1. majority
2. census
3. ethnic group
4. ethnocentrism
5. You should have written the answers to the questions you wrote on page 182 or three things you learned from the article.
6. Sample answer: Ethnocentrism could lead to prejudice and discrimination because people in one ethnic group would see the values and beliefs of another group as the wrong way to live.
7. Sample answer: The states with the highest concentration of minorities are different from the states with the largest increases in minorities.
8. **(2) Minority groups are spreading throughout the country.** According to the maps, the states with the highest concentration of minorities are not the states with the largest increases. Therefore, option 1 is incorrect. The maps show only state population, so option 3 is not supported. There is no evidence on the maps to support options 4 and 5.
9. **(4) The United States is home to many different ethnic groups.** All the other options suggest a prejudice that one culture is somehow superior to another.

10. **(2) people should learn not only about themselves but also about the contributions of other groups.** The other options stress unity over diversity.
11. There are many possible answers.

SECTION 26

PAGE 188

1–2. Answers should be things you knew before reading the article.
3. How Music Grows and Changes
4. Diffusion of African-American Music
5. Jazz and Other Cultures
6. Manu Dibango and Dizzy Gillespie are shown in the photos.
7–9. Questions should be things you expected the article to answer.

PAGE 189

Two reasons why music today is different are new technology and the changing of cultural traits.

PAGE 191

Dizzy Gillespie, the African American, is wearing African clothing. Manu Dibango, the African, is wearing American or Western clothing.

PAGES 192–193

1. cultural trait
2. diffusion
3. adapting
4. traditions
5. acculturated
6. You should have written the answers to the questions you wrote on page 188 or three things you learned from the article.
7. Spirituals are African in their rhythms and melodies. But they are American in their language and their content.
8. **(2) American restaurants create new French-bread pizzas and bagel pizzas.** According to the article, *adapt* means "to change to fit in a certain culture." Option 2 is the only option that shows how pizza has been changed to some American ways. The other options are incorrect because they show that pizza has been borrowed but not adapted.

9. **(2) Dizzy Gillespie wears African-style clothing.** According to the article, traditions, like the African clothing, are cultural traits handed down through the generations. Options 1, 4, and 5 are examples of acculturation. Option 3 is an example of cultural borrowing.
10. **(1) improvisation** According to the article, musicians rarely play jazz the same way twice. Their playing is often affected by moods. Feelings of sadness cause musicians to play the blues. The other options are elements of jazz, but they were not the most important in the creation of the blues.
11. There are many possible answers.

UNIT 5 REVIEW

PAGE 194

1. Grant says, "But you always know who you are, from the day you're born to the day you die."
2. Jumper keeps Seminole traditions alive through storytelling.
3. **(2) Efforts to assimilate may fail, but Native Americans have succeeded in the United States.** Option 1 is incorrect because the article gives examples of the ways two Native Americans have succeeded. Options 3 and 5 are not discussed in the article. Option 4 is incorrect because they both borrowed and adapted cultural traits.

PAGE 195

4. The child sees herself as a flower.
5. The classmate who sees her as a tree comes closest to seeing the girl as she sees herself.
6. **(1) People who belong to the same culture do not always see things in the same way.** There is no evidence that the children are of different cultures so option 2 is incorrect. The cartoon suggests that people read body language in very different ways. Therefore option 3 is incorrect. Option 4 may be true, but it is not a logical conclusion that can be drawn from the cartoon. The child is definitely communicating so option 5 is incorrect.

7. **(3) Attitudes about work are changing for men and women.** Options 1 and 2 are incorrect. The article states the opposite. Attitudes are changing for men and women so options 4 and 5 are incorrect.

8. **(1) Women are gentler and more caring than men.** Although she might agree with one or more of the other options, those beliefs are not reflected in her comments. As a result, options 2–5 are incorrect.

PAGE 197

9. The leader is the speaker. In this case it is the President of the United States.

10. He is standing in the center of a large group. The group is standing and applauding.

11. **(1) standing and applauding.** Option 2 may suggest respect for the event, not necessarily the speaker. Option 4 is a sign of disrespect. There is no evidence in the photograph to support options 3 or 5.

POSTTEST

PAGE 198

1. channels
2. Heavy rains in the highlands caused the annual flooding.
3. **(1) without the river, the whole country would be a desert.** Options 2–4 are true but only option 1 refers to the entire country of Egypt. There is no evidence in the article to support option 5.

PAGE 199

4. Most tropical climates are found between about 20° North and 20° South.
5. **(2) dry climate.**

PAGE 200

6. All three are women who took part in a battle.
7. **(2) some women have already proved themselves in combat.** According to the article, women have taken part in battle, so option 1 is wrong. Option 3 may be true, but it is not a conclusion that can be drawn from the article. There is no evidence in the article to support options 4 and 5.

PAGE 201

8. The men and boys were looking at the job postings at a labor agency.
9. **(3) many jobs were available in other parts of the country.** Option 1 is incorrect or the agency would not have been crowded. Option 2 is incorrect because none of the jobs were local and there was a large crowd outside the agency. Few jobs advertised require special skills. Most of the jobs required only physical strength, so option 4 is incorrect. The large number of boys at the agency suggests that option 5 is incorrect.
10. **(3) young, single men with no family responsibilities** The location of the jobs probably made those jobs unattractive to anyone with young children, so option 1 is incorrect. Children would not want to leave their families, so option 2 is incorrect. The physical nature of the jobs suggests that option 4 is incorrect. Some, but not all, people from other countries might have been interested so option 5 is incorrect.

PAGE 202

11. clearance
12. on sale
13. **(2) A new brand of shoes is brought in and sold at a low price.** According to the article, bringing in new items and selling them at a low price is a promotional sale. Option 1 is an example of items on sale. Option 3 is an example of a clearance sale. Option 4 is not a sale. Option 5 is a sale price, but the type of sale is not stated.

PAGE 203

14. Sales grew fastest in the first part of the decade, 1980–1984.
15. The sales dropped the next year, 1985.

16. **(2) the market for personal computers boomed in the early 1980s.** The market grew rapidly from 1980 to 1984. It peaked in 1990, so options 1, 3, and 4 are incorrect. Option 5 is not supported by the graph.

PAGE 204

17. **(3) A man in a wheelchair cannot get to work because he cannot get into the subway station.** According to the article, trains must be accessible to people with disabilities. Option 1 is not discriminatory. The law says alcoholics are covered only if they are in a treatment program. The woman in option 2 was not rejected because of her disability. She was turned down because she did not have the skills needed to do the job. In option 4, the reason the woman was dismissed had nothing to do with her disability. Option 5 is not discriminatory since a company does not have to comply with the law if it can show that it can't afford the special equipment.

18. **(3) If a business proves hardship, it does not have to obey the law.** According to the article, unless a business can prove hardship, it must comply with the law. Therefore, options 1, 2, 4, and 5 are incorrect.

PAGE 205

19. Cities spend most of their money on environment/housing and public safety.

20. **(5) all of the above** Option 1 has to do with public safety. Option 2 is part of education. Option 3 is a social service. Option 4 deals with transportation.

21. **(5) transportation** Buses are a form of transportation. The other options are incorrect since they do not deal with transportation issues.

PAGE 206

22. cross-cultural communication
23. The real-estate agent tries to establish trust.
24. **(1) The way houses are sold is changing as the population changes.** Option 2 is incorrect since the opposite is true. There is no evidence in the article to support options 3 and 5. Option 4 is incorrect because the article did not compare real-estate agents to other business people.

PAGE 207

25. occupation
26. The woman's job is mother or homemaker.
27. **(4) Being a woman, homemaker, and mother is a full-time job.** Options 1, 2, 3, and 5 cannot be inferred at all from the cartoon. By the woman's response to the question, you can infer that taking care of the house and children leaves time for little else.
28. **(3) that a woman's place is in the home.** There is no evidence to support options 1, 2, and 5. Since it is the woman who is home, option 4 is incorrect.

Acknowledgments *(continued from page ii)*

p. 6
Motor Vehicle Manufacturers Association of the United States, Inc. for statistics from "World Motor Vehicle Production." Reprinted by permission.

p. 10
The NEW YORKER Magazine for drawing by B. Tobey; © 1982 The New Yorker Magazine, Inc.

p. 106
L.F.P., Inc. for statistics from TRADING CARDS Magazine, August, 1991. Reprinted by permission.

p. 118
U. S. NEWS AND WORLD REPORT for excerpt from issue dated 7/16/90. Reprinted by permission.

p. 119
Time, Inc. for excerpt from FORTUNE, March 26, 1990. Copyright © 1990 by Time, Inc. Reprinted by permission.

p. 130
Randy Wicks for his cartoon from THE SIGNAL. Reprinted by permission.

p. 131
Communications Channels, Inc. for excerpt from AMERICAN CITY AND COUNTRY, March, 1991, p. 19, "Encouraging Recycling by Charging More for Garbage," by Lynn Scarlett. Reprinted by permission.

p. 148
CLEVELAND PLAIN DEALER for excerpt, "A caring man finds his nitch as advanced," by Brian Albrecht. First published in The Plain Dealer, Aug. 20, 1991.

p. 148
Felix Wright of the Minnesota Vikings for use of his quotation in THE CLEVELAND PLAIN DEALER, Nov. 3, 1990.

p. 154
Union Leader Corp. for cartoon by Bob Dix. Reprinted by permission.

p. 155
STAR TRIBUNE for cartoon by Steve Sack. Reprinted by permission.

p. 161
STAR TRIBUNE for cartoon by Roy Justus. Reprinted by permission.

p. 172
Dr. Kyle Pruett for his quotation from NEWSWEEK, May 1990. Reprinted by permission.

p. 172
Bunny Hoest for cartoon, "Okay . . . Heads . . ." © 1991; Reprinted courtesy of Bunny Hoest and PARADE Magazine.

p. 177
Dan Hurley for quotation from "Think-Healthy Tips" from PARENTS Magazine, March 1990. Reprinted by permission.

p. 177
Courtesy VOGUE. Copyright © 1985 by the Conde Nast Publications Inc.

p. 185
Mexican-American Legal and Educational Defense Fund for quotation by Antonia Hernandez. Reprinted by permission.

p. 195
The NEW YORKER Magazine for drawing by C. E. Martin; © 1961, 1989 The New Yorker
Magazine, Inc.

p. 201
Walter Rosenblum for photograph by Louis Hine from AMERICA AND LOUIS HINE. Copyright ©
1977 by Aperture, Inc. Reprinted by permission.

p. 203
Computer and Business Equipment Manufacturers' Association for statistics from "Sales of
Microcomputers, 1980–1990." Reprinted by permission.

p. 207
The NEW YORKER Magazine for drawing by Chon Day; © 1940, 1968 The New Yorker Magazine,
Inc.

Glossary

A

acculturation to borrow and adapt cultural traits from other cultures

adapt to change something to fit one's culture

adolescence the period of human life ranging approximately from the ages of 13 to 19

allies friends or countries that help each other

amendment an addition or change

annual percentage rate (APR) the percent of interest a lender charges each year for every $100 borrowed

anthropologist a scientist who studies the cultures created by different societies. An anthropologist also studies how the cultures affect the people who live in them.

anthropology the study of cultures and how they affect the people who live in them.

anxiety reaction a type of human behavior in which a person acts in a nervous manner during a social situation

apply to take information from one situation and use it in another situation

apprentice someone who learns a trade from an expert called a master

APR see annual percentage rate

aquifer an underground source of water

assimilate to give up one's culture to be like the majority

B

bait and switch a deceptive selling practice in which an item is advertised at a low price, but the customer is pressured into buying something more expensive

bar graph a graph often used to make comparisons

behavioral science the study of people and groups and the ways they act

bill a proposal for a law

Bill of Rights the first ten amendments to the United States Constitution. These amendments list the rights of individuals.

blues a type of jazz music that is sad or "blue"

body language unspoken communication such as smiles, nods, and posture

boycott to refuse to use a service or buy a certain item in protest against something

brand a mark burned onto an animal's skin to show who owns it

budget a detailed plan showing the earnings and expenses of a person or family over a period of time

business cycle the shifting of an economy from growth to recession and back to growth

buyers' market an economic situation in which there are far more goods available than there are buyers to purchase them

C

campaign a series of events designed to get people to vote a certain way

candidate a person running for political office

cartoon a picture that expresses the artist's point of view on a certain subject

cash crop a crop grown to sell, rather than to feed a farmer's family

cause tells why something happened

census a counting of all the people in a country

CentCom see Central Command

Central Command (CentCom) a military unit that is responsible for military activities in certain countries

chain referrals a selling practice in which customers are told they will get a reduced price or a free gift if they refer other customers

channel a trench dug to allow water flow

child labor the practice of using children as workers

circle graph a graph used to compare amounts. A circle graph is also known as a pie chart.

citizen 1) a person who is born in a country or who takes an oath of allegiance to that country 2) a person who has lived in a city, county, or state for a specified length of time

civil rights liberties available to citizens, including the right to be treated equally

civil war a war between people who live in the same country

clearance sale a sale in which the store lowers its prices on a certain item in order to sell its entire supply of it

climate the usual weather of a region over a long period of time

closed posture body language that shows the listener is unhappy with the speaker

coalition a group whose members have joined together to meet a goal

cold war a war fought mainly with words and money. Each side in a cold war is prepared to do actual battle if the need arises.

collaboration to work together, as when people of other cultures make music together

colonist a person who moves to a settlement that is ruled by that person's home country

colony a settlement or group of settlements far from the home country

communicate to exchange information

compare to tell how people, events, or things are alike

conclusion a logical judgment made from facts

Confederacy the southern states during the Civil War. The Confederacy was called the South, as well.

Congress the elected representatives in the law-making branch of the government

conserve to use something wisely

constitution a plan for a government

consumer a person who buys and uses goods and services

consumer confidence the way buyers feel about the economy

context 1) the rest of the words in a sentence 2) one particular situation

continental climate a climate that is found inland, away from a large body of water

contract a legal document between two or more people

contrast to show the difference between people, events, and things

cooperative farmers who join together to ensure the best quality and price for their crops

corporation a business that is owned by stockholders

crisis a time of extreme difficulty resulting in critical changes

cross-cultural communication the understanding that all cultures have their own sense of what they like or don't like

crude untreated oil

cultural behavior behavior that is learned from the way of life into which someone is born

cultural trait something special which distinguishes one person's way of life from another person's

culture a way of life

current water in motion

D

debt money that is owed

deceptive selling a selling practice that misleads the buyer

Declaration of Independence the document approved by the Second Continental Congress on July 4, 1776. It told the world that the 13 American colonies were free from England's rule.

defense industry companies that produce military supplies

demand the amount of goods or services consumers are willing to buy at a certain price at a given time

democracy a system of government in which the power to make choices belongs to the people. People exercise their power in a democracy through free elections.

depression a severe recession that lasts for a very long time

desalination plant a place where special machines take salt out of seawater. The seawater can then be used for drinking and watering crops.

details small pieces of information that explain or support the main idea

deter to prevent

diagram a drawing that often shows steps in a process with arrows showing how one step leads to another

dictator someone who has total power over a country

diffusion the spread of cultural traits

discrimination unequal and unfair treatment of a person or group

drought a long period of time when there is little or no rain

due process the right to a fair trial

E

economics the study of how people use their resources to meet their needs

economist a person who studies how people manage their resources

economy a country's system for managing its resources

effect tells what happened as a result of the cause

Eighth Amendment the addition to the United States Constitution that outlaws cruel and unusual punishment

elastic supply an amount of goods or services that increases or decreases as prices change

elevation the height of the land

Emancipation Proclamation the statement made by President Abraham Lincoln freeing all slaves in states fighting against the United States during the Civil War

endorse to support

entrepreneur someone who turns ideas into goods and services

environment all of the living and nonliving things that make up a place

environmentalist a person who wants laws to control pollution and to protect wildlife, rivers, lakes, and other resources

Environmental Protection Agency (EPA) a government agency that sets guidelines on how the environment can best be used and protected

EPA see Environmental Protection Agency

equator an imaginary circle exactly halfway between the North and South poles

ethnic group a group of people linked by race, language, religion, or culture

ethnocentrism the belief that a certain way of life is the natural and right way to live

expense money that is paid out

explorer a person who travels in order to make discoveries

exporter a business that sells its goods to other countries

exports the goods produced in one country and sold in other countries

F

fact a statement about something that actually happened or actually exists

faulty not correct

federal law a law that applies to the whole country

federal system a system in which governing is divided between the state government and the government of the entire country

Fifth Amendment the addition to the United States Constitution that states that someone cannot be brought to trial unless a formal charge has been made

finance charge the cost of a loan

First Amendment an addition to the United States Constitution that gives people the right to hold public meetings, rallies, and parades

fixed expenses payments that stay the same month after month

flexible expenses bills that vary from month to month

free enterprise system an economic system in which buyers affect which goods and services are produced

G

gender stereotype a general idea about how all men or all women behave

geographer a person who studies the relationship between people and places on Earth

geography the study of Earth's surface and the relationship between people and places

gestures body movements, such as with the hands or eyes

glaciers huge masses of ice that flow slowly over the land

glossary an alphabetical listing of important words and their definitions located at the end of a text

governor the chief executive of a state

graph a special kind of drawing that is used to compare information

groundwater an underground source of water. Examples include springs, wells, ponds, and aquifers.

gun-control laws legal limits set by the government on the sale of guns to the public

H

hasty generalization a broad statement based on little or no evidence

hazardous waste something thrown away that is harmful to the environment

high latitudes the two regions that are near the North and South poles

highland climate a climate affected by high elevations, including mountains

historical map a map that shows what happened at a particular place and time in the past

history the study of the past and the way people are connected to past events

House of Representatives a lawmaking group in a state or the nation. It is often referred to as the House.

iceberg a huge block of ice that has broken off from a glacier

implied not stated

importer a business that buys goods from other countries

imports the goods brought into a country from another country

improvisation in music, to change or make up a tune as it is being played

incentive a reason for an action

independent free and self-governing

indicted formally charged with a crime

industry factories

inelastic supply an amount of a good or service that cannot change no matter what happens to a price

inference the use of information to figure out things that are not actually stated

inflation a time when prices are rising

innate something in a person from birth

installment plan an arrangement to make payments over a specific period of time

instinct something that does not have to be taught, such as eating and sleeping

interest rate the amount of money paid for borrowing money

international having to do with two or more countries

interned to be sent to a prison camp and forced to stay there

intimate distance a zone that extends from actual contact between people to about 18 inches apart

iron curtain an invisible barrier that separated Soviet-controlled countries of Eastern Europe from the democratic countries of Western Europe

irrigate to bring water to crops

jazz a type of music, featuring syncopation and improvisation

justice a judge who serves on the Supreme Court

L

labor force all of the people who are capable of being employed

landfill a place where trash is buried under thin layers of earth

latitude lines on a map or globe used to measure the distance north or south of the equator

line graph a graph using lines to show how something increases or decreases over time

loan 1) a sum of money that is borrowed 2) to lend money

lobby to attempt to get lawmakers to see an issue in a certain way

logic a method of reasoning in which the truth of one statement depends on the truth of an earlier statement

longitude lines on a map or globe that reach from pole to pole and are used to measure distances to the east and west

low latitudes the region between $23\frac{1}{2}°$N and $23\frac{1}{2}°$S, also known as the tropics

Loyalist an American who remained loyal to England at the time of the American Revolution

M

main idea the topic of a paragraph

majority an amount that is more than half of the total

map key explains what each symbol on the map means

map scale used to figure out real distances on a map

map symbols lines, dots, colors, or pictures used to tell about places

marine climate a climate affected by an ocean

market a place where buyers and sellers meet. A market determines the goods and services that will be produced.

mayor the chief executive of a town or city

media agencies of communication such as television, radio, newspapers, and magazines

meridians see longitude

methane a colorless, odorless gas that burns easily

middle latitudes the climatic region that is located between the tropics and the polar regions

minority an amount that is less than half of the total

minstrel someone who sings, dances, and tells jokes

minutemen American colonists who could be ready to fight at a minute's notice

multinational worldwide

N

natural boundary something in nature, such as a mountain range or a river, that separates one area from another

net income money left after taxes are paid

neutral to refuse to be on one side or the other

nominate to choose a candidate to run for an elected office

nonrenewable resource something people need from Earth that will not last forever. Oil is an example of a nonrenewable resource.

O

oasis a place in the desert with an underground spring for water

open posture body language that shows a listener supports the speaker

opinion a statement that expresses what a person or group of people think or believe about a fact

opportunity cost the cost of choosing one thing over another

ordinance a law or regulation

orientation the direction in which people turn their bodies, especially the head

P

PAC see political action committee

parallels of latitude the lines on the maps used to measure distances from the equator in degrees (°)

paramount the most important

Parliament Great Britain's group of lawmakers

Patriot an American who wanted to be free from England at the time of the American Revolution

peer an equal

peninsula a piece of land surrounded on three sides by water

permit a document that gives permission

personal distance a zone between people that ranges from about 18 inches to four feet

pie chart a circle graph in which amounts are made to look like slices of a pie

pilgrim someone who makes a long journey for religious reasons

point of view how someone feels or thinks

polar climates regions with high latitudes near the North and South poles

political action committee (PAC) a group that gives money to candidates that have interests similar to its own

political cartoon a picture that expresses an opinion about an issue

political map a map that focuses on showing boundaries between countries

political party a group of people who have similar ideas about public issues. The political party works together to put its ideas into effect.

political scientist a person who studies politics and government

population map a map that shows where people live

posture the way people stand or sit

prairie a large area covered with tall, thick grass

predicting outcomes trying to figure out what will happen next

previewing to look over printed material quickly, without reading it completely

price the amount of money a consumer pays for goods

profit to make money by selling something at a higher price than the original cost

promotional sale reduced prices on items brought into a store especially for the sale

prosper to become rich or successful

psychologist a scientist who studies why individuals behave the way they do

psychology the study of individual behavior

public distance a zone between people that is over 12 feet away

R

raw materials base materials used to make goods

recession a time when business activity slows

recycle to remake or clean something so that it may be used again in some way

reformers people who work to change things for the better

regiment a large military group

region an area that is different in some way from the places around it

register to enroll by completing a form telling such things as name, address, and date of birth

repeal to take back or do away with something

republic a state

resource any part of an environment that people can use to meet their needs

resource map a map that uses symbols to show the resources of a region

revolution 1) a complete circle 2) a sudden change in political organization

rights see civil rights

run-off agriculture a method of farming in which a system of trenches carries water to terraced land

S

sanction a refusal to trade with a certain country

scarce a limited supply of something that is in demand

Second Amendment an addition to the United States Constitution that gives individuals the right to own guns

segregate to separate the races

self-defense to protect oneself

sellers' market an economic situation in which there are far more buyers wanting to buy goods than there are products to sell

Senate a lawmaking group of a state or the nation

sequence the order of events

service industries businesses that sell services by employing people who meet the needs of other people

Seventh Amendment the addition to the United States Constitution that gives those accused of a crime the right to a trial by jury

Sixth Amendment the addition to the United States Constitution that gives those accused of a crime the right to a speedy trial

social distance a zone between people that ranges from about four to twelve feet

social network relationships including casual and close friends

socialization the process by which people learn to fit into their culture

socializing agent a person or group who shapes someone's values, beliefs, or behavior

society groups linked by political, social, and economic ties

sociologist a scientist who studies group behavior

sociology the study of group behavior

special pricing a selling practice in which the buyer is told to buy now because the price will soon rise

state assembly a lawmaking group that makes decisions on a state level

status a level in society

steppe a dry grassland in which the grass grows in short, thin clumps

stereotype a general idea about how all people within a group or culture behave

stockholder a person who owns shares in a company

summarize to condense or shorten a larger amount of information into a few sentences

supply the amount of goods and services sellers are willing to offer at certain prices at a given time

supporting statements details that lead to a conclusion

Supreme Court the justices appointed by the president who interpret the Constitution

syncopation the stress of the weak rather than the strong beat in music

T

table a type of graph that organizes information in columns and rows

tax money a government collects from its people in order to provide public services

technology the tools and methods used to increase production

temperate climates mild climates in the middle latitudes

terraces large, flat steps of earth

timeline an illustration that shows when a series of events took place and the order in which they occurred

topic sentence the sentence that contains the main idea in a paragraph

tradition a cultural trait passed from one generation to the next

tropics the region between the two points of Earth receiving direct sunlight. The tropics are also known as the low latitudes.

U

unemployment rate the percent of workers in the labor force without jobs

Union the northern states during the Civil War. The Union was called the North, as well.

V

values things people feel are important, beautiful, or worthwhile

vegetation the plant life that grows naturally in an area

veto to refuse to sign into law

W

weather changes in wind, temperature, and/or precipitation over short periods of time

Index